T0295613

Strategic Tourism Planning for Communities

BUILDING THE FUTURE OF TOURISM

Series Editor: Anukrati Sharma

The world is entering the Third Millennium in which great changes are expected in all areas of human interest, life, and activity. These changes have been brought on by past and present man-made events, which have had both positive and negative consequences. The coming millennium will be marked by significant social, political, demographic, and technological changes and will definitely differ from the last century. The future will bring more leisure time, a higher standard of living, and a better quality of life for us all. This series examines recent and the most probable changes and gives a wide range of visionary insights as well as operational takeaways.

Forthcoming Volumes

Meaningful Tourism: Strategies and Futuristic Development
Pankaj Kumar Tyagi, Vipin Nadda, and Ajit Kumar Singh

Emerald Handbook of Tourism Economics and Sustainable Development
Ahmed Imran Hunjra and Anukrati Sharma

Value Proposition for Tourism "Co-opetition": Cases and Tools
Adriana Fumi Chim Miki and Rui Augusto da Costa

Dark Tourism: Theory, Interpretation and Attraction
Anukrati Sharma, Shruti Arora, and Parag Shukla

Strategic Tourism Planning for Communities: Restructuring and Rebranding

EDITED BY

ANUKRATI SHARMA

University of Kota, India

AND

SHRUTI ARORA

University of Kota, India

United Kingdom – North America – Japan – India – Malaysia – China

Emerald Publishing Limited
Emerald Publishing, Floor 5, Northspring, 21-23 Wellington Street, Leeds LS1 4DL

First edition 2024

British Library Cataloguing in Publication Data
A catalogue record for this book is available from the British Library

ISBN: 978-1-83549-016-7 (Print)
ISBN: 978-1-83549-015-0 (Online)
ISBN: 978-1-83549-017-4 (Epub)

INVESTOR IN PEOPLE

To our parents, who planted the seed of knowledge in our mind and nurtured it, who gave us the gift of dreams and the ability to realize them.
Last but not least to our wonderful contributors and readers.

Contents

About the Editors

Dr Anukrati Sharma is the *Head* and Associate Professor of the Department of Commerce and Management at the University of Kota (a State Govt. University) in Kota, Rajasthan, India. She is the *Director* of the Skill Development Center of the same university. She is also *Dean* (Honorary) of two faculties, Tourism and Hospitality and Aviation and Aerospace at Rajasthan Skill University (a Govt. State University) in Jaipur. In 2015, she received a Research Award from the University Grants Commission (UGC), New Delhi, for her project "Analysis of the Status of Tourism in Hadoti and Shekhawati Region/Circuit (Rajasthan): Opportunities, Challenges, and Future Prospects." Her doctorate from the University of Rajasthan is in Tourism Marketing, and she completed her dissertation research on Tourism in Rajasthan – Progress & Prospects. She has two postgraduate degree specialties – one in International Business (Master of International Business) and the other in Business Administration (Master of Commerce). Her special interest areas are Tourism, Tourism Marketing, Strategic Management, and International Business Management. She is appointed as the *Official Partner of the BRICS Funded Project for the years 2022−2024*. Dr Sharma is a *Routledge featured author*. Dr Sharma is the *Book Series Editor for "Building the Future of Tourism" published by Emerald Publishing, UK*. She is also the *Book Series Editor of "Routledge Insights in Tourism Series," Routledge, UK*. She also serves as *Book Series Editor for "Perspectives and Anthropology in Tourism and Hospitality (PATH)," Apple Academic Press (CRC Press a Taylor and Francis Group)*. She has edited books on Tourism – Opportunities and Ventures, on Maximizing Business Performance and Efficiency through Intelligent Systems, under IGI Global (*Scopus Indexded*), *Tourism Sustainable Tourism Development Futuristic Approaches under Apple Academic Press (CRC Press a Taylor and Francis Group), USA*, under the series Advances in Hospitality and Tourism and book titled *Tourism Events in Asia Marketing and Development Routledge, USA*, under Advances in Events Research Series, *Sustainable Destination Branding and Marketing: Strategies for Tourism Development under CABI*, UK, Future of Tourism: An Asian Perspective, under *Springer, Singapore, Over-tourism* as Destination Risk: Impacts and Solutions *Emerald Publishing, UK*, under the Tourism Security – Safety Series, Over-tourism, Technology Solutions and Decimated Destinations, *Springer, Singapore*, Event Tourism in Asian Countries: Challenges and Prospects under *Apple Academic Press (Taylor and Francis Group), USA* and The Emerald Handbook of ICT in Tourism and Hospitality under *Emerald Publishing, UK*. She also authored a book entitled "Event

Management and Marketing Theory, Practical Approaches and Planning." Another book she wrote is entitled "International Best Practice in Event Management," and it was published by *United Kingdom Event Industry Academy Ltd and Prasetiya Mulya Publishing, Indonesia*. Her current projects include editing a book on "COVID-19 and Tourism Sustainability: Ethics, Responsibilities, Challenges and New Directions" *for Routledge, USA*, "Festivals and Event Tourism: Building Resilience and Promoting Sustainability" for *CABI, UK*, The Emerald Handbook of Destination Recovery in Tourism and Hospitality, *Emerald Publishing, UK*, COVID-19 and the Tourism Industry: Sustainability, Resilience & New Directions *Routledge, UK*, Event Tourism & Sustainable Community Development: Advances, Effects and Implications, *Apple Academic Press, USA*, Crisis, Resilience and Recovery in Tourism and Hospitality *Springer Nature, Singapore*, Dynamics of Tourism Industry Post-Pandemic and Disasters, *Apple Academic Press, USA*, and Resilient and Sustainable Destinations after Disaster: Challenges and Strategies, *Emerald Publishing, UK*. She is also working on a *Major Research Project under Mahatma Gandhi National Council of Rural Education, Ministry of Human Resource Development Government of India*. A member of 7 professional bodies, she has attended a number of national and international conferences and presented 45 papers. She has been invited as Keynote, Speaker, and Panel member by different countries such as Sri Lanka, Uzbekistan, Nepal, and Turkey. She has been invited as Visiting Professor at Kazakhstan and Uzbekistan.

Dr Shruti Arora is currently working as an Assistant Professor (Guest Faculty) in the Department of Commerce and Management, University of Kota, Kota, Rajasthan, India, and has an experience of 14 years in education industry. Her core subjects are Marketing, General Management, International Business and Customer Relationship Management. She has attended various international conferences, and her publication includes various chapters in edited books like Routledge, Emerald, and Springer and research papers in National and International UGC approved and peer-reviewed journals. She has authored a book on "Event Management and Marketing: Theory, Practical Approaches and Planning" with ISBN: 978-93-86608-61-1 in 2018 and two edited book under Apple Academic Press, CRC Press. She is working as a Co-PI with Dr Anukrati Sharma on a major research project under Mahatma Gandhi National Council of Rural Education, Ministry of Human Resource Development Government of India. *She is appointed as the BRICS Community of Practice (CoP) Researcher for promoting cross-BRICS nations'* collaborations in co-authorship, co-supervision, co-examining, co-publishing in DHET and SCOPUS Accredited Journals, co-conferencing participation and hosting rotating BRICS workshops, seminars and guest lectures in the academic years 2023 and 2024. The term "Food Walk Tourism" is included in *Encyclopedia of Tourism Management and Marketing, editor in Chief, Professor Dimitrios Buhalis: Bournemouth University*, Edward Elgar Publishing Limited, ISBN: 9781800377479, e-ISBN: 9781800377486 in 2022.

About the Contributors

Shakil Ahmed, currently studying at Forestry and Wood Technology Discipline of Khulna University, Bangladesh. He intends to pursue a career in nature-based tourism. His passion is to help the local community by ensuring sustainable forest management. Participatory forest management, nature-based tourism, and wildlife management are some of his research interests. He enjoys participating in voluntary work and has volunteered for a number of organizations, including Bangladesh Youth Initiative (BYI), Forestry and Wood Technology Club, and Bangladesh Tourism Board.

R. S. S. W. Arachchi graduated from Sabaragamuwa University of Sri Lanka before receiving his Master's degree from Colombo University, Sri Lanka, and PhD degree from Management and Science University in Malaysia. He is currently working as a Professor in Tourism Management at the Department of Tourism Management, Faculty of Management Studies, Sabaragamuwa University of Sri Lanka, Belihuloya. He was involved in various administrative activities at the university and contributed his service to various government and private sector tourism projects as a consultant and a resource person in various workshops. His major teaching and research areas are ecotourism, community-based tourism, sustainable tourism development, responsible tourism, environment and tourism resources and homestay tourism in Asian Countries. He has published nearly 40 articles in well-recognized journals both in Sri Lanka and overseas. Prof Arachchi is an editorial board member of the *Journal of Tourism and Hospitality Management, International Journal of Education Humanities and Social Science* and a member of Global Association for Humanities and Social Science Research. Prof Arachchi is also a leading consultant in sustainable tourism, community-based eco-tourism and regulatory advice, curriculum development and quality parameters development projects in Sri Lanka.

Manpreet Arora, Senior Assistant Professor of Management in the School of Commerce and Management Studies, Central University of Himachal Pradesh Dharamshala, India. Her areas of research interest include Accounting and Finance, Strategic Management, Entrepreneurship, Qualitative Research, Case Study Development, Communication Skills, and Microfinance. She has been guiding research at the doctoral level and has worked in the area of Microfinance. Having published more than 25 papers in various journals of national and international repute (including SCOPUS, WOS, and Category Journals), she has also worked as a Content Developer of MHRD "e-PG Pathshala" Project and

xiv   *About the Contributors*

OER's for IGNOU. She has written 30 book chapters in national as well as international books/handbooks/volumes published with Routledge, CABI, Apple Academic Press, IGI, Taylor and Francis and latest with Springer Nature, etc. With four edited books in her credit, she is a persistent researcher in the field of Management.

Elif BAK ATEŞ, born in Ordu in 1989. She received her Bachelor's degree from Nevşehir University and her Master's and Doctorate degrees in Tourism Management from Mersin University. Between 2014 and 2020, she worked as a Research Assistant at Mersin University, Faculty of Tourism, Department of Tourism Management. She became a Professional tourist guide in English language in 2019. It is an active tourist guide affiliated to Trabzon Guides Chamber. Her research areas are intercultural communication, sustainable tourism, and tourist guidance. She has national and international book chapters and articles in national journals. She presented oral and full text papers in many national and international congresses.

Arup Kumar Baksi is working as a Professor in the Department of Management and Business Administration, Aliah University, Kolkata, West Bengal, India. Prof Baksi has 22 years of academic and four years of corporate experience. He has published more than 100 research papers in various national and international journals of repute and 31 book chapters. Prof Baksi is engaged as reviewer of several international journals published by reputed publishers. He has accomplished research projects funded by All India Council of Technical Education, ICSSR and State and Central Universities. He has developed MOOC modules for the SWAYAM portal of UGC. Prof Baksi has conducted a number of Research Methodology courses sponsored by ICSSR, SPSS, etc. and has enacted as a Resource Person in State and Central Universities across India.

Orhan Batman, Professor at the Department of Tourism and Hotel Management at Sakarya University of Applied Sciences. He earned his Bachelor's and Master's degree from Balıkesir University. He earned a PhD degree from the Department of Organization And Business Policy at Istanbul University. In Tourism and Management field, he has more than 100 articles, proceedings and books. Until now, he has supervised 10 doctoral and almost 40 master theses. Some of his selected works include, tourism policy and strategy; philosophy, theory, applications of Halal tourism; hotel management, international hotel management.

Gül ERKOL BAYRAM, Associate Professor in School of Tourism and Hotel Management, Department of Tour Guiding, University of Sinop, Sinop, Turkey. Her doctorate is in Tourism Management from the Sakarya University, Turkey, and she completed her dissertation research on Tour Guiding in Turkey. Her core subjects are tourism, tour guiding, tourism policy and planning, and women studies. Erkol Bayram has also worked as a Professional Tour Guide in the tourism sector. She has many book chapters and articles in national and international arena. She has been invited for many talks/lectures/panel discussions by different universities.

Sarah Chauhan, Researcher (NET-JRF-2019) in the Department of Tourism, Hospitality and Management Studies, Jamia Millia Islamia University, New Delhi, India, in the field of Tourism with a specialization in Museology. She gets her inspiration from current and past events pertaining to Museums and Heritage since her schooling days. A budding scholar, she is looking forward to more opportunities in the near future to promote the Indian culture in the field of Tourism. She is a member of ICOM and ICOMOS; both the fields are contributing towards the development of culture and heritage at the national and international level. She also served as a mentor to NET-JRF aspirants. She has attended many conferences in the field of Tourism, Museums and Heritage. Sarah is quite passionate about arts and history while keeping in mind her background. She did her Bachelor's in History from St Stephens College and Master's in Museology from the National Museum Institute and has been associated with these fields ever since.

Vaishali Dhiman, Research Scholar in HPKVBS, in the School of Commerce and Management Studies, Central University of Himachal Pradesh Dharamshala, India. She is working in the area of Entrepreneurship and Incubation. Her areas of interest include various dimensions of entrepreneurship, start-ups, venture creation, incubation, and creativity.

Ankit Dhiraj is currently a Senior Research Fellow at the School of Hotel Management and Tourism, Lovely Professional University, Punjab, India. He has completed his regular three years Bachelor's degree in Business Management from Magadh University Bodhgaya, a Masters's in Tourism Management from Alagappa University, Tamil Nadu and pursuing PhD in Tourism Management at the School of Hotel Management and Tourism, Lovely Professional University, Punjab, India. His area of research interest is Buddhist tourism, wellness tourism and sustainable practices. He has experience working with different universities in India as a business development associate. Ankit Dhiraj has also participated in various national and international conferences, seminars and research workshops. He has published more than 10 research papers in Scopus Indexed, UGC Approved and peer-reviewed Journals.

Kyialbek Dyikanov, PhD candidate and part-time lecturer at Kyrgyz – Turkish Manas University and General Director of LLC Bars International in Kyrgyz Republic. He completed his MBA degree in Cyprus International University (North Cyprus). His research interests are tourism, entrepreneurship and marketing.

Saanchi Grover, Lecturer of GRD Group of Colleges Punjab teaching hotel management subjects' inclusion of front office, food safety and commodities and a PhD Research Scholar of Lovely Professional University Punjab and an author of reputed publications in edited books alongside UGC care listed journals as well as a professional member of tourism and hospitality conferences and workshops and have separate knowledge of hotel and travel industry.

Md Wasiul Islam, a Professor of Forestry and Wood Technology Discipline of Khulna University, Bangladesh. He has accomplished his PhD from Business School (Tourism Cluster) of The University of Queensland, Australia, where he conducted research titled "Adaptive co-management as an approach to tourism destination governance – a case of protected areas in Bangladesh." Before his PhD, Prof Wasiul completed his second MSc in Master of Science in Forest and Nature Conservation (Minor in Leisure, Tourism and Environment) from the Wageningen University and Research Center, the Netherlands. He has done his first MSc and BSc from Forestry and Wood Technology Discipline, Khulna University. He has working experience in Bangladesh Forest Department where he was involved in several research projects on nature-based tourism and wildlife management. His research interests include participatory protected area management (particularly comanagement approach), governance, social learning, nature conservation, and nature-based tourism.

Orpha Jane, born at Gorontalo, October 6th, 1970. She has graduated from Parahyangan Catholique University (Unpar) for her Bachelor's, Padjadjaran University (Unpad) for her Master's and Indonesia University (UI) for her Doctoral program. From 1996 until now, she has taught and facilitated the Student Undergraduate and Graduate Program of Business Administration Department Faculty of Social and Political Unpar in Strategic Management. Besides that, she also taught and facilitated students in Digital Transformation and Business Global topics. As a lecturer's primary duty, she is doing research and community service on those topics frequently. Jane also has been responsible for managerial assignments for around 10 years at Unpar.

S. P. M. B. Jayakody, an undergraduate of the Department of Tourism Studies at UvaWellassa University, currently reading BBM in Hospitality, Tourism and Events Management, has a keen interest in sustainable tourism and inclusive tourism to be integrated with Destination Management of which his major research specialization domains are. With his aspirations to serve world tourism to switch onto sustainability, he continues to further his studies to bring more sustainable discussions to the table.

Sanjeev Kumar, Professor and Head of Department (HOD) of Lovely Professional University Punjab. Having 18 years of experience in industry and academic with research orientation, publish research paper in Scopus listed journals, attended more than 15–17 conferences and Co-editor of Journal in LPU and care list journal.

Raisa Tasnim Mahin, a senior student of Forestry and Wood Technology Discipline of Khulna University, Bangladesh. She is a positive and creative individual who loves to take challenges and is very enthusiastic about learning and discovering new things. She loves nature and enjoys working for the environment, wildlife, collaborative forest management, and tourism. Her research interest is nature-based tourism. She has done some volunteer work for several organizations as well as worked as a research assistant for a nature-based tourism project. She has a great passion for writing and is able to deliver a consistent approach throughout a challenging period of development.

Azamat Maksüdünov, Assistant Professor at Kyrgyz Turkish Manas University, Department of Management, Faculty of Economics and Management. Dr Maksüdünov received his MS and PhD degree in Business Administration from the Kyrgyz – Turkish Manas University. He carried out his doctoral thesis on service marketing and service quality. His research interests are in the fields of service marketing, tourism marketing, e-marketing and entrepreneurship. He has also visited foreign universities as a researcher including Entrepreneurship Development Institute of India, Sivas Cumhuriyet University, Turkey, Potsdam University of Applied Sciences, Germany, Florida Atlantic University, USA. He gives lectures both to undergraduate and graduate levels and has many publications in national and international peer-reviewed journals and conference proceedings.

Hüseyin Pamukçu, Bachelor's degree from Mustafa Kemal University in 2011 and his Master's degree from Afyon Kocatepe University in 2014 and his doctorate from Sakarya University 2017. He started his academic career at Kastamonu University in 2013. He started to work as a Research Assistant in 2013 and as a Doctor Lecturer in 2018 in the Department of Tourism Management of the Faculty of Tourism at the University of Kastamonu. As of February 2021, he has continued his studies at the Faculty of Tourism, University of Afyon Kocatepe as Assist Professor. In May 2021, he was successful in the Inter-University Board exam and received the title of Associate Professor. Pamukçu, who continues to work as an Associate Professor in the Department of Gastronomy and Culinary Arts at the same university, is married and has two children.

P. G. S. S. Pattiyagedara, Lecturer at the Department of Tourism Studies, Faculty of Management, UvaWellassa University of Sri Lanka. She obtained her first degree from UvaWellassa University Sri Lanka with a titled, BBM (Special) in Hospitality, Tourism and Event Management with second-class upper division honors. Currently, she is delivering lectures to the undergraduates following BBM in Hospitality Tourism and Events Management Degree Program. Her main research specialization areas are Sustainable Tourism, Responsible Tourism and Destination Marketing and Management.

I. Gde Pitana, Professor in Tourism Science at Udayana University, Bali, Indonesia. His background education is Socioeconomic Department in Faculty of Agriculture Udayana University (1984), Master's degree at Department of Sociology, Ateneo de Manila University, Manila, Philippines (1989), and a Doctoral degree at Department of Social Anthropology, the Australian National University, Canberra, Australia (1998). He got some strategic positions in the Ministry of Tourism and Creative Economy of the Republic of Indonesia from 2005 to 2019. One of his strategic positions was as a deputy of the minister in international tourism marketing development (2015–2018). He has already written some academic articles and books. One of his books was published in 2021 with the title: "*PariwisataSpiritual DalamTeori dan Aplikasi* (Spiritual Tourism on Theory and Application)."

R. L. T. D. S. Rajapakshe, an Ayurvedic Medical Officer currently serving as a Medical Officer in Sabaragamuwa Province, Sri Lanka. She holds a Bachelor of Ayurveda Medicine and Surgery (BAMS second Class Upper) degree from the Institute of Indigenous Medicine, University of Colombo, Sri Lanka and a postgraduate Diploma in Shalyathantra from Gampaha Wickramarachchi Ayurveda University, Sri Lanka. Currently, she is an undergraduate in Master of Ayurvedic Hospital Management degree at the Sabaragamuwa University of Sri Lanka. Her areas of interest are Ayurveda, Shalyathantra, Wellness tourism, and Ayurveda tourism.

Dr Subhashree Sanyal is currently serving as an Assistant Professor at the Dept. of Social Work at Visva-Bharati Santiniketan. She has been a Social Work Academic and Practitioner for the last 14 years with over 10 years of teaching experience in different Central Universities of India. Dr Sanyal has published widely in distinguished books and journals and with widely known houses like Sage, Routledge, Oxford and Springer. A number of Government Projects, Collaborations and numerable workshops and seminars add to her academic credit. She has been one of the few leading in the field of mental health and social work in teaching research and practice for the last few years in Eastern India. Dr Sanyal is passionate about poetry and music. She enjoys reading as her hobby and traveling. She currently lives and works in Santiniketan, West Bengal.

Ömer Saraç, Bachelor's degree from Mustafa Kemal University in 2011 and his Master's degree from Kastamonu University in 2017 and his doctorate from Sakarya University of Applied Sciences in 2020. He started his academic career as a Lecturer at Kastamonu University CideRıfatIlgaz Vocational School in 2015. After receiving his doctorate, he continued his career at Sakarya University of Applied Sciences. He is currently working as an Asst Prof Dr in the Department of Tourism Management of the Faculty of Tourism at the Sakarya University of Applied Sciences. Throughout his academic career, the author has attended many national and international symposiums and congresses. The author has book and book chapter authorship as well as national/international articles published in various journals.

I. Made Sarjana, Researcher at the Center of Excellence in Tourism at Udayana University, Bali, Indonesia. His background education is Socioeconomic Department in Faculty of Agriculture Udayana University (1997), Master's degree in Master Program in Leisure, Tourism and Environment Wageningen University and Research (MLE-WUR) the Netherlands (2011), and Doctoral Department of Tourism Faculty Udayana University (2021). Therefore, he has focused on integrating agriculture and tourism as a theme or core study for years. Before joining as a lecturer or researcher at Udayana University, he worked as a journalist for Bali Post Daily. As an impact of job experience acculturation as a researcher and journalist, he prefers to use qualitative methods in his research projects. He has already written some academic articles and books. One of his books was published in 2020 with the title: "*Agrowisata: Pariwisata Berbasis Pertanian* (Agritourism: Tourism Based on Agriculture)."

Sofia Devi Shamurailatpam holds a PhD in Economics with specialization in the area of Banking and Financial Economics. Currently, she is serving as an Assistant Professor in the Department of Banking and Insurance, Faculty of Commerce, the Maharaja Sayajirao University of Baroda. She has published several research papers in her credit and authored a book entitled "Banking Reforms in India: Consolidation, Restructuring and Performance," published by Palgrave Macmillan, UK (2017). Her major research area of interests includes Economics of Banking, Financial Economics, Economics of Gender, Agricultural Economics and Development Economics particularly Contemporary issues on Sustainability.

Parag S. Shukla holds a PhD degree in Commerce and Business Management with focus on Strategic Marketing in the area of "Retailing." He has been working as an Assistant Professor in the Maharaja Sayajirao University of Baroda since 2009. He has presented and published many research papers in contemporary areas of Marketing in National and International Journals. He is also an author in a book entitled "Retail Shoppers' Behavior in Brick and Mortar Stores – A Strategic Marketing Approach" which is published by a reputed publisher. His major research area of interests includes Retailing, Services Marketing and Consumer Behavior to name a few.

Priya Sodani (Choudhary) has done her graduation from Mumbai University, Mumbai, and MBA (IB) and PhD from University of Kota, Kota. She was the gold medalist in Master's in International Business in 2009, University of Kota, Kota. Currently, she is working as a Guest Faculty, Department of Commerce and Management, University of Kota, Kota. Earlier, Dr Sodani has worked as a Lecturer in Modi Institute of Management and Technology, Kota, and also worked as a Guest Faculty of Business Administration in J.D.B. Govt Commerce Girls College, Kota. She has work experience in corporate field for 3 years and education field for 11 years. She is a member of the Indian Accounting Association, Kota Branch. She has contributed 11 research articles to various national and international repute journals. She has presented eight papers in national and international conferences and seminars. Dr Sodani is the author of "Indian women in Economic World," which was published in the year 2018. She has participated in many national and international webinars. She is an active member of social groups – Bharat Vikas Parishad, Rotary Padmini, Upasana Welfare society.

Nusrat Yasmeen, Assistant Professor in the Department of Tourism and Hospitality Management, Jamia Millia Islamia, New Delhi, India. She completed her PhD from Jamia Millia Islamia in Medical Tourism. She also did MPhil in Social Culture of Delhi. She is currently a member of the Faculty Committee and PhD program coordinator in the department. She is supervising the students in the diversity of tourism to date. She obtains life membership in Indian Tourism Congress, Indian Hospitality Congress and Rajasthan History Congress. Other than this, she also has a keen interest in topics related to arts, history, culture and heritage too.

Betül Yılmazer, Bachelor's degree from Kocaeli University, Department of Gastronomy and Culinary Arts in 2021. She continues her Master's degree in Tourism Management at Sakarya University of Applied Sciences. Yılmazer conducts studies on sustainable tourism and carrying capacity in tourism. She is married and has two children.

Preface

Traditionally, strategic planning has been used for tangible products and not for intangible services like hospitality or tourism.

The new dynamics have altered the working of the service sector, and strategic planning now plays an important role. Numerous nations have long used tourism as a tool for development, from the national to the local level. To succeed, tourism must be strategically planned within a community framework. The viability of a destination is greatly influenced by its tourism strategy.

There is no doubt that external factors have a significant impact on the tourism industry, as the COVID-19 crisis serves to remind us. There is a search for new branding and organizational strategies among destination marketing organizations (DMOs) throughout the globe. They need to plan strategically for upcoming economic, political, and cultural changes. Planning strategically and executing it effectively is essential not only to overcome immediate obstacles but also to establish, enhance, and maintain a destination's competitiveness throughout the long recovery period. As urban and rural communities seek to increase revenue sources by developing or reviving tourist hot spots, rebranding and restructuring tourist attractions are becoming more common. In today's world, tourism cannot be complete without the involvement of the locals. It gives the tourist a distinctive experience in addition to enhancing the livelihood chances for the local population. Encouragement of local community engagement is a key component of tourism development because it is essential to the long-term viability of the sector.

There are many topics included in this edited book, including sustainable tourism planning, community festivals, culture, community development, local communities, COVID-19 impact on the tourism Industry, Ayurvedic wellness, revitalizing community-based tourism, and applications of smart transportation systems to tourism. Creating this edited book was primarily aimed at spreading knowledge about the "Strategic Tourism Planning for Communities: Restructuring and Rebranding."

This book is the culmination of the meticulous efforts of many minds from India, Sri Lanka, Turkey, Indonesia, Kyrgyzstan, and Bangladesh. We wish to thank all the contributors for their hard work.

Dr Anukrati Sharma
Dr Shruti Arora

Acknowledgment

We want to acknowledge this book under the major research project entitled "Rural Community Development and Engagement through Rural Tourism: Strategies of Strengthening the Capacity of Rajasthan's Villages" under Mahatma Gandhi National Council of Rural Education (MGNCRE), Department of Higher Education, Ministry of Education, Government of India.

Chapter 1

Local Community Participation and Sustainability of Tourism – A Content Analysis

Anukrati Sharma and Shruti Arora

University of Kota, India

Abstract

This chapter investigates the concept and relationship between community pride, involvement, and participation needs in the sustainable tourism development. The study will also try to find out how local communities are involved in various activities and practices for the development of the sustainable tourism. Local community participation in tourism activities has become one of the major principles of sustainable tourism. As tourism is a people-oriented industry, its major functions depend on human resources. A significant number of communities depend on tourism as a primary source of income. Tourism contributes to the growth of a community because it creates a lot of jobs in the various industries associated with tourism.

Keywords: Community involvement; community participation; local community; tourism industry; sustainable tourism

Introduction

Nowadays, one of the foremost sources of income is tourism. It creates job opportunities, earns foreign currency, aids in the construction of infrastructure, and even supports the economy in rural areas. One of the industries with the highest international growth rates, according to tourism literature, is tourism. This is as a consequence of the fact that it brings in billions of dollars every year. Through foreign exchange investment, tourism also makes significant contributions to the economy of the host country (Othman et al., 2012). Additionally, it has a diversity of effects on how the locals conduct their life. In addition to

Strategic Tourism Planning for Communities, 1–10

Copyright © 2024 Anukrati Sharma and Shruti Arora

Published under exclusive licence by Emerald Publishing Limited

doi:10.1108/978-1-83549-015-020241001

meeting the needs of tourists and investors, developing sustainable tourism also considers the requirements of local communities that are immediately impacted by the growth of the tourism industry. In order to achieve sustainable economic, social, cultural, and environmental growth, local community involvement becomes a crucial component of tourism development. However, the majority of local communities in developing nations have few opportunities to contribute to the growth of tourism. Gilmour and Fisher (1991) claim that rather than referring to residents of a particular location, "a community can be defined as a set of persons having mutually recognized interest in the resources of that area" and sustainability of tourism is defined as all forms of tourist-related activities, management, and development that uphold the integrity of the environment, the economy, and society while ensuring the preservation of natural and cultural resources. While safeguarding and enhancing potential for the future, it satisfies the requirements of visitors and host communities in the present. India is often referred to as a tourist ecstasy because of its stunning natural and cultural landscapes. Travelers may benefit from community involvement in their natural experiences by being familiar with local customs, getting involved in cultural pursuits, and having the chance to enjoy nature and the natural ecosystem. Participation of the local community in tourist planning and related activities not only results in support for the tourism business but also plays a key role in attaining sustainable tourism development (Cole, 2006).

Review of Literature

It is impossible to develop any tourism site without involving the local population, and it is not a simple assignment for any kind of agency. In an ideal world, government should play a key role in tourist growth as well as pay attention to environmental and cultural preservation. Prioritizing local communities' interests should be the top priority (Palimbunga, 2018). According to research by Thestane (2019), the community must be involved in tourism planning, decision-making, implementation, and evaluation. Therefore, it is essential to change the paradigm of tourism growth from one that is capitalist-destructive and top-down to one that is bottom-up, ensures justice and the welfare of people, and is sustainable. Sustainable tourism is an initiative to develop tourism that has less detrimental influence on the environment and local culture and fosters a future-focused economic distribution that benefits the neighborhood (Joobi & Satheesh, 2017). The success of the tour depends on improved community leadership, sustain and participation of local administrative systems, strategic plans, comprehension, coordination, and cooperation between local leaders and business owners, support and participation of local administrative bodies, harmonization and teamwork of local business owners, participation in information supply and technological support, efficient convention and tourism bureaus, and community support (Nagarjuna, 2015). Active local community participation in tourist development is necessary to achieve sustainability goals and improve local welfare (Ertuna & Kirbas, 2012). The potential of the tourism business may be destroyed if local community objectives and capacities do not line up with tourism development and planning. Participation of the local community is typically regarded as a key factor in the success of tourism projects (Breugel, 2013). The term "participation in tourism" refers to the proactive involvement of an individual or group of individuals (consciously) in tourism programs from decision-making, planning, implementation, monitoring, evaluation, and problem-solving, with full knowledge that the program or tourism activities will benefit those who participate. In a community within the tourist area, participation from the local community enables sustainable tourism growth. Similar to how tourism has evolved into a travel-related industry that helps a nation's economy, it also enables local communities to provide visitors with the chance to experience and learn about their culture, thereby promoting their own heritage and past (López-Guzmán et al., 2011). According to Kamarudin (2013), community involvement is crucial for the development of the tourism industry because it enables various stakeholders to forge solid political leadership and a shared understanding of the issues at hand. The delegates also offer suggestions for how to foster active community involvement. Researchers have shown that although tourism brings many positive impacts, it can also cause the loss of sustainability in terms of economic, environmental, and social value of the site, especially if it is not properly planned (Adamson & Bromiley, 2008). Local communities are defined by Scherl and Edwards (2007) as groupings of individuals with a shared identity and who may participate in a variety of connected livelihood activities. Additionally, they point out that local populations frequently have customary rights pertaining to the region and its natural resources as well as a solid connection to the region on a cultural, social, economic, and spiritual level. According to Aref et al. (2010), a community is a cluster of people who live or work in the same region and share certain common cultures or interests. The decisions made on tourism should be focused on these residents (Choi & Sirakaya, 2005). Locals can be crucial in the promotion of a destination since they are far more familiar with the local tourism product than outsiders are. In order to obtain the best support from host communities, it is decisive to engross them in the development of tourism in a more favorable way. According to Dodds and Butler (2010), tourism is a complex system with many stakeholders, and community involvement in the form of community-based tourism can aid these communities in achieving sustainable tourist growth.

Communities therefore need to be aware of both internal and external constraints on local participation. With the awareness of its economic role in supporting stagnant economies and its capacity to unify local community inhabitants, tourism is becoming more and more recognized as a crucial community tool (Fennell, 2003). At the local level, tourism provided chances for employment and revenue that were direct, indirect, and induced, promoting regional and local economic growth (Aref, 2010; Coccossis, 2004). Tourism development, according to Godfrey and Clarke (2000), is a continuous process. It is best used as an addition to a local community's efforts to improve because it is not an economic panacea (Godfrey & Clarke, 2000). Local engagement promotes community empowerment, decision-making, and the recognition of issues and challenges unique to the area (France, 2003). Basically, the involvement of the local community is crucial to this industry because it guarantees tourists have an outstanding vacation while also allowing the community to profit from tourists' visits.

Objective of the Study

- Emphasize the importance of local communities for the growth of sustainable tourism.
- To become familiar with various Indian local groups that promotes tourism.
- To be aware of the obstacles or difficulties that local community engagement faces.
- Advice on how localities might promote tourism in the area.

Methodology

The study analyses literature in the form of journal articles, research papers, blogs, newspapers, and other forms using the content analysis method.

Various journal databases and search engines, including UGC, Scopus, Science Direct, and Taylor and Francis, were used to compile research articles, news stories, and blogs that were published between 2000 and 2022 for the analysis.

Role of Local Communities for Sustainable Tourism Development

One of the key components of tourism development is local community involvement because it is essential to the long-term viability of the tourism sector.

Involving the local community offers significant benefits for the people' lifestyle, as well as for the natural, cultural, and traditional characteristics that make the area attractive to tourists. By promoting local ownership of guide services, transportation, lodging, restaurants, handicrafts, and local product stores, local engagement can stop the leaking of foreign currency. Homestay or agro-tourism vacations boost local participation even more because they give visitors an enriching alternative to the mass market. To increase people's trust and confidence in tourist development, the local community must be involved in decision- and policymaking processes. The community's involvement guarantees that plans and service delivery are improved while encouraging a sense of community involvement among those who share a similar goal.

The concept of sustainable development is considered to be one of the most fundamental ideas. It aims to lessen the conflict, discord, and environmental degradation that may arise from interactions and overlaps between the tourism industry, tourists, and local communities on the one hand, and the environment and the environment on the other. Therefore, community participation and goodwill are essential for the success of tourism growth. Making residents feel welcome to express their opinions and collecting various viewpoints from everyone who wishes to engage are the two main goals of community involvement.

There are various roles played by local community (as shown below in Table 1.1) like:

Table 1.1. Types of Community Participation (Role Play by Local Community).

1. *Passive Participation (Compliance):* People engage in passive participation when administration makes unilateral announcements informing them of upcoming events or past ones. Only external professionals should have access to the information.	2. *Information Sharing:* Participants don't have the chance to make decisions; instead, they respond to questions posed by extractive researchers utilizing questionnaire surveys or other similar methods.
3. *Material Incentives:* People engage by contributing resources, such as labor, in exchange for food, money, or other material incentives; this is sometimes referred to as participation, but when the incentives run out, people have no vested interest in continuing the behaviors.	4. *Participation in Consultation:* People participate by being consulted, and an outsider hears the opinions and may change them in light of the responses, but they do not share in the decision-making process.
5. *Interactive Participation (Co-Learning):* Participants engage in cooperative analysis, the creation of action plans, and the construction or improvement of regional institutions. Participation is viewed as a right, not just a way to carry out a project's objectives.	6. *Functional Participation (Cooperation):* After significant decisions have been made, people participate by establishing teams to carry out predefined project-related goals.

Source: Compiled by authors.

Community members' participation is crucial for a successful representative democracy generally (shown in Fig. 1.1). Public engagement is crucial for people's empowerment in a democracy. Therefore, local communities would not only have the chance to speak up for themselves but also have the chance to participate actively, own stakes in certain projects, and show less opposition to novel ideas and plans. Local communities can also contribute fresh, innovative concepts that could lead to more profitable economic endeavors.

Fig. 1.1.   Importance of Community Participation in Tourism.
Source: Compiled by authors.

Few Examples of Local Communities of India Involved in Tourism Development

By staying in homestays or farm stays and partaking in activities like crafting and cooking together, storytelling, and village tours, tourists can experience local life as it is lived by locals. To promote tourism in local or regional areas that are rich in traditional, performing and visual arts and crafts, food or cuisines, their living patterns, etc., new destinations are formed and new brands are produced, such as:

- Darap, a small village in West Sikkim, is proud to be a part of Sikkim's most comprehensive limboo culture legacy. There are adventurous activities available, including trekking and excursions.
- East Sikkim (a little village called Pastanga) – Rhododendrons, orchids, and diverse bird species are among the area's top attractions. Mountain biking and trekking are also available.
- Uttarakhand (Goat Village) – This area is known for its earthen Garhwali huts with views of the mountains, where organic farming and agriculture, including goat breeding, are practiced.
- Odisha (South Koraput district: Pottery Village) – Visitors can explore the village at their own pace, go to the potters' colony and learn pottery, take nature hikes in the nearby hills, interact with the local tribal women (who, if approached, will perform beautiful singing and dancing), and discover how to make local cuisine.
Here, community-based homestays are rather widespread.
- Himachal Pradesh (Pragpur – Heritage Village) – For those who are more active, there are delightful nature hikes, picnics by the Beas, water sports at Nadaun, or rides on the charming Kangra Valley narrow gauge train, for which the evening signal is still illuminated by an oil lamp. It is marketed as an illustration of local involvement in tourism and is perfect for village land tourism.
- Kerala – Homestays have been established by villagers for visitors in the village of Mothakkara, which is in the Wayanad district. To perform for tourists, women drummers studied the Chenda art style of Kerala. Additionally, mini

ceramic workshops for the travelers were organized. During the village trip, some of the village families serve traditional meals to the visitors.

- Ladakh (a little village called Tarchit) – The women were clad in their vibrant traditional clothing, known as kos. "Om mani padme hum" was repeated by village elders as they spun prayer wheels in their hands slowly and rhythmically, a fantastic illustration of how to coexist with nature. Snow leopards are stunning, uncommon wild cats that are well-represented in this area. Communities are also given encouragement to create homestays so that visitors can experience the Ladakhi people's warm hospitality and traditional way of life.
- Madhaya Pradesh (little regions like Malwa, Nimar, and Mahakaushal) – This region highlights the distinctive culture of its native and tribal populations. Tourists are provided with luxurious house stays designed specifically for them. In addition to experiencing the local cuisine, cooking techniques, dress, dialect, rituals and customs, traditions, traditional modes of transportation, jewelry, makeup, musical instruments, traditional healing systems, art, spirituality, fairs and festivals, rural games, ways of preserving food, customs, and hospitality, they also go on excursions throughout the village.
- Districts of Jhansi, Jalaun, Lalitpur, Chitrakoot, Banda, Hamirpur, and Mahoba in Uttar Pradesh's Bundelkhand area – It boasts robust traditions, culture, and ethnicity, including Rai dance and Bundeli music performances by the locals. It is also well renowned for its handlooms and textile industry, where tourists may buy handcrafted goods like handmade paper.
- Gujarat (a typical Indian village called Baradpani) – The homestays are comfortable to stay in because they are composed of mud, cow dung, and wood. Without air conditioning or ceiling fans, it is tolerable to stay inside all year round because to the heating and cooling effects of cow dung. On a chulha, the indoor kitchen is where most meals are prepared (traditional firewood kiln). The settlement, which is tucked away in the Sahayadri Mountains, is a veritable haven for nature lovers, complete with flowing streams and organic farms.

Few examples of local based community–based tourism experiences can be like cooking and tasting local food, visiting a local market, working on the field, experiencing the coffee process, fishing or sailing with locals, biking tour around the village, handcrafting or painting.

Barriers to Local Community Participation

While community involvement was crucial in the development of a destination, it is also evident that many tourist sites, despite having enormous tourism potential, are still undeveloped and the community does not take the initiative to get involved in procedures related to tourism. According to research by Azah et al. (2014), there are both internal (cultural hurdles) and external (operational and structural) impediments that prevent community engagement in the development of tourism. According to Tosun (2000), there are numerous barriers to community participation in many developing nations, including paternalism, racism, clientele, a lack of knowledge and resources, a lack of financial support, and other structural issues. These obstacles make it difficult to carry out the actual process of community participation. The welfare of the local population in the tourist sites is not, however, always guaranteed by the growth of tourism in different locations. This is due to the fact that many locations are still managed by capitalists who are primarily from outside the tourism region (Sidiq & Resnawaty, 2019). While theoretically local community involvement in tourism is thought to be able to accomplish the development of sustainable tourism destinations, in reality there are many difficulties and obstacles (Campbell, 1999; Dogra & Gupta, 2012; Scheyvens, 2002; Shah & Gupta, 2000). Few barriers to local community participation (as shown below in Fig. 1.2).

Suggestions to Develop Sustainable Tourism Through Local Community Involvement

There are numerous things to keep in mind and pay special attention to while promoting local tourism with the support of the local community. It's crucial that both the local population and the visitor have a good time. Communities can play a significant role in the growth of the tourism industry. The idea of sustainable development has been proposed for improvement of community life quality in order to encourage community engagement (Lo & Janta, 2020). The authors make the following recommendations for the growth of local sustainable tourism:

- development and bolstering of community language proficiency and technical tourism management skills;
- offering financial aid to community groups so they can carry out tourism-related projects;
- training qualified workers for the tourism industry, including tour guides, restaurants, and hotels;
- educating the populace about the advantages of tourism while offering coaching and training;
- creation of initiatives to inspire and motivate the locals to support tourism-related activities in the area;
- official community participation in the local tourism industry's planning processes.

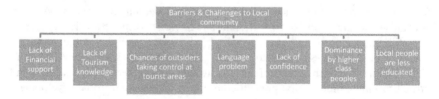

Fig. 1.2.   Barriers to Local Community Participation.
Source: Compiled by authors.

Conclusion

Our analysis leads us to the conclusion that community involvement in tourism development is essential if it is founded on the conviction that the community is best equipped to determine what is required. When the community is involved in all aspects of the tourism development stage, including planning, decision-making, implementation, and oversight of development initiatives, full involvement is achieved. Tourists go mostly to experience local communities, their way of life, and the goods that make up other cultures. In several areas, including tour guides, languages, communication, and expressing viewpoints, the local population's skills are still lacking.

References

Adamson, D., & Bromiley, R. (2008). *Community empowerment in practice: Lessons from communities first*. Joseph Rowntree Foundation.

Aref, F. (2010). Residents' attitudes towards tourism impacts: A case study of Shiraz, Iran. *Tourism Analysis, 15*(2), 253–261.

Aref, F., Gill, S. S., & Farshid, A. (2010). Tourism development in local communities: As a community development approach. *Journal of American Science, 6*, 155–161.

Azah, N., Azman, I., & Ibrahim, Y. (2014). Barriers to community participation in tourism development in Island destination. *Tourism, Leisure and Global Change, 1*, 90–105.

Breugel, L. V. (2013). *Community-based tourism: Local participation and perceived impacts a comparative study between two communities in Thailand*. Master's thesis. http://tourismlibrary.tat.or.th/medias/RU0232/RU0232_fulltext.pdf

Campbell, L. M. (1999). Ecotourism in rural developing communities. *Annals of Tourism Research, 26*, 534–553.

Choi, H. S., & Sirakaya, E. (2005). Measuring residents' attitude toward sustainable tourism: Development of sustainable tourism attitude scale. *Journal of Travel Research, 43*, 380–394.

Coccossis, H. (2004). *Sustainable tourism and carrying capacity*. Ashgate Publishing.

Cole, S. (2006). Cultural tourism, community participation and empowerment. In *Cultural tourism in a changing world politics, participation and (Re) presentation politics, participation and (Re) presentation* (pp. 89–99). Channel View Publications.

Dodds, R., & Butler, R. (2010). Barriers to implementing sustainable tourism policy in mass tourism destinations. *Tourismos: An International Multidisciplinary Journal of Tourism, 5*(1), 35–53.

Dogra, R., & Gupta, A. (2012). Barriers to community participation in tourism development: Empirical evidence from a rural destination. *South Asian Journal of Tourism and Heritage, 5*, 131–142.

Ertuna, B., & Kirbas, G. (2012). Local community involvement in rural tourism development: The case of Kastamonu, Turkey. *PASOS. Revista de Turismo y Patrimonio Cultural, 10*(2), 17–24.

Fennell, D. A. (2003). *Ecotourism: An introduction* (2nd ed.). Routledge.

France, L. (2003). Local participation in tourism in the West Indian Islands. In B. Faulkner, E. Laws, & G. Moscardo (Eds.), *Embracing and managing change in tourism* (pp. 257–268). Routledge.

Gilmour, D. A., & Fisher, R. J. (1991). *Villagers, forests and foresters: The philosophy, process and practices of community forestry in Nepal.* Sahyogi Press.

Godfrey, K., & Clarke, J. (2000). *The tourism development handbook: A practical approach to planning and marketing.* Continuum.

Joobi, V. P., & Satheesh, E. K. (2017). Local community participation in responsible tourism – A case of Kumarakam Panchayath in Kerala. *International Journal of Current Research in Multidisciplinary, 2*(11), 05–11.

Kamarudin, K. H. (2013). *Local stakeholders participation in developing sustainable Community Based Rural Tourism (CBRT): The case of three villages in the East Coast of Malaysia* (pp. 33–40). International Conference on Tourism Development.

Lo, Y. C., & Janta, P. (2020). Resident's perspective on developing community-based tourism – A qualitative study of Muen Ngoen Kong community, Chiang Mai, Thailand. *Frontiers in Psychology.* https://doi.org/10.3389/fpsyg.2020.01493

López-Guzmán, T., Borges, O., & Cerezo, J. M. (2011). Community-based tourism and local socio-economic development: A case study in Cape Verde. *African Journal of Business Management, 5*, 1608–1617.

Nagarjuna, G. (2015). Local community involvement in tourism: A content analysis of websites of wildlife resorts. *Atna Journal of Tourism Studies, 10*(1) https://doi.org/10.12727/ajts.13.2

Othman, R., Salleh, N. H., & Sarmidi, T. (2012). Analysis of causal relationship between tourism development, economic growth and foreign direct investment: An ardl approach. *Journal of Applied Sciences, 12*(12), 1245–1254. https://doi.org/10.3923/jas.2012.1245.1254

Palimbunga, I. P. (2018). Keterlibatan masyarakat dalam pengembangan pariwisata di desa wisata Tablanusu, Papua. *Jurnal Master Pariwisata (JUMPA), 05*(01), 93–210.

Scherl, L. M., & Edwards, S. (2007). Tourism, indigenous and local communities and protected areas in developing nations. In R. Bushell, & P. F. J. Eagles (Eds.), *Tourism and protected areas: Benefits beyond boundaries.* CABI International.

Scheyvens, R. (2002). *Tourism for development; empowering communities.* Prentice Hall.

Shah, K., & Gupta, V. (2000). *Tourism, the poor and other stakeholders: Experience in Asia this edited version.* Russell Press Ltd.

Sidiq, A. J., & Resnawaty, R. (2019). Pengembangan desa wisata berbasis partisipasi masyarakat lokal di desa wisata Linggarjati Kuningan, Jawa Barat. *Proc KS: Riset dan PKM, 4*(1), 38–44.

Thestane, R. M. (2019). Local community participation in tourism development: The case of Kaste villages in Lestoho. *Athens Journal of Tourism, 6*(2), 123–140.

Tosun, C. (2000). Limits to community participation in the tourism development process in developing countries. *Tourism Management, 21*, 613–633.

Chapter 2

Community Perception on Tourism Development: A Case Study of Riverston, Matale, Sri Lanka

S. P. M. B. Jayakody[a], R. S. S. W. Arachchi[b] and P. G. S. S. Pattiyagedara[a]

[a]Uva Wellassa University, Sri Lanka
[b]Sabaragamuwa University of Sri Lanka, Sri Lanka

Abstract

Riverston, Sri Lanka, is famous for its natural and cultural significance. The tourism industry is emerging there and expanding with more community engagement. Riverston being a community-based tourism site, this study aimed at discovering the perception of the Riverston community on tourism development further focusing on the market opportunities, challenges, and strategies for the way forward. Data were collected from the Riverston area community who engage in tourism through in-depth interviews with semi-structured questions, and the sample was selected based on the purposive sampling technique. Data were analyzed through content analysis. The findings disclosed that challenging the authentic culture, traditional livelihood shifting toward tourism, lack of awareness and knowledge of the tourism industry among the community, the impact of legal restrictions on the community, and lack of education are the sociocultural challenges for the community on tourism development. The Riverston area is getting developed in terms of infrastructure with tourism development, and that benefits the living conditions of the community. Further, results indicated forest conversation policies had impacted the community's living in high magnitude. It persuades people to move away from agriculture to the tourism sector. In addition, the timely need for a well-planned sustainable tourism approach and awareness from ground-level tourism practitioners was underscored by the data set.

Strategic Tourism Planning for Communities, 11–21
Copyright © 2024 S. P. M. B. Jayakody, R. S. S. W. Arachchi and P. G. S. S. Pattiyagedara
Published under exclusive licence by Emerald Publishing Limited
doi:10.1108/978-1-83549-015-020241002

Keywords: Community perception; sustainability; tourism development; market opportunities; challenges and strategies

Introduction

The tourism business is currently one of the world's largest and fastest-expanding service sectors. Many changes are occurring in tourism's numerous aspects due to its dynamic character. The tourism industry's growing impacts expanded to other economic sectors, increasing the country's macroeconomic performance. It contributes to economic prosperity by creating job opportunities, increasing national income, and improving the country's balance of payments, for example. Tourism contributes greatly to the gross domestic product (GDP) of developing nations, both directly and indirectly. Furthermore, it contributes significantly to poverty reduction and regional development in poor nations (Hausmann et al., 2009).

Sri Lanka is a tropical island, and its natural environment is famed for its great scenic beauty and diversity and has a rich environment to engage with the tourism development. For the rural social context, Sri Lanka had before colonization, Sri Lanka has a rural cultural asset that can be utilized as a form of cultural tourism, rural cultural tourism. In certain rustic areas of Sri Lanka, in the countryside, still rural social context is visible, particularly in the villages around the Knuckles range as well. The Knuckles forest range is one of Sri Lanka's most important tropical rainforests. The Knuckles range and its surrounding massif is without a doubt the most picturesque area of Sri Lanka's highlands, including some of the island's most rugged, stunning, and breathtaking mountain landscapes. The Knuckles Peaks are known locally as Dumbara, which means "mountains shrouded in mist" (Bandaratillake, 2005). Riverston is one of the villages located in the Knuckles range. Riverston, Sri Lanka, is famous for its natural and cultural significance. The tourism industry is emerging there and expanding with more community engagement.

Forest formations, a broad range of rare and indigenous flora and wildlife, and some spectacular Sri Lankan mountain views may all be found in the Knuckles National Heritage and Wilderness area. It's a hiker's and mountain biker's dream, with several hilly paths that take you across clear rivers, through deep woods, past rushing waterfalls and beautiful tea plantations, and along terraced rice fields. However, policymakers and responsible individuals have paid less attention to the exploitation of precious resources as a means of improving rural livelihoods.

In such a context, this study aims at the community's perception of tourism development in Riverston, Matale, Sri Lanka. This will open up more avenues for tourism development and community engagement through more tourism concepts, to fill the above vacuum in Sri Lanka. The research objectives have been formulated by catering to the selected tourism destination, Riverston, Matale, Sri Lanka, as follows:

- to identify the community perception of tourism development in Riverston, Matale, Sri Lanka;
- to identify the strategies to overcome challenges in tourism development in Riverston, Matale, Sri Lanka.

Literature Review

Community Perception

Individual experiences are linked to a collective experience through the idea of "community perception." The meaning of the perception is defined as "the process by which each individual selects, organizes, and evaluates sensory stimulations from the external environment to provide meaningful experiences for himself or herself," (Atmadja & Sills, 2016). Andriotis (2003) has pointed out the importance of a community's attitudes and perceptions toward tourism through a factor analysis under a few key dimensions such as economic benefit, cultural and infrastructural, environmental, overall benefit, development options, family benefits, spending and investment, leakage, and outside intervention. It has revealed that the community does not accept tourism just because of the economic benefit but also the restoration of historical, cultural, and infrastructural activities that go hand in hand with enhancing the destination image. In addition, it has also been found that socially and environmentally concerned families perceive that they have not gained a significant benefit from tourism development since they highly consider the environmental cost incurred by tourism expansion.

Tourism Development

Tourism development refers to the finest service execution in the tour, travel, and transportation sectors. Tourism agents give a complete comfort-level zone in hotels, food tailored to your preferences, and a whole journey within your budget. It's also known as an increase in the number of tourist services supplied by tourism agents. Tourist development refers to anything created by a tourism agency in this industry (Miles, 2018). Tourism is currently one of Sri Lanka's most important sectors in Sri Lanka. The famed beaches in the southern and eastern portions of the nation, historical heritage sites in the center of the country, and hotels in the mountainous areas of the country is the island's main tourist attractions (Aslam, 2011). Further development of tourism in fact to the small and medium-sized enterprises (SMEs), particularly in developing nations, contributes significantly to both GDP and employment.

Community Perception on Tourism Development

According to social exchange theory (Lankford & Howard, 2004), residents are more likely to have a favorable attitude toward tourism activities if they perceive bigger economic gains or personal benefits from tourism in their areas. Investigating the host community's perceptions of tourism is important because it influences their behavior toward tourism (Andriotis, 2003). As a result, before planning and managing sustainable tourism, a good understanding of the host community's attitudes and interests is required. According to the literature on residents' opinions of tourism, inhabitants' levels of support for tourism development are dependent on their contentment with the quality of life in the destination as a result of tourism (Andereck & Nayaupane, 2011). Many studies have led to the development of quality-of-life indicators. Economic indicators such as income, tax, and prices; environmental indicators such as cleanliness, peace, and safety; and social–cultural indicators such as community identity and recreational opportunities for residents are all examples of tourism-specific indicators of quality of life in the literature (Woo et al., 2015). Community-based tourism is an indigenous effort, that should be aimed at individual and community well-being, communities frequently lack financial resources and capacities, and community-based tourism faces marketing or market access challenges. (Giampiccoli & Saayman, 2018). The word "community" in community-based tourism must be understood to mean disadvantaged or marginalized community members of society (Tasci et al., 2013). Another important aspect of the community perception of tourism is that disadvantaged communities should be the beneficiaries: they should have control over, ownership of, and management of community-based development (Nataraja & Devidasan, 2014).

Community Perception on Tourism Development in Riverston, Matale, Sri Lanka

Local visitation has been consistently growing in Knuckles and Riverston over the past 5 years, with local visitors arriving at the Illukkumbura/Pitawala Panthana/Atanwala/Walpolamulla, entry point exceeding 70,000 people in 2017 (a 253% increase from 2013). Foreign tourists represent an exponentially smaller number of visitors to Knuckles and Riverston conservation rainforest, accounting for just 1.2% of all visitors in 2017. Some of the major reasons for the small number of foreign visitors include a lack of adequate tourism lodging (accommodation) in the region and a lack of awareness in regards to the natural and cultural attractions Knuckles Conservation Forest has to offer both issues that will need to be addressed to promote foreign tourists' visitation.

From the creation of plans through the implementation of management prescriptions, the Riverston Range is managed with a high level of community engagement. Through community-based groups, they participate in forest conservation, enrichment planting, and other management operations. Participation in ecotourism activities is also organized with community-based groups in mind. The new mechanisms safeguard the forest while also benefiting local villages through employment and having their voices heard in decision-making. There are 77 settlements in the area, and it offers a lot of potential for nature-based tourism and pleasure (Bandaratillake, 2005). Still, a key issue in the community residing in

Riverston Range is the poverty that has been coupled with remoteness and the lack of infrastructural facilities in the area.

Methodology

The study focused on the community's perception of tourism development in Riverston, Matale, Sri Lanka. The population of this study is all the community and stakeholders who live in the Riverston area. To achieve research objectives, 10 community residents and stakeholders were selected purposively for the sample. The semi-structured direct interviews were conducted to gain stakeholders' perceptions of tourism development in Riverston. This research is based on the qualitative research approach. Collected data were analyzed by using content analysis methods.

Results and Discussion

Identify the Community Perception of Tourism Development in Riverston, Matale, Sri Lanka

The first objective of the study was to identify the community's perception of sociocultural habitat and changes with tourism development in Riverston, Matale. The community's perception of sociocultural habitat and changes in Riverston is mainly due to tourism development. Seven respondents out of the 09 have mentioned there were different changes in their cultural image, traditional livelihood, and daily traditional lifestyle of the community. The rustic and rural livelihood of the community has been changed with new trends. Due to the changes in traditional livelihood, the authenticity of the village also changed. The main social problem many respondents have mentioned is the drug addiction of the young generation in the area.

> As we have heard young community take drugs nowadays. They like to maintain relationships with travellers and visitors. People used to be odd people who had a when-behaved culture. Now it's all destroyed because of the politics. Politicians try to fulfil their requirements. (Respondent 07, Personal communication, 2022)

The majority of the respondents highlighted it is clear that the community in Riverston has an idea about tourism and the ability to integrate tourism with most of the aspects bound with life. They have understood the value of historical, cultural, and natural heritage for the tourism industry and why Riverston is special to promote as a tourist destination in Sri Lanka.

Tourism can combine everything. So, this is a business in which everyone should work together. Everyone has to work collaboratively to get an advantage from tourism. (Respondent 02, Personal communication, 2022)

The daily traditional lifestyle of the community has been interrupted due to forest conservation laws. People lost their lands and income sources as a result. Further, they have mentioned a way of living which has then shut down with rules and regulations imposed by the government to ban chena and cardamom cultivation in this area through the Forest Conservation Act. Despite banning chena and cardamom cultivations, results also indicate that legislative actions have been made to conserve the Knuckles Forest range where Riverston stands. The area is designated as a climatic reserve and a conservation forest. It is a national biosphere reserve now. All the communities in the forest area are prohibited by the law.

Cardamom cultivation especially happened in areas like; Atanwala, Pitawala, Gonamada, and KMP Forest likewise. But forest conservation laws under the past president banned Cardamom and Chena cultivation. (Respondent 09, Personal communication, 2022)

Based on the ideas on community perception about education and how it affects their children's future and how education harmonizes with tourism development, Riverston being a rural site with the least facilities, the community is less experienced because they are framed to that social and geographical context. For its natural and cultural value, even though tourism emerged, the community who work as tourism service providers have a lesser knowledge and understanding of the industry as well as their hospitality management skills. According to the findings, the literacy rate of the community in Riverston is at a lower level and the tendency for higher education in this area is lesser. The educational qualifications of the community are also lesser compared to other areas of Sri Lanka.

Today, the community in Riverston is more engaged in tourism, but at the same time, they have been hit by unexpected issues occurred as the COVID-19 pandemic and the Easter bomb attack which affected the tourism industry in a high magnitude. Due to overdependence on tourism by the community drifting apart from the traditional way of living, the impact of these sudden issues on their lives is huge. The results also explain that the community has understood by experience the uncertainty of tourist income.

The tourism in the Riverston area is still blooming. So, if we take it as a percentage, nearly 70% of the people in this area are involved in tourism activities directly or indirectly. With the pandemic situation, they have been adopting their old lifestyle again. (Respondent 06, Personal communication, 2022)

Due to the tourism development in Riverston, income sources and occupational opportunities were created in the community. Along with women's employment, self-employment level has been increased, which has helped the community to be financially stable. Results also state the impact of tourism emergence on urban migration of the rural community. Fruit, trickle and honey vendors, lunch packet and candy vendors, herbal drink and toddy vendors, and food and lodging vendors are all highlighted. Food and beverage vendors derive 80% of their income directly from tourism. Hotels and villas managers, cooks, kitchen helpers, stewards, cleaners, gardeners, maintainers, securities, and night and day weathermen are some employment opportunities that create tourism development in the area. Other than that, construction officers, construction laborers, storekeepers, etc., are some other jobs that were generated because of the uprising of the tourism industry. It also provides an opportunity for small and medium entrepreneurs to start businesses related to the tourism sector.

> Women make up the majority of self-employed economically mobilized as the area's tourism improves. …self-employment in the tourism industry in the Riverston area. …opportunity for them to improve their financial situation. (Respondent 01, Personal communication, 2022)

According to the responses of the community, the researcher has identified that Riverston is dominated by local tourists. The main reason for the poof arrival of foreigners is the lack of infrastructure. The road access, quality accommodation and lodging options in the Riverston area are limited, there is no large hotels, no proper service, etc., but with the development of tourism, some positive things also happened. The development of public sanitary facilities in the Pitawala Patana area, Thelgamu Oya area, Sera Ella area, regional road developments and nearby village bridge repair projects are some of them. The researchers have identified that most of the visitors who come to the Riverston area are local visitors. Hence, souvenirs and handicraft stalls are not very profitable. When talking about the entrepreneurs, the fruit, treacle and honey vendors, lunch packet and candy vendors, herbal drink and toddy vendors, and food and lodging vendors are all highlighted, and they bloom with the development of the tourism industry.

The results of the study further indicate that the community in Riverston does not have a clear idea about sustainability and sustainable tourist products. Further, they have not yet recognized the need to go sustainable just trying to earn their living. Thus, they have not focused on sustainable tourism management or businesses. The data set also suggests that due to the lack of knowledge about sustainable tourism and the value of a sustainable way of living, the tourism service providers in the Riverston community do not think of eco-friendly practices or any waste management plan. Even though Riverston is a rich natural heritage site, the community has no knowledge and understanding of the biodiversity and the endemic flora and fauna in the area. Since the Riverston area is a highly sensitive bio-diversity area, cutting trees is prohibited. However, Illegal tree-cutting and construction are happening in the area due to the political influence.

> The majority of the community doesn't have a proper idea about how sustainability should harmonize with tourism development. Most of the hotel owners, as well as the service staff, don't have an idea about how to do business sustainably. They don't have proper knowledge of how to manage a business sustainably. (Respondent 02, Personal communication, 2022)

According to the findings, the researchers have further identified that in the Riverston area, the laws under forest conservation are higher. Because of that, now most of the forest area is under control. But earlier people cut down trees to build new buildings. Based on the responses of the respondents, the findings of the study and a summary of the contents can be illustrated by the researchers in Table 2.1.

Table 2.1. Content Visualization of the Interviews.

The community perception of tourism development in Riverston, Matale, Sri Lanka	
Sociocultural	Culture, image, and traditional livelihood
	Awareness and knowledge about the industry
	Legal restrictions
	Education
Economic	Impact on livelihood and living standards
	Income sources and occupational opportunities
	Infrastructure and SME
Environment	Sustainable approach
	Impact on forest conservation

Identify the Strategies to Overcome Challenges in the Tourism Industry in Riverston, Matale, Sri Lanka

According to the community perception and findings, the researchers have identified four main issues that have arisen with the tourism development in the Riverston area, and the community has suggested a few strategies to overcome them. The four main issues that arise are minimum opportunities for jobs for the local community, lack of economy and infrastructure in the Riverston area, lack of knowledge about the tourism industry, how it works, biodiversity and forest conservation, and no proper mechanism to improve destination products and visitor experience and to improve destination image.

According to the findings, the researchers have further observed that the local community is not getting enough job opportunities with tourism development. But they are getting some opportunities like souvenir selling, selling of food parcels, providing accommodation, and local tour guide services. So, the community proposed some suggestions. Some of them are that the government should have a proper mechanism to train the local tour guides, and they should be trained under the guidance of the wildlife department. Then local tour guides need proper and professional equipment. The other point is when appointing the guides, they should give priority to the residents. And they are suggesting that the residents who do retail business need proper places and loan facilities to carry on the business. In a data-gathering interview with unemployed youth, they stated that they desire to engage in self-employment related to tourism in the area. This is an opportunity for them to improve their financial situation. It will have a good impact on reducing rural–urban migration and community youth unrest.

According to the findings, the main reasons for the poor arrival of foreigners are a lack of infrastructure, lack of road access, contented accommodations, and satisfying service. On the one hand, bad infrastructure facilities diminish tourism demand in the area, while on the other, infrastructures have a direct impact on livelihood development.

The community in Riverston does not have the required hospitality management knowledge, understanding, guest handling skills, and marketing knowledge to develop the tourism industry there. Therefore, it suggests that training programs that would address the knowledge and skills gap of the tourism practitioners in Riverston would serve their best to develop tourism. Results also mention the need to upgrade the guiding knowledge and skills, language skills of the children or the school leavers or anyone interested in tour guiding in Riverston, the reason being the lack of education due to lack of tendency for education in childhood. The community also lacks knowledge about biodiversity, the value or importance of natural heritage, and an understanding of the need for biodiversity conservation. Being Riverston a more sensitive natural destination, it is a must to fill those gaps to educate the tourism service providers in Riverston about a sustainable way of doing business.

Further, there is no proper mechanism to improve destination products and visitor experience to enhance destination image. And they need access to those places, and to do that, it should develop the infrastructure facilities like roads, car parks, safe lockers, etc. The people who provide the accommodation service, need good knowledge and awareness about the business and to handle guests without any complaints. There should be more opportunities to do adventure activities in that area, so it needs to develop infrastructure for that. There should be a place to rent out camping, hiking, and trekking equipment. There should be programs for tourists to experience cultural livelihood, like cooking classes, village tours, and village house tours. To build up the image of the destination, the local community who live in the Riverston area must need good directions. Accommodation providers need good awareness to provide a good experience and excellent service to their customers. People need a very good understanding and awareness of the biodiversity importance in that area and how to give value to that environment.

Conclusion

According to the findings, the researchers identified that earlier residents in Riverston do cardamom, tea, chena, paddy, and vegetable cultivation. But after the 1990s, people in that area shifted to other industries like garment jobs, retail shops, government jobs, etc. With the uprising of tourism, new occupation opportunities have arisen. So, most locals are now shifting to the tourism industry. The finding suggested that residents who live in the Riverston area have some knowledge about the tourism industry. But they don't know how to provide standard service in the hotels and guiding service. The literacy rate of the community in Riverston is at a lower level, and the tendency for higher education in this area is lesser. The educational qualifications of the community are also lesser compared to other areas of Sri Lanka. The results found that due to the lack of knowledge about sustainable tourism and the value of a sustainable way of living, the tourism service providers in the Riverston community do not think of eco-friendly practices or any waste management plan.

Objective two of this study is to identify the strategies to overcome challenges in the tourism industry in Riverston, Matale, Sri Lanka. According to the community perception and findings, the researchers have identified four main issues that have arisen with the tourism development in the Riverston area and the community has suggested a few strategies to overcome them. There are minimum opportunities in jobs for the local community, a lack of economy and infrastructure in the Riverston area, a lack of knowledge about the tourism industry, how it works, bio-diversity and forest conservation, and no proper mechanism to improve destination products and visitor experience and to improve destination image. Under the discussion on minimum opportunities in jobs for the local community proposed some suggestions. Some of them have mentioned that the government should have a proper mechanism to train local tour guides. It should be done under the guidance of the Wildlife Department. Then local tour guides need proper and professional equipment. Further residents who do retail business need proper places and loan facilities to carry on the business. It will have a good impact on reducing rural–urban migration and community youth unrest and improve their financial situation. The development of the infrastructure also caused the tourism development of the Riverston area. Training programs that would address the knowledge and skills gap of tourism practitioners are more important.

References

Andereck, K. L., & Nayaupane, G. P. (2011). Exploring the nature of tourism and quality of life perception among residents. *Journal of Travel Research*, *50*(3), 248–260.

Andriotis, K. (2003). Tourism in crete, A form of modernisation. *Current Issues in Tourism*, *6*(1), 23–53.

Aslam, M. S. (2011, February). The role of alternative tourism for sustainable rural development (Sinhala). *Economic Review - Colombo People's Bank Publication*, 28–35.

Atmadja, S. S., & Sills, E. O. (2016). What is a "community perception" of REDD+? A systematic review of how perceptions of REDD+ have been elicited and reported in the literature. *PLoS One*, *11*(11), e0155636. https://doi.org/10.1371/journal.pone.0155636

Bandaratillake, H. (2005). In P. B. Durst, C. Brown, H. D. Tacio, & M. Ishikawa (Eds.), *In search of excellence: Exemplary forest management in Asia and the Pacific; The Knuckles range: Protecting livelihoods, protecting forests*. RAP Publication.

Giampiccoli, A., & Saayman, M. (2018). Community-based tourism development model and community participation. *African Journal of Hospitality, Tourism and Leisure, 7*(4), 1–27.

Hausmann, R., Tyson, L. D., & Zahidi, S. (2009). *Global gender gap report*. World Economic Forum. http://www3.weforum.org/docs/WEF_GenderGap_Report_2010.pdf

Lankford, S. V., & Howard, D. R. (2004). Developing a tourism impact attitude scale. *Annals of Tourism Research, 21*(1), 121–139.

Miles, D. (2018). *Travel agent: Holiday, tours and travels package provider*. Quora. https://www.quora.com/What-is-tourism-development

Nataraja, T. C., & Devidasan, S. D. (2014). Community-based tourism: A case study on the potential of Shivanahalli village. *Compass, 1*(2), 67–75.

Tasci, A. D. S., Semrad, K. J., & Yilmaz, S. S. (2013). *Community-based tourism finding the equilibrium in COMCEC context: Setting the pathway for the future*. COMCEC, Coordination Office.

Woo, E., Kim, H., & Uysal, M. (2015). Life satisfaction and support for tourism development. *Annals of Tourism Research, 50*, 84–97.

Chapter 3

Branding Intangible Cultural Heritage: A Root Reinforcement Model for Tourism Resurgence With Indigenous Doll Making

Arup Kumar Baksi[a] *and Subhashree Sanyal*[b]

[a]Aliah University, India
[b]Visva-Bharati, India

Abstract

Intangible cultural heritage (ICH) can be a valuable tourism asset for both government and local communities. Due to the fragmented nature of ICH data, it becomes difficult for the researchers to comprehend its impact on the psychology of the interacting tourists. Prior research has shown that traditional crafts and craftsmanship as ICH could be used to promote a place. However, ICH has scarcely been considered as a place branding element. The study apprehends that branding places with ICH will not only upscale the place in terms of ethno-cultural significance but also will integrate the visiting population with the ICH and thereby ensure knowledge propagation and preservation and reinforce the cultural roots. The study proposes a reflective brand model in the context of ICH of Natungram, a village known for its legacy of craftsmanship of wooden dolls. The study used crossover analysis framework (CAF), as a part of causal mixed-method research design, to inquire into the complex psyche of the tourists while interacting with the ICH and the artisans at Natungram. Three distinct brand elements were identified through a qualitative thematic content analysis, namely subjective vitality, authentic experience, and experiential quality. The brand model was tested for its impact on the behavioral pattern of the tourists by using appropriate quantitative method. The results confirmed both direct and partially mediated effects of the brand elements on the tourist behavior. In future, the model could be extrapolated spatiotemporally for places of ICH significance.

Keywords: Intangible cultural heritage; branding; artisan; craft; tourists

Strategic Tourism Planning for Communities, 23–50
Copyright © 2024 Arup Kumar Baksi and Subhashree Sanyal
Published under exclusive licence by Emerald Publishing Limited
doi:10.1108/978-1-83549-015-020241004

Introduction

Culture is the cumulative concept that envelopes knowledge, belief, customs, practices, and any other habits acquired by people as members of society. Culture and heritage, in the social context, has a rooted connotation of the past which is being carried over. It functions as a generic reference to the places framed in temporal terms (Dallen & Boyd, 2006). Culturally drenched place brand, has at its core, a set of values, namely esthetic, symbolic, atmospheric, and emotional wrapped around ethnic, heritage, and archeological foundation (Smith et al., 2010). Such incongruent value bundles are often mobilized and transformed through cultural tourism and its extensions in broader social fields.

The implications of intangible cultural heritage (ICH) have been well recognized from the perspective of cultural immersion and place branding. The ICH not only embeds the abstract elements, namely the practices, expressions, knowledge, and skill sets, but also has its tangible spread in the form of artifacts, objects, and cultural spaces. The United Nations Educational, Scientific, and Cultural Organization (UNESCO) drafted the Recommendation on the Safeguarding of Traditional Culture and Folklore as the first international legal instrument regarding ICH in 1989. Owing to folklore's restricted implications, UNESCO, in 2003, incorporated five dimensions of ICH:

(1) oral expressions and traditions (including language as a vehicle of ICH);
(2) performing arts;
(3) rituals, festivals, and social practices;
(4) knowledge and practices focusing nature and the universe;
(5) traditional and transgenerational craftsmanship.

Postulated to create conditions conducive to personal and social transformation necessary for a radical dynamism in transformative tourism (Kirillova et al., 2017a, 2017b; Lean, 2016; Lean et al., 2014; Reisinger, 2013, 2015; Soulard et al., 2019), researchers have zeroed their focus on branding ICH to reignite emotional connectivity of the tourists with cultural and heritage repository of a destination in post-disruptive phases. Branding cultural forms and heritage practices require root reinforcement as the process attempts to embed emotion and transform it into an economic offer. In post-COVID-19 scenario, regenerative tourism economy is presumed to witness "conscious travel" based on place-driven cultural assimilation. In the context of tourism research, branding of ICH has been understudied, though the significance of the process to evoke travel decision and propagate an immersive experience is undeniable.

The National list of ICH published by the Ministry of Culture, Govt. of India has state-wise representations of traditional practices of culture and knowledge associated with it. The state of West Bengal has its own exclusive list, namely *Manosa Gaan (Bankura), Deoal Chitra and Alpana (Purulia, Birbhum and Paschim Midnapore), Kushan Gaan (North Bengal), Durga Puja, Chhau Dance (Purulia), Sowa-Rigpa (Darjeeling, Kalimpong), Gaudiya Nritya (Nadia) and Bonbibir Pala (South 24 Parganas – The Sundarbans).* The certification of such

ICH was done based on UNESCO's (2003) recommendation. Some of these places which host this ICH have become vibrant tourist destinations. However, there are many more cultural practices in West Bengal that are quite prominent and lend support to the ethnic existence of habitat. These forms of traditional knowledge and associated cultural practices are part of the ICH reservoir and can be used as branding attributes to promote these places hosting such cultural assets.

Literature Review and Theoretical Framework

Cultural Effects on Brand Perceptions

Approaching the cultural heritage from branding perspective requires under-standing of the principles proposed for its conceptualization by the International Cultural Tourism Committee (2002). The operational framework for branding based on culture has heritage consumers' experiences at its core. This cultural heritage consumer passes through the interconnected stages of the heritage cycle proposed by Thurley (2005). The Anholt Ipsos Nation Brand Index (AINBI) uses perceived cultural and heritage identity to measure nation brands since 2008. Brand perceptions are constructed out of culturally constituted brand architecture and are transferred through brand interactions and transactions. The diverse mix of value that distinguishes cultural tourism is increasingly channeled through branding efforts and has been acknowledged as an approach that draws on traditional ways of differentiation and signaling the unique culture-driven ele-ments that make a place appealing to prospective tourists (Cai et al., 2009). Tourism industry operators, like those in other commercial sectors, see branding as the primary means by which the economic value of tourism circulates, repro-duces, and becomes available for exclusionary regimes to capture new rents. Branding, on the other hand, appears to structure value much beyond the realm of economic trade. As cultural tourism gets infused with the logic of branding along different dimensions, they offer a productive angle from which to approach and better understand the dynamics of value in tourism. The value creation process balances the economic and symbolic identity of a place having significant cultural corpus and heritage spread. The interdependency of economic and symbolic value has become increasingly apparent in recent years as governments, development agencies, marketing professionals, and others assess and seek to capitalize upon the value of culture in concrete terms (Comaroff & Comaroff, 2009; Mortensen, 2009a, 2009b; Yudice, 2003). In cultural tourism, this notion of value typically manifests in the transactional exchange involving culture-based performances and experiences, crafts, cuisines, access to protected areas, heritage sites and other assets, and for all allied services that facilitate visiting place-based destinations. This model posits value as a differentiating dimension in the context of ethnic identity, cultural embeddedness, and heritage roots while developing the reflective branded form of cultural tourism.

Recent research on anthropological theories have observed a resurgence in the study of culture-based value-proposition that focuses on the dynamic approaches to how value is created, negotiated, and translated across domains and through complex acts of exchange (Eiss & Pedersen, 2002; Graeber, 2001; Miller, 2008). This approach propagates "value" as "constellation of action" (Ferry, 2013) which has been institutionalized as culture-based branding. Place brands must be culturally relatable to the target visitors as studies found that culturally similar aspects are instrumental in forming perceptual images of places (Ng et al., 2007). Poria et al. (2006) conducted a study in a heritage site in Amsterdam and observed that promotion of place based on its cultural and heritage assets trigger a sense of belongingness exhibited among the tourists in the form of greater interest to learn about the culture, emotional involvement and passing on the legacy to their children. Cultural and emotional elements, are thus, posited as significant to develop brand image for places with cultural heritage. Kerstetter et al. (2001) suggested that niche visitors within the heritage tourism market have a higher level of prior knowledge, which could explain their higher probability of branded perception of culturally rich places. Several studies were also taken up to assess the impact of UNESCO World Heritage (WH) branding effort. Su and Lin (2014) found that inflow of tourists increases once the places are enlisted as UNESCO WH sites. This suggested that WH listing enacted as a brand-envelopment for those places. Prior information regarding enlistment of places in UNESCO WH also stimulated choice of visitation and positive referrals. This notion could be supported with the results of a study by Moscardo et al. (2001) whereby they found that more than 90% of sampled tourists had prior knowledge that the Great Barrier Reef of Australia was on the UNESCO WH list. Adie et al. (2018) identified two site-specific criteria (with 10 criterion), namely, environmental and cultural, to assess the impact of the tourists' brand perception of places (USA, Serbia, and Morocco) based on cultural identity.

The theoretical pool of place branding has seen a number of models. However, almost all models have tangible elements (tourism products and offers) at the core of the brand architecture. Balakrishnan and Kerr (2013) developed the four-dimensional place brand model with deciding, designing, delivering and determining as the dimensions. Prior to this Kerr and Braithwaite (2011) outlined culture, reputation and strategic alliance as key performance indicators for a place brand. The Brand Prizm model of Kapferer (2013) was also used to explain place branding with six dimensional factors. The Experience Theory by Wang (2000), which observed authenticity of experience as the major value perception while interacting with abstract cultural resources, could provide a surrogated support to the construction of a ICH-based brand model. Going by Leiper (1990), "at least one generating marker is necessary, referring to some kind of phenomenon that acts as a primary nucleus, before an individual can become motivated to set off on a touristic trip". ICH can be a potent marker of uniqueness for a place that could be transformed into a branded entity. Cultural heritage, its preservation, restoration, and promotion, represents a determinant of branding, competitiveness and soft power. The increasing flow of cultural and heritage explorers are inducing cultural wrap-up of places to form their brand images on one hand and to make it sustainable and resilient on the other. Increasing demand for culturally enriched establishments are prompting the place administrators and marketers to make their places interesting to be discovered, explored, experienced and enjoyed.

ICH and Place Branding – A Reflective Branding Perspective

Literature has examined the possibilities, specificities, and hazards of place branding in depth (Anholt, 2007; Braun, 2008; Govers & Go, 2009; Lucarelli & Berg, 2011). The complexity involved in embedding a place as a branded entity (Julier, 2005; Kavaratzis & Ashworth, 2005) and the lack of control over this entity (Braun, 2008; Hankinson, 2004; Van den Berg & Braun, 1999) have surfaced in various research. Multisensory branding frameworks were tried out to capture the essence of a place as a brand element. Prior research has also argued that a standardized model of place branding is difficult to adopt considering the uniqueness associated with different places (Kavaratzis & Kalandides, 2015). Legacy-based place branding has shifted from a finance-driven approach toward a more social and inclusive one (Boisen et al., 2018; Braun et al., 2013). Places, with its cultural roots and ethnic spreads, are a complex system which integrates the stakeholders with the core offer. Place branding related to urban establishments is a dynamic process and can be considered as a major challenge (Maitland, 2019). Rural areas, with cultural heritage (both tangible and intangible) provide opportunities for authentic, unspoiled, transgenerational practices/rituals/festivals (Mitropoulou & Spilanis, 2020; Timothy, 2005). The perceptual identity of these kind of rural establishments are influenced by its cultural heritage and traditions which can be used as branding elements (Waitt, 2000). Creativity and creative entrepreneurship that fosters patronization of culture-based craft practices, traditional festivals, etc., are linked with the identity of a place and could play a significant role in place branding (Bagwell, 2008; Bonarou et al., 2019; Sarantakou et al., 2018).

ICH provides a cultural content to a place that can be used for constructing the brand narratives. ICH also transforms place branding by shifting the focus from visual interactions to experiential bliss (González, 2008). The ICH repository can lend credibility and an assurance of experiential quality and authenticity to cultural experiences. This could be considered as a new dimension in place branding. Since ICH takes form through an evolutionary intervention of the people involved as craftsmen or artisans, a major cog-in-the-wheel in the place brand concept. Artisans play a significant role in the value addition. Conceptually, a brand is stretched beyond its product-centered reality. For culturally shaped products, namely crafts, the artisans share a functional purpose with the brands (Arvidsson, 2006; Upadhyay, 2018). The vehicular impact of artisan in the storytelling aspects of culture and its transgenerational practice could be impactful in shaping an ICH brand specific to a place. The value of an artisan is reflected in the brand concept which essentially has culture and heritage at its core.

Natungram – The Doll Village

Natungram, a remote village in the district of Purba Bardhaman, West Bengal, India, has evolved as a hub of transgenerational practice of wooden crafts. The wave of Bhakti movement in Bengal during the 15th century introduced the figurines of *Gour & Nitai*, a pair of male dolls with their hands outstretched over their heads in a dancing pose. They represent Sri Chaitanya

Mahaprabhu (Gour) and his close disciple Nityananda. Another divine doll, Gopinath, the guardian deity of Agradwip, a town near the Bardhaman-Nadia border. Probably, it was the royal influence (Burdwan is a former royal kingdom of Bengal) that introduced the making of soldier dolls. As a homage to the patronization by the king of Bardhaman, the artisans made the idols popularly known as the "raja-rani" pair. But the most popular is the *pair of owlets*, with its origin rooted in the Hindu religion as many Hindu families still worship a pair of painted wooden owls to seek the blessings of Lakshmi, the goddess of wealth. The owls are painted with bright red, green and yellow on a white base, with black used to paint the eyes and other features. The pair of owlets symbolizes the branded content of the ICH carried over by almost three hundred households in Natungram as their primary livelihood. The artisans are the Hindus having the surname as *Bhaskar*, meaning sculptor or *Sutradhar*, meaning the story teller. Natungram has been identified as the "doll village". Inflow of tourists has increased considerable over the last decade or so. The State Government has formed a handicraft cluster along with a training workshop and a guest house to accommodate tourists. The traditional craftsmanship is continuing with the introduction of new artifacts which are in great demand in both domestic and overseas market. The tourists could identify Natungram as the dolls' village and the produce as the Natungram doll (Fig. 3.1). Therefore, the place branding has, in its core, the practice and

Fig. 3.1.   Glimpses of Artisans at Work in Natungram and the Products.

acknowledgment of ICH and the crafts as the tangible output. The tourists could interact with the artisans and their family members in their own homes and could see them producing an artwork from the scratch. The manner in which branding serves to organize resources in Natungram under particular cultural forms, namely, delimiting value for focused sets of experience, lived space, narratives of ICH, and cultural discourses, deserve much more attention.

Methodology

The study used a crossover analysis framework (CAF) developed by Hitchcock and Onwuegbuzie (2020) to study the multilayered inquiry (e.g., related to experiential nature of the study) into social phenomenon. CAF is used as a sequential causal mixed-method design that aims to integrate two mono-methods, namely qualitative and quantitative, to generate meta inferences based on vertical mixed data analysis.

The qualitative phase of the study was grounded on phenomenology and hermeneutics, needs to navigate the ontological, epistemological, and axiological positions, as well as the momentous issue of meaning (Dahlberg & Dahlberg, 2019). Interpretative phenomenological analysis (IPA) was used to identify the dimensional distribution of a reflective place brand with ICH as the core brand element (Larkin et al., 2006; Reid et al., 2005; Todorova, 2011). This study had underlining of hermeneutic, existential, and ontological posits in tune with the Heidegger's philosophy, and concerned with probing the lived experiential meanings and understanding of the social world, from an ontological perspective. The reflective brand model as the root reinforcer is framed through an interpretivist epistemology that converged upon intentionality, intersubjectivity, and hermeneutics. The study used the concept of Kapferer's Brand Identity Prism model for extrapolation into the metaphorical representation of ICH. The study posited "branding" as a context-bound phenomena with ICH as the core element. The perception of the respondents regarding the ICH-induced branding was apprehended to be multilayered with each perceptual layer forming a linkage with the subsequent layer. The researchers had to assign meaning and interpretation on iterative basis, thereby constructing the "'whole" from "parts". The notion of branding, in this study, has been approached from a deep-seated meta-cognitive orientation whereby the hermeneutic circle, dialogic transactions, and process of interpretations lead to a fusion of horizons.

The study used phenomenological interviews to gather thick descriptions of lived-in experience of interacting with ICH and the manner in which a pre-reflective, preconscious mode of branded entity shaped up. These interviews were targeted to generate textual content based on in-depth interactions and collect comprehensive descriptions (Giorgi, 1997). Semi-structured questionnaires (schedule) were used with probing questions to supplement additional information mining. Participants were free to talk and expand without interrupting. Taking cue from the conversation the researchers summarized, rephrased, probed, and asked follow-up questions and whether there was anything further (Dahlberg & Dahlberg, 2020).

The study intended to capture the subjective vitality and authenticity experience evoking from the interaction with indigenous doll making and collecting them as souvenirs. These two notions were presumed to be the root reinforcers of ICH. Empirical studies governing branding of ICH remain scarce and inconclusive. Additionally, those studies did not consider embedding brand-ignition triggers within the cultural repository to recover culture-based tourism under disruptive conditions. Hence, this study adopted application-based literature-mining using MaxQda to identify proximity brand elements for immersive cultural experience and ICH (Canli et al., 2017; Hajdas, 2017; Pasquinelli, 2017). Necessary measurement constructs were extrapolated from previous studies (Li et al., 2016; Su et al., 2020). The study identified was conducted in Natungram (district-Purba Bardhaman) in West Bengal, India, which is strongly rooted on transgenerational practice of doll and idol making. The study was conducted in two phases. The first phase used a qualitative method to develop the brand model, was from November 2019 to March 2020. The second phase used a quantitative method to test the model, was conducted between November 2021 and March 2022. Purposive sampling technique was used to locate artisans involved in doll making in the study areas and tourists interacting with this indigenous practice. Pilot study was carried out for content validity. The instruments were checked for internal reliability, dimensionality, and validated by applying appropriate statistical techniques.

Lemeshow formula was used for the highly volatile tourist population The tourist population has high volatility in terms of their visitation to Natungram and hence cannot be clearly defined (finite) at a given point of time. Therefore, the sampling plan for the study used the following equation (Levy & Lemeshow, 2013):

$$n = \frac{Z\alpha^2 x P x Q}{L^2}$$

where,

n = sample size required
$Z\alpha$ = standard distribution with α at 5% = 1.96
P = Prevalence of Outcome, 50% for unknown population
Q = 1−P
L = Level of accuracy, 10%

Therefore, the required sample size for the study was computed as:

$$n = \frac{(1.96)^2 x (0.5) x (0.5)}{(0.1)^2} = 96.4$$

The minimum sample size required from each population was 97. The study decided to fix the sample size to 100.

Data Analysis

In-depth interview transcripts, generated from the artisans, were analyzed using the thematic content analysis. MAXQda was used as the application tool. Thematic content analysis helped organizing the data into categories based on initial classification around certain criteria. Initial surface-level analysis allowed the researchers to identify the major words/terminologies/phrases. A lexical search was conducted to identify the contexts in which such words/terminologies/phrases were used by the respondents. The coding system was developed as per Morgan and Hoffman (2018). An evaluative and scaling content analysis (Kuckartz, 2014; Mayring, 2019) was deployed to add evaluative codes for measurement. A total of 330 coded segments were created with 14 codes and 5 subcodes. Fig. 3.2 exhibited different code levels in the coding system.

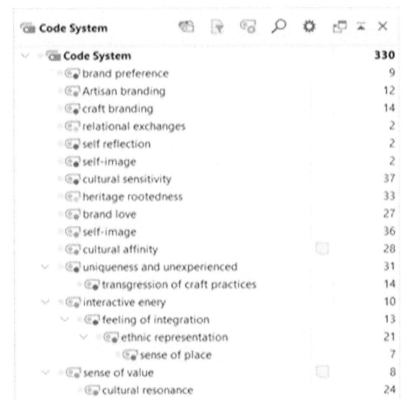

Fig. 3.2.   The Code System in MAXQda.

After exploring the responses pertaining to brand perception elements based on ICH among the 21 interviewees using the lexical search and then automatically coding the search hits along with their surrounding paragraphs, the Code Matrix Browser function was used in MAXQda to create a "Interviewee X Topic matrix" which revealed the distribution of codes across the 21 participants. The largest nodes were displayed with the codes, namely "heritage rootedness," "cultural sensitivity," "brand love" and "self-image" followed by "uniqueness and unexperienced," "feeling of integration," "cultural affinity," "transgression of craft practices," "ethnic representation," and "cultural resonance." The Complex Coding Query function was used to assess the intersectionality of codes across the responses. 124 auto-paraphrased quotations were identified with intersectionality of the codes, namely "heritage rootedness," "cultural sensitivity," "uniqueness and unexperienced," "cultural affinity," "transgression of craft practices," "ethnic representation" "self-image," "brand love," and "cultural resonance." The intersectionality confirmed the pattern distribution of response among the participants in the interview process. The Code Configuration tool was used to identify the combinatorial occurrence of codes which could be used for dimensional/clustering function. Fig. 3.2 exhibited the code configuration results. The major combinations observed for clustering were "cultural sensitivity + heritage rootedness" (8.1%), "uniqueness and unexperienced + cultural affinity" (3.7%), "brand love + self-image" (3.7%), "brand love + cultural affinity" (3.7%), "cultural sensitivity + self-image" (3.1%), "heritage rootedness + cultural resonance" (2.5%), "cultural sensitivity + brand love" (2.5%), "ethnic representation +cultural resonance" (1.9%), and "brand love + heritage rootedness" (1.9%).

We used the MAXMaps to visualize the code co-occurrences and to identify the networks. Hermeneutic interpretation was used as we constructed two networks (Figs. 3.3 and 3.4) to fix the dimensions based on interlinkages and simultaneous occurrence of the codes. The code co-occurrence map depicted in Fig. 3.3 established a three-dimensional code-cluster structure with "feeling of integration," "cultural affinity," and "interactive energy" at the apex of the network.

Fig. 3.4 depicted a four-dimensional code-cluster with "relational exchange", "interactive energy", "feeling of integration", and "self-image" at the vertex.

Based on the code co-occurrence models, we postulated the dimensional structure of a reflective brand model with ICH as the core element. Three dimensions were assigned, namely subjective vitality, experiential quality, and authentic experience. Vitality is a kind of energy evoking from the self and having a causal relationship with the internal perception of the self (Deci & Ryan, 1985). Subjective vitality has not been conceptualized as a form of energy, but it refers to the energy that can be felt while interacting with intangible culture and heritage. We observed that Fredrickson (2000) argued that vitality refers to a positive emotion that enhances individual's cognitive and learning skills. Altunel and Koçak (2017) also pointed out that vitality impacts the quality of experience.

Code Co-occurrence Model (Code Occurrence)

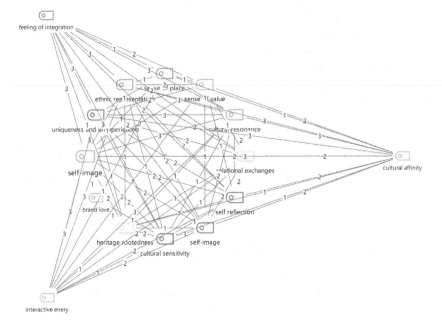

Fig. 3.3.   Code Co-occurrence Map-1.

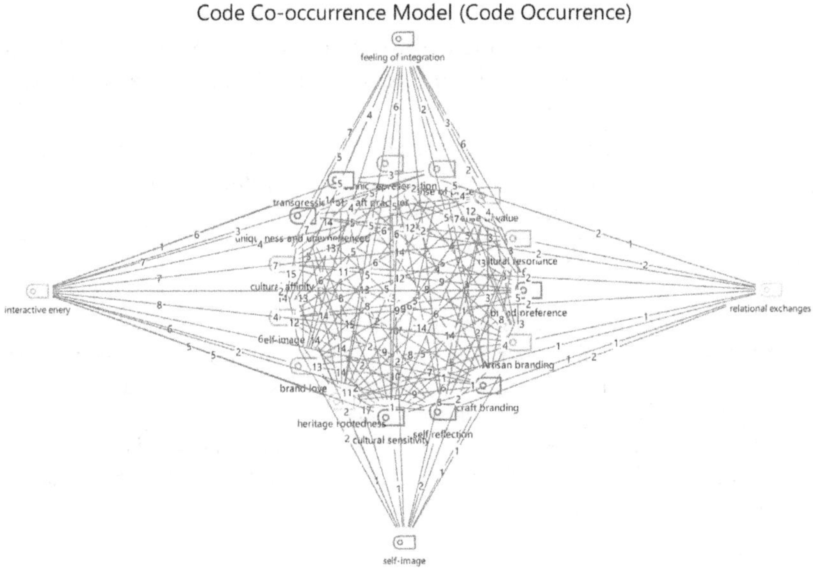

Code Co-occurrence Model (Code Occurrence)

Fig. 3.4.   Code Co-occurrence Map-2.

Few studies (Chen & Chen, 2010; Su et al., 2020) have indicated a relationship between the experiential quality of the heritage tourists and their behavioral pattern. Jin et al. (2013) have found that the quality of the interaction as a determinant of behavioral intention of the tourists. Moon et al. (2013) observed that the place brand image could play a mediating role in the relationship between quality of the experience and the behavioral intention of the tourists. Altunel and Koçak (2017) found that cultural tourists tend to form a behavioral pattern based on the quality of their interactive experiences. Authenticity experience, in the context of ICH-based interactions, has been identified as an important trend in cultural tourism (Kolar & Zabkar, 2010). Authenticity of experience has been considered to be extremely important in the context of cultural and heritage tourism (Su et al., 2020) as authentic experience has emerged as an incentive to perceive place image and assign place identity (Poria et al., 2004). Studies have also shown that authentic experience has a positive and significant impact on experiential quality (Girish & Chen, 2017; Li et al., 2016). Lee and Phau (2018) and Wong et al. (2018) observed that tourists' perception of authenticity was deterministic of the value perception of tourists with regard to place image. Table 3.1 displayed the proposed dimensions of the reflective brand model.

Table 3.1. Proposed Dimensions of the Reflective Brand Model.

Proposed Dimensions	Codes
Subjective vitality	Interactive energy, feeling of integration, cultural resonance
Authentic experience	Cultural rootedness, cultural sensitivity, cultural affinity, brand love, brand preference, self-image, transgression of craft practices
Experiential quality	Sense of value, sense of place, artisan branding, craft branding, ethnic representation, uniqueness and unexperienced, self-reflection

We applied the two-case model to visualize the extent to which codes, e.g., relevant topics, occur in two cases. The frequencies of the codes can be produced per case, and their memos can also be integrated. With the two-case model, we could contrast the proposed dimensions. Since we have proposed three dimensions, we constructed three sets of two-case models and applied the hermeneutic interpretation to conceive the whole reflective brand model. Figs. 3.5–3.7 represented the two-case models.

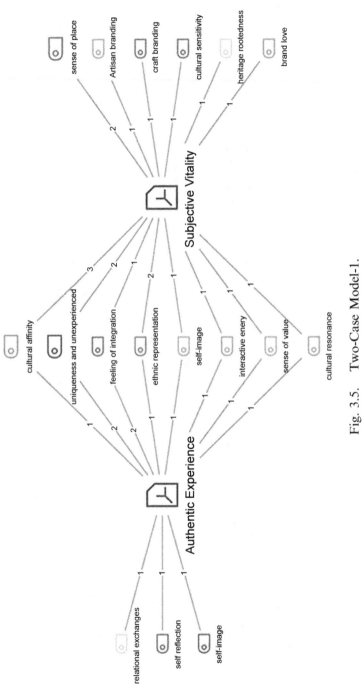

Fig. 3.5.   Two-Case Model-1.

Fig. 3.6.   Two-Case Model-2.

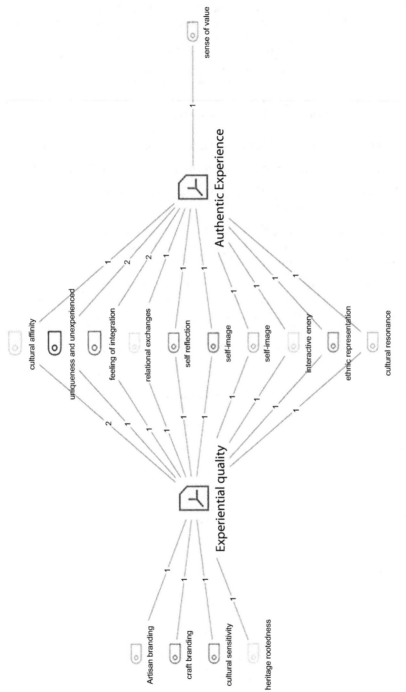

Fig. 3.7.   Two-Case Model-3.

The second phase of the study was conducted to validate the proposed reflective brand model. 100 tourists were interviewed with a structured questionnaire. The measurement of each construct used a Likert 5-point scale (1 = strongly disagree, 5 = strongly agree). Subjective vitality included 3 scale items, authenticity experience used 4 scale items, and experiential quality had 6 scale items. The behavioral pattern of the tourists was measured with a 4-item construct. Based on the apprehended relationship between the major variables (identified brand elements), five hypotheses were framed:

H1. Subjective vitality (SubVitl) influences experiential quality (ExpQual).

H2. Subjective vitality (SubVitl) impacts authenticity experience (AuthExp).

H3. Subjective vitality (SubVitl) influences ICH postinteraction behavioral pattern of tourists (BhvPtrn).

H4. Authenticity experience (AuthExp) plays a mediating role in the relationship between experiential quality (ExpQual) and ICH postinteraction behavioral pattern of tourists (BhvPtrn).

H5. Experiential quality (ExpQual) plays a mediating role in the relationship between subjective vitality (SubVitl) and ICH postinteraction behavioral pattern of tourists (BhvPtrn).

The demographic details of the participants were displayed in Table 3.2.

Table 3.2. Demographic Profile of the Participants.

Demographic	Frequency	Percentage
Gender		
Male	59	59
Female	41	41
Age		
18–25	14	14
>25 ≤ 35	16	16
>35 ≤ 45	29	29
>45 ≤ 55	18	18
>55	23	23
Education		
High school	07	07
Undergraduate	59	59
Postgraduate	34	34

Table 3.2. *(Continued)*

Demographic	Frequency	Percentage
Occupation		
Student	16	16
Service holder	67	67
Professionals	17	17

Common method variance assessment was used to check whether the data can be further analyzed. The Corrected Item-Total Correlation (CITC) of each dimension was tested, eliminating the inappropriate items, and then the reliability test is carried out. The measurement model was analyzed by Amos 23.0 for confirmatory factor analysis (CFA), combined with reliability and convergence validity analysis to determine model modifications, if required. The overall structural model is tested by using structural equation modeling (SEM). The possible mediating effects of experiential quality and authentic experience were tested. The Bootstrap method is used to analyze possible mediating effects. Table 3.3 summarized the result of the CFA.

Table 3.3. Summary of Confirmatory Factor Analysis.

Construct/Scale-Items	Factor Loadings	T-Value	Alpha Value	CR	AVE
Subjective Vitality (SubVitl)					
I feel energetic while interacting with ICH of Natungram and the practicing artisans.	0.816		0.839	0.876	0.639
I feel integrated with the local ICH of Natungram and the practicing artisans.	0.789	12.367			
I feel like culturally resonate with the local ICH of Natungram and the practicing artisans.	0.801	14.092			
Authentic Experience (AuthExp)					
I experience cultural rootedness while interacting with ICH of Natungram and the practicing artisans.	0.811		0.845	0.849	0.679
I experience cultural affinity while interacting with ICH of Natungram and the practicing artisans.	0.798	12.783			

(Continued)

Table 3.3. *(Continued)*

Construct/Scale-Items	Factor Loadings	T-Value	Alpha Value	CR	AVE
I feel brand love while interacting with ICH of Natungram and the practicing artisans.	0.749	12.129			
I experience an enhancement of my self-image love while interacting with ICH of Natungram and the practicing artisans.	0.738	11.982			
Experiential Quality (ExpQual)					
I experience sense of value interacting with ICH of Natungram and the practicing artisans.	0.738		0.881	0.885	0.692
Interacting with ICH of Natungram and the practicing artisans gives me a feeling of ethnic integration.	0.780	12.217			
Interacting with ICH of Natungram and the practicing artisans gives me a feeling of uniqueness.	0.793	12.698			
I experience self-reflection while interacting with ICH of Natungram and the practicing artisans.	0.804	13.987			
I participated in the craft making process of Natungram.	0.839	14.871			
I participated in the interaction process with the artisans of Natungram.	0.763	12.091			
Behavioral Pattern (BhvPtrn)					
I would recommend visitation of Natungram based on its ICH.	0.711	12.002	0.855	0.862	0.598
I would like to come back to Natungram to interact with its ICH.	0.726	12.021			
I would say positive things about my experience I had in Natungram.	0.742	12.208			
I would like to stay in Natungram and experience a part of artisans' life.	0.777	12.749			

Note: CR – construct reliability, AVE – Average Variance Extracted.

Harman's (1976) single factor test method was used to determine if common method variance was an issue with the sample. The variance explained by the first factor obtained was 21.269%, which was lower than the standard of 50%. Therefore, common method variance was not found to be an issue. Cronbach's alpha ranged from 0.839 to 0.881, and the CITC was found to be > 0.5. Therefore, data reliability was established. From the results of Table 3.2, the factor loading of the scale items was >0.7, the value of composite reliability for each dimension was >0.7, and the average variance extracted (AVE) was >0.5.

CFA was used to analyze the reliability and validity of data (Anderson & Gerbing, 1988). Table 3.4 tabulated the model fit of the measurement model and was found in accordance with the standard recommended by Hair et al. (2010). The results showed in Table 3.5 revealed that the square root of each dimension AVE is higher than correlations among the corresponding latent variables providing evidence of discriminant validity.

Table 3.4. Results of the Model Fit.

Index	χ^2	df	χ^2/df	RMSEA	GFI	AGFI	CFI	IFI
CFA	292.319	172	1.699	0.039	0.915	0.907	0.967	0.966
Structural model	321.527	184	1.747	0.037	0.923	0.912	0.970	0.972
Fitted value			<3.0	<0.05	>0.900	>0.900	>0.900	>0.900

Table 3.5. Discriminant Validity.

Constructs	AVE	SubVitl	AuthExp	ExpQual	BhvPtrn
SubVitl	0.639	**0.799**			
AuthExp	0.679	0.213	**0.824**		
ExpQual	0.692	0.180	0.235	**0.831**	
BhvPtrn	0.598	0.203	0.312	0.281	**0.773**

Maximum likelihood method was used to measure the hypotheses of the model. The model fit for the structural model (Fig. 3.8) was found to be satisfactory (Hair et al., 2010). The structure parameter estimates were displayed in Table 3.6.

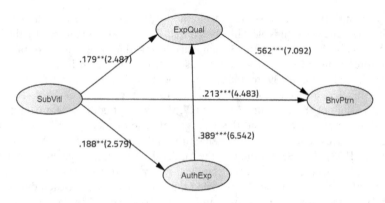

Fig. 3.8.   Structural Model With Path Coefficient.

Table 3.6. Structure Parameter Estimates.

Hypotheses Path	Estimate	Std.	S.E.	*T*-Value	*p* Value	Conclusion
SubVitl→AuthExp	0.219	0.188	0.091	2.837	0.006	Support
AuthExp→ExpQual	0.346	0.389	0.072	5.092	0.000	Support
SubVitl→ExpQual	0.182	0.179	0.065	2.062	0.008	Support
SubVitl→BhvPtrn	0.194	0.213	0.108	2.214	0.000	Support
ExpQual→BhvPtrn	0.486	0.562	0.087	6.742	0.000	Support

Bootstrap (Bootstrap = 5000) was used to measure the mediating effects:

• Mediating role of authenticity experience (AuthExp) in the relationship between experiential quality (ExpQual) and ICH-induced postinteraction behavioral pattern of tourists (BhvPtrn).
• Mediating role of experiential quality (ExpQual) in the relationship between Subjective vitality (SubVitl) and ICH-induced postinteraction behavioral pattern of tourists (BhvPtrn).

It was found that authenticity experience played the role of a partial mediator in the relationship between experiential quality and ICH postinteraction behavioral pattern of tourists. Similarly, experiential quality was also found to partially mediate the relationship between subjective vitality (SubVitl) and ICH-induced post-interaction behavioral pattern of tourists. The results are displayed in Table 3.7.

Table 3.7. Mediation Effect.

Path	Effects	Percentile 95% CI		Bias-Corrected Percentile 95% CI		Mediation Effect
SubVitl→ExpQual→BhvPtrn	Direct	0.179	0.334	0.692	0.329	0.683	Yes
	Indirect	0.138	0.012	0.279	0.009	0.189	
	Total	0.317	0.381	0.723	0.301	0.364	
SubVitl→AuthExp→ExpQual	Direct	0.188	0.421	0.877	0.397	0.734	Yes
	Indirect	0.095	0.007	0.193	0.004	0.178	
	Total	0.283	0.498	0.819	0.438	0.769	

Conclusion

The study posited ICH as a brand element for branding places with significant cultural and heritage rootedness. Culture has been postulated as a potent driver for the economic engine when it comes to place branding. The practice of transgenerational culture and the sense of pride associated with it enacts as a placebo for all such individuals who interact with it (Van den Berg & Russo, 2004). A good part of tourism theory has segregated destination branding from place branding. While destination branding concentrated purely on recreational tourism, place branding touched upon the spheres of life that are saturated with culture and heritage, ethnicity, knowledge pool, and events and festivals (Berács et al., 2006). The study used Natungram, a remote village in the district of Purba Bardhaman, West Bengal, India, as a case. The village has a legacy of producing wooden crafts, and the artisans have proudly taken it up as their primary livelihood. The motifs, colors, forms, textures, and materials used and the crafting itself have gone through the evolutionary phases but have remained rooted to the origin.

Theoretical Implication of the Study

The researchers identified three specific elements for place branding based on the ICH associated with the place, namely subjective vitality, authentic experience, and the experiential quality. At the core of this study, the researchers used the Kapferer's (2009) Brand Identity Prizm model and the four-dimensional place branding model (Balakrishnan & Kerr, 2013). The results of the qualitative phase of the study identified the artisans (code: artisan branding) and the attached persona (code: cultural sensitivity) as the constructed source and tourists (code: sense of place) as the constructed receivers. The externalization of the brand model was advocated through the physique, reflection, and relationship associated with the ICH, while the internalization has been reflected through self-image and brand love. The Kapferer's model was further extended and specified with subjective vitality as an intrinsic element and authentic experience and experiential quality as extrinsic elements. The study found subjective vitality impacting the behavioral pattern and intentions of the tourists which confirmed the kind of positive vibes that the tourists felt while interacting with the ICH of Natungram. The relationship between subjective vitality and behavioral pattern was found to be mediated by the experiential quality. This finding reinforced the observations of the previous researchers (Altunel & Koçak, 2017; Chen & Chen, 2010; Jin et al., 2013; Moon et al., 2013; Su et al., 2020). Authentic experience of the tourists was also found as a potent mediator which, on one hand, mediates the relationship between subjective vitality and experiential quality and, on the other hand, churns out a mediated mediation model whereby it impacts the relationship between subjective vitality and behavioral pattern through experiential quality. These results resonated with the observations made by the researchers regarding the implications of authentic experience in the context of cultural tourism (Kolar & Zabkar, 2010). It also confirmed the findings of Girish and Chen (2017) who observed that authentic experience had a significant impact on experiential quality. From place branding point of view, the study found enough support to induct "tourists perception of authenticity" as an extrinsic dimension to the reflective brand model based on ICH. The notion received conformity from the studies of Lee and Phau (2018) and Wong et al. (2018) who found that tourists' perception of authenticity was deterministic of the value perception of tourists with regard to place image. The concept of artisan branding has also been taken forward as the theory of experiential value and socially responsible consumption were reinforced. A previous study conducted by Upadhyay (2018) found positive and significant relationship between craft-brand experiential value and self-brand connection which in turn impacted behavioral pattern. The present study extended this notion and found that not only the experiential quality but also the energy felt through such experiences (subjective vitality) were instrumental in shaping behavioral pattern. Further, the brand model of Natungram (dolls) will enact as a reinforcer of the cultural roots.

Industry Implication of the Study

Place branding rather than destination branding has emerged as the differentiator to lure visitors. However, place branding concept is limited to places having significant uniqueness and exclusivity which could be seamlessly integrated as an experiential offer with the basic tourism product. Archeological establishments, ethnic existence, transgenerational cultural practices, and heritage spread are, therefore, assimilated as attributional differentiators for place branding. Villages like Natungram which are located far from the urban centers attract considerable number of tourists based on their cultural and heritage legacy. The initial brand effect could be felt based on the word-of-mouth and subsequent advocacy by the tourists who experienced the interaction with the ICH. With the increase in the flow of tourists, the economic scaffold of Natungram has strengthened considerably. The destination marketing organizations (DMOs) are positioning Natungram as the "doll village" in spatiotemporal sense. The artisans are earning decently for all their hard work, and a community cluster has grown up to foster tourism activities. ICH branding could be the new panacea for cultural preservation.

Limitation of the Study

The study was limited to a single case, namely Natungram. There are several places across India with ICH and which draw perennial visitation. Future studies could be conducted in those places with the identified brand model to test its transferability and generalizability. The designed brand model could be expanded to cross-cultural brand equity perspective.

References

Adie, B. A., Hall, C. M., & Prayag, G. (2018). World Heritage as a placebo brand: A comparative analysis of three sites and marketing implications. *Journal of Sustainable Tourism, 26*(3), 399–415. https://doi.org/10.1080/09669582.2017.1359277

Altunel, M., & Koçak, Ö. (2017). The roles of subjective vitality, involvement, experience quality, and satisfaction in tourists' behavioral intentions. *European Journal of Tourism Research, 16*, 233–251. https://doi.org/10.54055/ejtr.v16i.287

Anderson, J. C., & Gerbing, D. W. (1988). Structural equation modeling in practice: A review and recommended two-step approach. *Psychological Bulletin, 103*(3), 411.

Anholt, S. (2007). *Competitive identity: The new brand management for countries, regions and cities.* Palgrave-Macmillan. https://doi.org/10.1057/9780230627772

Arvidsson, A. (2006). *Brands: Meaning and value in media culture.* Psychology Press.

Bagwell, S. (2008). Creative clusters and city growth. *Creative Industries Journal, 1*(1), 31–46.

Balakrishnan, M. S., & Kerr, G. (2013). The 4D model of place brand management. *Branded spaces*, 31–42. https://doi.org/10.1007/978-3-658-01561-9_2

Berács, J., Clifton, R., Davidson, H., Johnston, Y., Lodge, C., Melissen, & Wästberg, O. (2006). How has place branding developed during the year that place branding has been in publication? *Place Branding, 2*(1), 6–17.

Boisen, M., Terlouw, K., Groote, P., & Couwenberg, O. (2018). Reframing place promotion, place marketing, and place branding-moving beyond conceptual confusion. *Cities, 80*, 4–11. https://doi.org/10.1016/j.cities.2017.08.021

Bonarou, C., Tsartas, P., & Sarantakou, E. (2019). E-storytelling and wine tourism branding: Insights from the "wine roads of Northern Greece". In *Wine tourism destination management and marketing* (pp. 77–98). Palgrave Macmillan.

Braun, E. (2008). *City marketing: Towards an integrated approach.* ERIM PhD Series in Research and Management, 142. Erasmus Research Institute of Management (ERIM), Rotterdam.

Braun, E., Kavaratzis, M., & Zenker, S. (2013). My city – My brand: The different roles of residents in place branding. *Journal of Place Management and Development, 6*(4), 77–89. https://doi.org/10.1108/17538331311306087

Cai, L., Gartner, W. C., & Munar, A. M. (Eds.). (2009). *Tourism branding: Communities in action.* Emerald Publishing Limited.

Canli, Z., Hayran, C., & Sarial-Abi, G. (2017). Culture and branding. In *Cross cultural issues in consumer science and consumer psychology: Current perspectives and future directions* (pp. 129–147). https://doi.org/10.1007/978-3-319-65091-3_8

Chen, C.-F., & Chen, F.-S. (2010). Experience quality, perceived value, satisfaction and behavioral intentions for heritage tourists. *Tourism Management, 31*(1), 29–35. https://doi.org/10.1016/j.tourman.2009.02.008

Comaroff, J., & Comaroff, J. (2009). *Ethnicity, Inc.* Chicago University Press.

Dallen, T., & Boyd, S. (2006). Heritage tourism in the 21st century: Valued traditions and new perspectives. *Journal of Heritage Tourism, 1*(1), 1–16.

Dahlberg, H., & Dahlberg, K. (2019). The question of meaning—A momentous issue for qualitative research. *International Journal of Qualitative Studies on Health and Well-Being, 14*(1), 1598723.

Dahlberg, H., & Dahlberg, K. (2020). Open and reflective lifeworld research: A third way. *Qualitative Inquiry, 26*(5), 458–464. https://doi.org/10.1177/1077800419836696

Deci, E. L., & Ryan, R. M. (1985). The general causality orientations scale: Self-determination in personality. *Journal of Research in Personality, 19*(2), 109–134. https://doi.org/10.1016/0092-6566(85)90023-6

Eiss, P., & Pedersen, D. (2002). Introduction: Values of value. *Cultural Anthropology, 17*(3), 283–290.

Ferry, E. (2013). *Minerals, collecting, and value across the US-Mexico border.* Indiana University Press.

Fredrickson, B. L. (2000). Cultivating positive emotions to optimize health and well-being. *Prevention & Treatment, 3*(1), 1a. https://doi.org/10.1037/1522-3736.3.1.31a

Giorgi, A. (1997). The theory, practice, and evaluation of phenomenological method as a qualitative research practice procedure. *Journal of Phenomenological Psychology, 28*(2), 235–260. https://search.proquest.com/docview/211498419?accountid=12860

Girish, V., & Chen, C.-F. (2017). Authenticity, experience, and loyalty in the festival context: Evidence from the San Fermin festival, Spain. *Current Issues in Tourism, 20*(15), 1551–1556. https://doi.org/10.1080/13683500.2017.1296821

González, M. V. (2008). Intangible heritage tourism and identity. *Tourism Management, 29*(4), 807–810.

Govers, R., & Go, F. (2009). *Place branding: Virtual and physical identities, glocal, imagined and experienced.* Palgrave-Macmillan.

Graeber, D. (2001). *Towards an anthropological theory of value.* Palgrave.

Hair, J. F., Black, W. C., Babin, B. J., & Anderson, R. E. (2010). *Multivariate data analysis* (7th ed.). Prentice Hall.

Hajdas, M. (2017). The impact of cultural branding on brand equity–Exploratory study. *Handel Wewnętrzny, 5*(370), 213–221.

Hankinson, G. (2004). Relational network brands: Towards a conceptual model of place brands. *Journal of Vacation Marketing, 10*(2), 109–121.

Harman, H. H. (1976). *Modern factor analysis.* University of Chicago Press.

Hitchcock, J. H., & Onwuegbuzie, A. J. (2020). Developing mixed methods crossover analysis approaches. *Journal of Mixed Methods Research, 14*(1), 63–83. https://doi.org/10.1177/15586898198417

Jin, N., Lee, H., & Lee, S. (2013). Event quality, perceived value, destination image, and behavioral intention of sports events: The case of the IAAF World Championship, Daegu, 2011. *Asia Pacific Journal of Tourism Research, 18*(8), 849–864. https://doi.org/10.1080/10941665.2012.711336

Julier, G. (2005). Urban design spaces and the production of aesthetic consent. *Urban Studies, 42*, 5–6, 689–888.

Kapferer, J. N. (2009). Kapferer's brand-identity prism model. *European Institute for Brand Management, 24.*

Kavaratzis, M., & Ashworth, G. J. (2005). City branding: An effective assertion of identity or a transitory marketing trick? *Tijdschrift voor economische en sociale geografie, 96*(5), 506–514.

Kavaratzis, M., & Kalandides, A. (2015). Rethinking the place brand: The interactive formation of place brands and the role of participatory place branding. *Environment and Planning A, 47*(6), 1368–1382.

Kerr, G., & Braithwaite, B. (2011). A framework for preparing and implementing economic development plans for local government areas in Australia. In *ANZRSAI Conference* (pp. 6–9). December.

Kerstetter, D. L., Confer, J. J., & Graefe, A. R. (2001). An exploration of the specialization concept within the context of heritage tourism. *Journal of Travel Research, 39*(3), 267–274.

Kirillova, K., Lehto, X., & Cai, L. (2017a). Existential authenticity and anxiety as outcomes: The tourist in the experience economy. *International Journal of Tourism Research, 19*(1), 13–26.

Kirillova, K. X., Lehto, X., & Cai, L. (2017b). What triggers transformative tourism experiences? *Tourism Recreation Research, 42*(4), 498–511. https://www.tandfonline.com/doi/abs/10.1080/02508281.2017.1342349?journalCode=rtrr20

Kolar, T., & Zabkar, V. (2010). A consumer-based model of authenticity: An oxymoron or the foundation of cultural heritage marketing? *Tourism Management, 31*(5), 652–664. https://doi.org/10.1016/j.tourman.2009.07.010

Kuckartz, U. (2014). *Qualitative text analysis: A guide to methods, practice and using software.* Sage.

Larkin, M., Watts, S., & Clifton, E. (2006). Giving voice and making sense in interpretative phenomenological analysis. *Qualitative Research in Psychology, 3*(2), 102–120.

Lean, G. (2016). *Transformative travel in a mobile world.* CABI.

Lean, G., Staiff, R., & Waterton, E. (Eds.). (2014). *Travel and transformation. Current development in the geographies of leisure series.* Ashgate Publishing.

Lee, S., & Phau, I. (2018). Young tourists' perceptions of authenticity, perceived value and satisfaction: The case of Little India, Singapore. *Young Consumers, 19*(1), 70–86. https://doi.org/10.1108/YC-07-2017-00714

Leiper, N. (1990). Tourist attraction systems. *Annals of Tourism Research, 17*, 367–384. https://doi.org/10.1016/0160-7383(90)90004-B

Levy, P. S., & Lemeshow, S. (2013). *Sampling of populations: Methods and applications.* John Wiley & Sons. http://doi.org/10.1002/9780470374597

Li, X., Shen, H., & Wen, H. (2016). A study on tourists' perceived authenticity towards experience quality and behavior intention of cultural heritage in Macao. *International Journal of Marketing Studies, 8*(4), 117–123. https://doi.org/10.5539/ijms.v8n4

Lucarelli, A., & Berg, P. O. (2011). City branding: A state-of-the-art review of the research domain. *Journal of Place Management and Development, 4*(1), 9–27. https://doi.org/10.1108/17538331111117133

Maitland, R. (2019). Extending the frontiers of city tourism: Suburbs and the real London. In *Destination London* (p. 15). http://doi.org/10.16997/book35.b

Mayring, P. (2019). Qualitative content analysis: Demarcation, varieties, developments. In *Forum: Qualitative Social Research* (Vol. 20, No. 3, pp. 1–26). Freie Universität Berlin. https://doi.org/10.17169/fqs-20.3.3343

Miller, D. (2008). The uses of value. *Geoforum, 39*, 1122–1132. http://doi.org/10.1016/j.geoforum.2006.03.009

Mitropoulou, A., & Spilanis, I. (2020). Towards a contemporary research agenda for island branding: Developments, challenges, and dynamics. *Place Branding and Public Diplomacy, 16*(4), 293–303. https://link.springer.com/article/10.1057/s41254-020-00181-4

Moon, K.-S., Ko, Y. J., Connaughton, D. P., & Lee, J.-H. (2013). A mediating role of destination image in the relationship between event quality, perceived value, and behavioral intention. *Journal of Sport & Tourism, 18*(1), 49–66. https://doi.org/10.1080/14775085.2013.799960

Morgan, D. L., & Hoffman, K. (2018). A system for coding the interaction in focus groups and dyadic interviews. *Qualitative Report, 23*(3), 519–531. https://doi.org/ 10.46743/2160-3715/2018.2733

Mortensen, L. (2009a). Producing Copán in the archaeology industry. In L. Mortensen & J. Hollowell (Eds.), *Ethnographies and archaeologies: Iterations of the past* (pp. 178–198). University Press of Florida.

Mortensen, L. (2009b). Copán past and present: Maya archaeological tourism and the Ch'orti' in Honduras. In B. Metz, C. McNeil, & K. Hull (Eds.), *The Ch'orti' region, past and present* (pp. 246–257). University Press of Florida.

Moscardo, G., Green, D., & Greenwood, T. (2001). How great is the Great Barrier Reef! Tourists' knowledge and understanding of the World Heritage status of the Great Barrier Reef. *Tourism Recreation Research, 26*(1), 19–25. http://doi.org/10. 1080/02508281.2001.11081173

Ng, S. I., Lee, J. A., & Soutar, G. N. (2007). Tourists' intention to visit a country: The impact of cultural distance. *Tourism Management, 28*(6), 1497–1506. https://doi. org/10.1016/j.tourman.2006.11.005

Pasquinelli, C. (2017). Tourism connectivity and spatial complexity: A widening bi-dimensional arena of urban tourism research. In *Tourism in the city: Towards an integrative agenda on urban tourism* (pp. 29–50).

Poria, Y., Butler, R., & Airey, D. (2004). Links between tourists, heritage, and reasons for visiting heritage sites. *Journal of Travel Research, 43*(1), 19–28.

Poria, Y., Reichel, A., & Biran, A. (2006). Heritage site management: Motivations and expectations. *Annals of Tourism Research, 33*(1), 162–178. https://doi.org/10. 1016/j.annals.2005.08.001

Reid, K., Flowers, P., & Larkin, M. (2005). Exploring lived experience. *The Psychologist. 18*(1), 20–23.

Reisinger, Y. (2013). *Transformational tourism: Tourist perspectives.* CABI.

Reisinger, Y. (2015). *Transformational tourism: Host perspectives.* CABI.

Sarantakou, E., Tsartas, P., & Bonarou, C. (2018). How new technologies influence the perception of Athens as a tourist and cultural destination. In *Innovative approaches to tourism and leisure* (Vol. 8, No. 3, pp. 169–172). https://doi.org/10. 1007/978-3-319-67603-6_12

Smith, G., Messenger, P., & Soderland, H. (Eds.). (2010). *Heritage values in contemporary society.* Left Coast. https://doi.org/10.4324/9781315427492

Soulard, J., McGehee, N. G., & Stern, M. (2019). Transformative tourism organizations and glocalization. *Annals of Tourism Research, 76*(2019), 91–104. https:// doi.org/10.1016/j.annals.2019.03.007

Su, X., Li, X., Chen, W., & Zeng, T. (2020). Subjective vitality, authenticity experience, and intangible cultural heritage tourism: An empirical study of the puppet show. *Journal of Travel & Tourism Marketing, 37*(2), 258–271. https://doi.org/10. 1080/10548408.2020.1740141

Su, Y. W., & Lin, H. L. (2014). Analysis of international tourist arrivals worldwide: The role of world heritage sites. *Tourism Management, 40*, 46–58. https://doi.org/ 10.1016/j.tourman.2013.04.005

Thurley, S. (2005). Into the future. Our strategy for 2005–2010. *Conservation Bulletin* [English Heritage], 49.

Timothy, D. J. (2005). Shopping tourism, retailing and leisure In *Shopping tourism, retailing and leisure*. Channel View Publications. https://doi.org/10.21832/ 9781873150610

Todorova, I. (2011). Explorations with interpretative phenomenological analysis in different socio-cultural contexts: Commentary on J. Smith: 'Evaluating the contribution of interpretative phenomenological analysis. *Health Psychology Review*, 5(1), 34–38. https://doi.org/10.1080/17437199.2010.520115

Upadhyay, A. (2018). Artisan branding: An emerging dimension for socially responsible brands. *International Journal of Management and Applied Science*, 4(6), 78–82.

Van den Berg, L., & Braun, E. (1999). Urban competitiveness, marketing and the need for organising capacity. *Urban Studies*, 36(5–6), 987–999. https://doi.org/10.1080/ 0042098993312

Van den Berg, L., & Russo, A. P. (2004). *The student city: Strategic planning for students' communities in EU cities*. Ashgate.

Waitt, G. (2000). Consuming heritage: Perceived historical authenticity. *Annals of Tourism Research*, 27(4), 835–862. https://doi.org/10.1016/S0160-7383(99)00115-2

Wang, N. (2000). *Tourism and modernity: A sociological analysis*. Pergamon Press.

Wong, I. A., Ji, M., & Liu, M. T. (2018). The effect of event supportive service environment and authenticity in the quality–value–satisfaction framework. *Journal of Hospitality & Tourism Research*, 42(4), 563–586. https://doi.org/10.1177/ 1096348015614957

Yudice, G. (2003). *The expediency of culture: The uses of culture in the global era*. Duke University Press.

Chapter 4

Strategic Entrepreneurship and Digital Transformation to Enhance the Tourism Performance Management

Orpha Jane

Parahyangan Catholic University, Indonesia

Abstract

This chapter delves into the enhancement of the tourism industry through strategic entrepreneurship (SE) and digital transformation. The potential of these methodologies in revolutionizing tourism development and management is emphasized. The Fourth Industrial Revolution, characterized by technologies such as the Internet of Things, big data, artificial intelligence (AI), cloud computing, augmented and virtual reality, and 3D printing, has permeated various sectors including governance and commerce.

This paradigm shift has also seeped into tourism, dubbed as Tourism 4.0 by Korze (2019). As highlighted by Peceny et al. (2019), the infusion of critical communication and information technologies, particularly augmented reality (AR) and virtual reality (VR), into the tourism sector can provide tourists with vivid previews or simulations of attractions. Such immersive experiences can influence travel decisions.

There's an evident rise in the integration of the Fourth Industrial Revolution's technologies in tourism. A prominent example is the adoption of these innovations in digital marketing strategies, especially on social media platforms (Zeng & Gerritsen, 2014; Leung et al., 2013). Given the profound impact of digital tech in molding a network-driven consumer behavior (Rogers, 2016), it becomes imperative for the tourism sector to undergo a comprehensive digital metamorphosis, paying heed to value chains and systems (Ismail et al., 2017).

Furthermore, the importance of SE cannot be overlooked (Ireland et al., 2003; Ireland & Webb 2007). It encapsulates an entity's prowess in seizing opportunities with apt strategies, ensuring the tourism industry remains resilient and thriving.

Strategic Tourism Planning for Communities, 51–62

Copyright © 2024 Orpha Jane

Published under exclusive licence by Emerald Publishing Limited

doi:10.1108/978-1-83549-015-020241005

Keywords: Strategic entrepreneurship; digital transformation; tourism performance; tourism management; Fourth Industrial Revolution

Introduction

Tourism is one of the sectors which had a specific influence by digitalization. Digitalization has significantly impacted the tourism sector in several specific ways. For example, social media platforms are now key for communication and promotional activities. Additionally, virtual and augmented reality technologies enhance tourists' experiences through virtual tours. Mobile applications serve as a digital interface, offering personalized services. Furthermore, the sector benefits from search engine optimization (SEO), influencer marketing, and data analytics to improve visibility, engage with a wider audience, and analyze consumer behavior and trends. With the potency of digitalization, tourism actors – business and government – should have designed and implemented a specific strategy to enhance tourism performance. To give some perspectives on the strategy, this chapter describes the importance of strategic entrepreneurship (SE) in developing digitalization in tourism.

Tourism in Digital Era

The digital era gained momentum when COVID-19 pandemic hit worldwide. One of the ways to control the spreading of the virus is by distance. People in all countries must do their routines such as work, study, shop, or even religious rituals digitally. As a result of the pandemic, there was a significant increase in internet communication, leading to greater usage of various digital platforms and services. This surge encompassed a wide range of tools and apps. For design, platforms like Canva became popular. Social media platforms such as Facebook, Instagram, and Twitter saw increased activity. Professional communication and collaboration tools, including Microsoft Teams and Zoom, became essential for remote work. E-commerce platforms like Amazon and Shopee experienced higher demand. Entertainment services, including YouTube and TikTok, saw more users seeking entertainment online. Moreover, transportation and travel services like Grab and Traveloka were also affected, adapting to the changing needs during the pandemic.

Those digital platforms show a vivid fact of today's digital landscape, emphasizing its expansive and all-encompassing nature. Each platform signifies a different facet of the online world, from entertainment and social connectivity to professional collaboration and e-commerce. Their presence together in a single image underscores how these platforms have become integral components of our daily lives (Jane, 2022).

In the current era, the lines between different digital services are blurring. For instance, a platform like "Instagram," once primarily for photo sharing, now offers shopping features, while "Zoom," which began as a tool for virtual meetings, is now used for social gatherings, webinars, and even online concerts. This interconnectedness suggests that modern life is not just influenced by these platforms but is deeply woven into them. They cater to our multifaceted needs, from work and learning to shopping, entertainment, and socializing, making them indispensable. As a result, these platforms are essential to the modern lifestyle, highlighting the central role of users within this digital ecosystem. It's a testament to how consumers today are not just passive recipients but active participants, curating their experiences and contributing to the digital zeitgeist. In essence, this underscores the profound impact and omnipresence of digital platforms in shaping contemporary lifestyles, cultures, and interactions.

While other sectors benefit from digitalization, the tourism industry has a different context, especially during the pandemic. Tourism has a tremendous effect since people have to distance themselves and stay at home as we realize that in 2020, all countries will be closed because of the virus. According to the United Nations World Tourism Organization (UNWTO), COVID-19 impacted tourism. The tourism industry is even more back than 30 years ago. From 2020 UNWTO report, we had a fact:

- The International Tourist Arrival metric reveals a sharp downturn in 2020, with a staggering 74% decrease in travelers compared to prior years.
- The global tourism industry experienced a loss of approximately 1 billion international tourist arrivals due to the pandemic's restrictions and fears.
- A monetary loss quantified at US$ 1.3 trillion in the tourism export sector, indicating the substantial economic blow the industry faced.
- The income loss being 11 times greater than what was experienced during the 2009 economic crisis.

The condition gives a challenge and an opportunity. The challenge is creating a new approach to the unique situation, such as distancing, health protocol, and other rules to prevent the virus. Meanwhile, the opportunity is to create digital tourism. Digitalization itself has a significant and positive contribution to tourism development.

Peceny et al. (2019) identify that tourism can also implement critical technology in information and communication; for example, VR – virtual reality – can help tourists decide which place or country they will visit. Alternatively, AR – augmented reality – will enhance the tourist experience, especially in heritage or adventure attractions.

Korze (2019) uses the Tourism 4.0 term to explain digitalization in tourism, specifically while trying to implement the new tourism ecosystem. It includes big data, robotization, artificial intelligence, mobile technologies, VR, and distributed ledger technologies.

Benyon et al. (2014) develop digital tourism as a powerful tool to create user experience (UX). The characteristics of tourism with many activities fit with the digitalization to enhance the tourist experience. Digitalization can increase tourist experience before the journey, during, and even more after the trip. According to Benyon, digital tourism is not a new concept because some online activities such as TripAdvisor, Expedia, official airline websites, and many more are examples of the implementation of digital tourism.

Besides focusing on digital technology, research in digital tourism is also related to social media, especially for information search, promotion, and facilitating tourist interaction.

Zeng and Gerritsen (2014) explored and analyzed 165 papers focusing on social media in tourism and concluded:

- tourist behavior – in planning the trip, attitude, perception, and intention toward ecotourism issues;
- the impact of social media content – economic, social, and cultural aspects – that influenced by tourist nationality;
- social media as a marketing and promotion tool;
- impact on knowledge and culture of tourism – it is primarily in the changing of consumption pattern of tourism as a digital tool.

   Research by Leung et al. (2013) on the same topic adds one aspect: a supplier's role in tourism. Using social media, suppliers run the promotion, distribution, management, or even the research function. The research compilation on tourism digitalization is organized and presented shown in Fig. 4.1.

Fig. 4.1.   Research Topic in Digital Tourism (Author).

Why Have to Transform

The phenomenon of digitalization is transforming and influencing consumer behavior. According to Rogers (2016), the concept of customer networks emphasizes the complex interactions between customers and companies. At the heart of these networks is the company, but there is also a strong emphasis on the vast web of connections that customers form not only with the company but also with each other. These interactions are facilitated through various digital touchpoints such as comments sections, platforms like Craigslist, blogs, social media sites like Twitter and YouTube, and online forums. The relationships, as symbolized by directional arrows, are reciprocal, emphasizing a two-way flow of communication. This concept emphasizes the interconnectedness of customers in the digital era, showcasing how they don't function in isolation but are constantly engaging with both the company and other customers across diverse platforms. Customers are not isolated and not as an aggregate target who receive the information about the product or services.

According to Rogers, the Network model is also related to the role of the customer as a connector. The customer is a node and a center connecting all the digital platforms. It is different from the previous era – the twentieth – in which the role of the customer is passive and considered in aggregate. In this era, customers act as advocates for the product or service. More specifically, Rogers identifies the characteristics of customers in this digital era: access, engage, customize, connect, and collaboration.

Access is a behavior that always wants to know everything around them, especially in a digital context. Engage means that consumers are active in spreading and evaluating products or services. With the characteristic of customize, customers seek to customize their experience using the product and service. Connect is related to the intention of the customer to share their experience, ideas, or opinion with other customers. Collaboration is related to the characteristic of customers as social humans that always want to work together.

Drawing inspiration from Rogers' Network Behavior and recognizing the dawn of the digital age, it's imperative for the tourism sector to recalibrate its strategies. Given the evident shift in consumer patterns, digital overhaul has become paramount for stakeholders in the tourism realm. The author underscores that "digital transformation" encompasses more than just marketing and promotions in the tourism industry. It signifies a holistic embrace of digital tools, encapsulating every facet, from the value chain to the entire value system.

In the context of digital transformation, authors suggest the conceptual framework developed by Ismail et al. (2017). The conceptual representation delves into two primary components of a business framework: the "Firm Value Chain" and the "Entire Value System." The following sentences are a description of the framework.

Firm Value Chain

Digital transformation in the value chain area refers to the incorporation of digital technologies into various stages of an organization's value chain to enhance efficiency, customer experience, and overall value generation. Ismail et al. explain that within the value chain, digital transformation primarily affects the Operational Element. This element highlights the systems and techniques a company uses in its everyday operations. It includes two main aspects: (1) operations/processes, which refer to the specific methods and routines the business follows, and (2) decision-making, which involves the strategies and reasoning used in the company's choice-making processes.

The outcomes or consequences stemming from the transformation process are in *Human Element*: This segment accentuates the integral role of individuals in influencing the trajectory of a business: (1) People: Refers to the collective workforce or team members and (2) Culture: Represents the set of shared values, norms, and beliefs that define and shape the organizational ambiance.

Entire Value System

Digital transformation in the value system refers to the comprehensive integration of digital technologies throughout the entire ecosystem in which a business operates, encompassing not just its internal value chain but also its external interactions and dependencies. The value system considers the broader network of activities beyond the individual company, including suppliers, distributors, and even the end consumers. It considers the interconnectedness and interdependencies among various stakeholders in the creation and delivery of value. Transformation embodies the evolution of strategies, factoring in external interactions and client perceptions (1) customer element: captures the essence of interactions and perceptions from the clientele's viewpoint, (2) customer experience: encompasses the holistic perception and interactions clients have with the company's offerings, (3) products/services: denotes the tangible or intangible items or solutions provided to the market.

The significance of the impact refers to the wide-ranging consequences of the transformation that go beyond the immediate confines of the organization. This includes two key areas: (1) the network element, which highlights the business's connections with other stakeholders and its position within a larger network, and (2) integrated value networks, which represent the mutually beneficial relationships and collaborations the organization engages in, both within its immediate environment and across the wider industry.

Applying the concepts of the value chain and value creation system to tourism presents challenges due to the sector's complexity. The tourism industry involves a wide range of participants, such as government entities, local communities, business owners, and media or educational institutions. Consequently, Porter's value chain model cannot be directly applied as is. However, the United Nations World Tourism Organization (UNWTO), as cited by Milicevic (2021), provides adapted frameworks or insights that are more suitable for addressing the unique aspects of the tourism industry. The model described is divided into two main sections: On the left side are the outbound activities, which occur in the tourist's home country and include both direct and indirect activities related to preparing for travel. The right side focuses on inbound activities, which take place in the destination country or location that the tourist intends to visit. This side typically encompasses all tourism-related activities, such as transportation, accommodation, food and beverage services, handicrafts, cultural attractions, leisure activities, and various support services. Infrastructure support, essential for facilitating these tourism activities, is illustrated at the bottom of the model. Meanwhile, support from indirect activities, like policies from the Tourism Ministry, contributions from the Chamber of Commerce, and services from the banking sector, are depicted at the top of the model.

Using the United Nations World Tourism Organization (UNWTO) Model and the framework provided by Ismail et al., the author presents a digital transformation framework specifically tailored for the tourism sector, as illustrated in Fig. 4.2.

The tourism industry's digital transformation may include both sides of the value chain, outbound and inbound, focusing on operational elements. The operational elements include the critical business processes and operations which will integrate with digitalization (Ismail et al., 2017). An outbound activity in the country of origin of tourism comprises all the key processes and operations of travel and booking organizations. Moreover, in outbound activities in the country destination, it covers all the key processes and operations of the transportation, accommodation, food and beverage, handcrafts, cultural asset, leisure, and support services as the consequences are the human element. It means that digitalization should trigger the need to enhance the qualification and standards of the people behind all the services in both inbound and outbound activities. The tourism organization should arrange a new company culture that facilitates a more flexible work environment and knowledge sharing (Ismail et al., 2017).

The transformation will cover the area of the value chain (inbound and outbound activities) and the area of the value-creating system, which is more specific on the customer side. In this process, the transformation will impact customer experiences. According to Ismail et al. (2017), the spectrum of digital transformation in customer experience encompasses improving customer understanding via analytics to facilitate seamless and enhanced engagement across all contact points with digitally improved communication tools. This transformation in customer experience not only alters a company's operations but also significantly impacts its interactions within its value networks, affecting how the company connects and collaborates with other entities in its ecosystem.

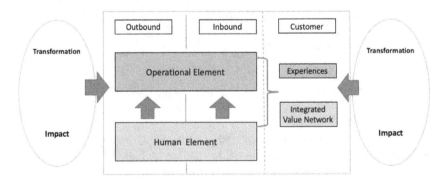

Fig. 4.2.   Digital Transformation Framework in Tourism Value
Chain and Value System (Author).

SE as a Competency to Enhance the Digital Adoption

As all the sectors have already implemented the digital transformation, the tourism actors (including Government) need to see these as a strategic agenda. Furthermore, at this point, one of the competencies that all actors must improve is the ability to respond strategically to market opportunities. This competency is called SE. It can be defined as the combination of entrepreneurship and strategic management to explore the new opportunity and exploit it to build and gain a competitive advantage. Ireland and Webb (2007) specify that SE will create value from the intersection between strategy aspects and entrepreneurship (Fig. 4.3). SE comprises two essential characteristics: opportunity-seeking activities as an entrepreneurship characteristic and advantage-seeking activities as a strategist characteristic (Utoyo, 2020).

By implementing exploration and exploitation-oriented SE, organizations can develop a consistent flow of innovation and continue to surpass their competitors in various forms, starting from new organizational forms, new products, new processes, new services, and others (Utoyo, 2020, p. 86). In addition, Ireland et al. (2003) argue that SE is something unique and constructive that can lead an organization to create prosperity through its four dimensions: entrepreneurial mindset, entrepreneurial culture, entrepreneurial leadership, managing resources strategically, applying creativity, and developing innovation. Further, they design

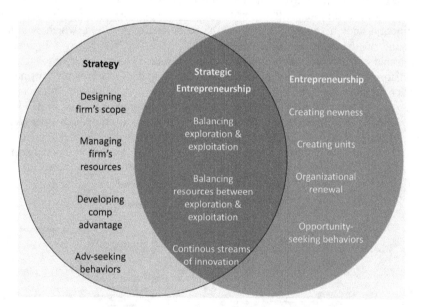

Fig. 4.3.   Strategic Entrepreneurship: A Value-Creating Intersection Between Strategy and Entrepreneurship. *Source:* Adapted from Ireland and Webb, 2007, by Utoyo (2020).

it as a model of strategic entrepreneurship: constructs and dimensions. The model contains various SE concepts from many researchers such as Covin and Miles (1999), Hitt et al. (2001), and Ireland et al. (2001).

The model of SE proposed by Ireland et al. in 2003, seeks to blend entrepreneurial actions and strategic management practices to achieve competitive advantage and wealth creation. The core of this model lies in understanding that entrepreneurship and strategic management, when combined, can lead to a firm's increased innovation, adaptability, and overall success.

Here are the main components and their interrelationships:

- Entrepreneurial mindset, culture, and leadership: the foundation of SE. It promotes a firm-wide belief in seeking new opportunities and being innovative. It emphasizes leadership that encourages risk-taking and adaptability.
- Resource orchestration: SE isn't just about spotting opportunities; it's also about utilizing and reallocating resources effectively to exploit these opportunities. This involves managing the firm's resources strategically, aligning them with the identified opportunities.
- Innovation: Entrepreneurs bring about innovations, whether in products, services, or processes. Combining this innovation with strategic insights allows firms to be unique in the marketplace and gain a competitive edge.
- Competitive advantage: By merging entrepreneurial actions with strategic practices, firms can establish a position of advantage in the market. This competitive position helps them differentiate from rivals and maintain sustainability in the long run.
- Wealth creation: the goal of SE. By leveraging opportunities with an effective strategy and innovation, firms can create value for stakeholders and generate increased wealth.

The model emphasizes the synergy between entrepreneurial actions and strategic management, advocating for their simultaneous implementation to ensure both opportunity exploration and exploitation. This combination is seen as key to driving firm growth, innovation, and achieving sustainable competitive advantage.

The model addresses that the entrepreneurial mindset, culture, and leadership are prerequisites for creativity and innovation to achieve a competitive advantage and create wealth. The digital transformation, which is a practical approach in this era for all sectors, including tourism, can be implemented only if all actors have or use the SE model. Therefore, we need all the tourism industry actors to implement or adapt the entrepreneurial mindset, culture, or leadership. Ireland et al. (2003, p. 968) define an entrepreneurial mindset as a growth-oriented perspective through which individuals promote flexibility, creativity, continuous innovation, and renewal. It includes the components: recognizing entrepreneurial opportunities, entrepreneurial alertness, actual options logic, and entrepreneurial framework.

An entrepreneurial mindset is a specific way of thinking, feeling, and acting that is oriented toward identifying and acting upon opportunities, while embracing the uncertainties of the future. It's what sets entrepreneurs apart, allowing them to innovate, take calculated risks, and drive change. Key components and traits of this mindset include: the *opportunity recognition* that is the ability to lookout for new possibilities; *risk tolerance*, behavior that comfortable with taking calculated risks; *innovativeness, adaptability, visionary*; *real options logic* a framework for evaluating and managing uncertainties and complexities in dealing with potential future opportunities and *entrepreneurial framework* that is specific mindset that allows individuals to identify and act upon opportunities, innovate, and navigate the challenges of starting and running a business. In essence, the entrepreneurial mindset is a unique blend of traits, beliefs, and behaviors that propel individuals toward entrepreneurial actions and success. It's not just about starting businesses; it's a way of approaching life's challenges and opportunities with enthusiasm, creativity, and tenacity.

The characteristics of an entrepreneurial culture, as described by Ireland et al. (2003), encompass traits such as fostering fresh ideas, promoting creativity, endorsing risk-taking, being understanding of failures, advocating for continuous learning, and constantly championing innovation in products, processes, and administration. In this vein, Ireland posits that leaders play a crucial role in cultivating this entrepreneurial culture, enabling the successful application of SE (p. 971). Furthermore, Ireland characterizes entrepreneurial leadership as the skill of strategically guiding others in the management of resources, balancing both the pursuit of opportunities and the quest for competitive advantages (Covin & Miles, 1999; Ireland & Hitt, 1999; Rowe, 2001 in Ireland et al., 2003).

Furthermore, the characteristics of entrepreneurial leadership can be described as follows:

- Fostering entrepreneurial abilities: enhancing human capital by nurturing individual attributes like agility, creativity, and strategic resource management skills.
- Safeguarding current business models: informing organizational members about the potential advantages of disruptive innovations, such as paving the way for new competitive edges.
- Understanding opportunities: articulating the significance of opportunities and how their utilization aligns with both the firm's and individuals' objectives.
- Challenging established norms: assessing the prevalent assumptions in the business world to ensure the firm is primed to pinpoint entrepreneurial prospects that add value.
- Re-evaluating fundamental queries: periodically revisiting core questions about market viability, company purpose, success criteria, and stakeholder relationships to discern opportunities and the strategic resource allocation to seize them.

• Bridging entrepreneurship and strategy: cultivating an environment where resources are utilized both strategically, targeting competitive advantages, and entrepreneurially, seeking out new opportunities.

Implication

In today's digital era, the paramount importance of digital transformation in tourism management cannot be overstated. This chapter's framework addresses key operational facets of the tourism sector, including travel and booking agencies, transportation, lodging, culinary experiences, handicrafts, destination assets, recreation, and auxiliary services. Introducing digitalization to these operational dimensions will inevitably influence the human aspect. However, the success of such initiatives hinges on the tourism industry's stakeholders embracing an entrepreneurial mindset, culture, and leadership.

Conclusion

Digital transformation in the tourism sector is a must and strategic agenda because the digitalization era is already happening. However, it will also help all actors achieve and create value for their customers (tourists). It is precise because now, the behavior of customers or tourists is a network behavior. Moreover, digital transformation entails the tourism sector's value chain and system. The value chain comprises inbound and outbound activities, while the value system is related to customers' experience. This chapter has concluded with an integrated framework to show how digitalization impacts the value chain and value system.

In addition, SE with specific traits: opportunities and advantage-seeking behavior (Ireland et al., 2003) is a competency that every actor in the tourism industry needs to master. This competency relates explicitly to entrepreneurial mindset, entrepreneurial culture, and leadership. The author believes that by using SE, the tourism industry will excel in anticipating and managing the tremendous change and create more value for the stakeholder.

References

Benyon, D., Quiley, A., O'Keefe, B., & Riva, G. (2014). Presence and digital tourism. *AI & Society, 29*(4), 521–529.

Covin, J. G., & Miles, M. P. (1999). Corporate entrepreneurship and the pursuit of competitive advantage. *Entrepreneurship Theory and Practice, 23*(3), 47–63.

Hitt, M. A., Bierman, L., Shimizu, K., & Kochhar, R. (2001). Direct and moderating effects of human capital on strategy and performance in professional service firms: A resource-based perspective. *Academy of Management Journal, 44*, 13–28.

Ireland, R. D., & Hitt, M. A. (1999). Achieving and maintaining strategic competitiveness in the 21st century: The role of strategic leadership. *Academy of Management Executive, 13*(1), 43–57.

Ireland, R. D., Hitt, M. A., Camp, S. M., & Sexton, D. L. (2001). Integrating entrepreneurship and strategic management action to create firm wealth. *Academy of Management Executive, 15*(1), 49–63.

Ireland, R. D., Hitt, M. A., & Sirmon, D. G. (2003). A model of strategic entrepreneurship: The construct and its dimensions. *Journal of Management, 29*(6), 963–989.

Ireland, R. D, & Webb, J. W. (2007). A cross-disciplinary exploration of entrepreneurship research. *Journal of Management, 33*, 891–927.

Ismail, M. H., Kater, M., & Zaki, M. (2017). *Digital business transformation and strategy: What do we know so far?* Cambridge Service Alliance.

Jane, O. (2022). *Strategic management +*. PT Refika Aditama.

Korze, S. Z. (2019). From industry 4.0 to tourism 4.0. *Innovative Issues and Approaches in Social Sciences, 12*(3).

Leung, D., Law, R., van Hoof, H., & Buhalis, D. (2013). Social media in tourism and hospitality: A literature review. *Journal of Travel & Tourism Marketing, 30*(1–2), 3–22.

Milicevic, K. (2021). *Tourism value chain and sustainability certification report.* Labelscape: Integration of Sustainability Labels into Mediterranean Tourism Policy.

Peceny, U. S., Urbancic, J., Mokorel, S., Kuralt, V., & Iljas, T. (2019). Tourism 4.0: Challenges in marketing paradigm shift. In *Consumer behavior and marketing.* IntechOpen.

Rogers, D. L. (2016). *Digital transformation playbook: Rethink your business for the digital age.* Columbia University Press.

Rowe, W. G. (2001). Creating wealth in organizations: The role of strategic leadership. *Academy of Management Executive, 15*(1), 81–94.

United Nations World of Tourism Organization (UNWTO). (2021). *Covid-19 and tourism report.*

Utoyo, I. (2020). *Hybrid company model: Cara menang di Era digital.* Rayyana Komunikasindo.

Zeng, B., & Gerritsen, R. (2014). What do we know about social media in tourism? A review. *Tourism Management Perspectives, 10*, 27–36.

Chapter 5

Microfinance as a Catalyst of Promoting SMEs for Rebuilding Communities: A Roadmap for Achieving SDGs Suggesting Policy Implications

Manpreet Arora

Central University of Himachal Pradesh, India

Abstract

Rebuilding communities in economically struggling places might mean taking steps to combat poverty and promote economic growth. This can entail boosting employment prospects, promoting small-town enterprises, and enhancing access to health care and education. The COVID-19 pandemic had a significant and all-encompassing influence on economy around the world. In order to craft a convincing case for the critical role that microfinance plays in promoting the expansion of small and medium-sized enterprises (SMEs) and, as a result, helping to rebuild communities and achieve the Sustainable Development Goals (SDGs), the author has used a thorough literature-based methodology in this chapter. This is an opinion-based chapter. In order to discover recurring themes and patterns connected to microfinance, SME development, and SDGs, the author has rigorously analyzed and integrated the data and insights offered in various sources. The presented thoughts and policy suggestions are built upon the findings of this literature research.

Keywords: Microfinance; SMEs; rebuilding communities; SDGs; policy implications; Sustainable Development Goals

Strategic Tourism Planning for Communities, 63–79
Copyright © 2024 Manpreet Arora
Published under exclusive licence by Emerald Publishing Limited
doi:10.1108/978-1-83549-015-020241006

Introduction

Rebuilding communities is the process of reviving and enhancing a specific place or community that has experienced difficulties, setbacks, or calamities. This concept can be used in variety of situations, such as disaster recovery, following natural catastrophes (such as hurricanes, earthquakes, and floods) or disasters caused by humans (such as conflicts, industrial accidents), communities are frequently rebuilt. Rebuilding in these situations entails fixing damaged buildings, restoring houses, and offering assistance to let the impacted people and families resume their regular lives. Rebuilding communities in economically struggling places might mean taking steps to combat poverty and promote economic growth. This can entail boosting employment prospects, promoting small-town enterprises, and enhancing access to health care and education. Rebuilding urban communities might involve reviving run-down, criminalized, or neglected neighborhoods. To develop a sense of belonging and pride, this can involve renovating or reusing buildings, enhancing public areas, and encouraging community interaction. Communities may also need to be rebuilt following social or political upheavals, such as civil wars or rifts within the community. In these situations, efforts frequently center on integration, settlement of disputes, and inclusivity and diversity promotion. Communities that have suffered from environmental degradation may need to be rebuilt using ecological restoration techniques and sustainable development methods to provide long-term resilience. Rebuilding communities can also apply to situations involving public health, such the aftermath of a pandemic. It might entail enhancing public health infrastructure, addressing issues with mental health and well-being, and strengthening healthcare systems. Depending on the particular needs and obstacles of each situation, the precise tactics and actions involved in rebuilding communities can differ significantly. To develop a thorough and long-lasting plan for reform, it typically needs cooperation between government agencies, nonprofit organizations, community leaders, and citizens. The ultimate objective is to build flourishing, resilient, and powerful communities that can face new challenges.

Growing Relevance of Rebuilding Communities After COVID-19

Following the COVID-19 pandemic, the idea of reconstructing economies became quite popular for a number of reasons:

The COVID-19 pandemic had a significant and all-encompassing influence on economy around the world (Cheng et al., 2022; Mukarram, 2020; Plzáková & Smeral, 2022; Roshana et al., 2020; Sidhu et al., 2020). Job losses, decreased economic activity, and, in many cases, recessionary conditions were caused by lockdowns, limits on commercial activities, and interruptions to global supply lines (Brodeur et al., 2021; Ibn-Mohammed et al., 2021; Jackson et al., 2020; Kumar et al., 2020; Laborde et al., 2021; Rasul et al., 2021; Shafi et al., 2020; Yu et al., 2021). As a result, it was urgent to handle the economic consequences and make up lost ground. Governments from all around the world put in place a variety of stimulus measures to lessen the pandemic's negative economic effects.

These included investments in healthcare infrastructure, assistance for enterprises, and financial aid to individuals. There have been discussions regarding how to handle the consequent debt and budgetary issues due to the size and extent of these interventions.

Further, the epidemic revealed weaknesses in a number of industries, including health care, supply networks, and hiring procedures. Rebuilding economies was viewed as a chance to not only recover but also to create more flexible and resilient systems that could withstand shocks in the future. The pandemic sped up digital transformation and innovation across a wide range of businesses, from telemedicine and online education to remote employment and e-commerce (Banga & te Velde, 2020; Brem et al., 2021; Datta & Nwankpa, 2021; Lund et al., 2021; Radu & Vodă, 2023; Shao et al., 2023; Yeganeh, 2021). Rebuilding economies provided an opportunity to take advantage of these developments and apply them to long-term economic plans. Existing social and economic inequality was made worse by COVID-19. As economies recovered, concerns about equity, accessible health care, social safety nets, and ethical workplace practices gained popularity as a way to address these inequalities. The pandemic's worldwide scope brought to light how intertwined economies are and how crucial cooperation on a global scale is. Discussions about reforming international trade, bolstering health systems, and assisting poor countries in their economic recovery were all part of the process of rebuilding economies. The epidemic acted as a wake-up call, highlighting the necessity of being ready for upcoming disasters, whether they are environmental, economic, or health-related. Discussions about improving crisis management and resilience mechanisms were part of the process of rebuilding economies.

Methodology

In order to craft a convincing case for the critical role that microfinance plays in promoting the expansion of small and medium-sized enterprises (SMEs) and, as a result, helping to rebuild communities and achieve the Sustainable Development Goals (SDGs), the author has used a thorough methodology in this chapter. The study starts with a thorough analysis of academic papers, studies, and policy documents from reliable sources like scholarly journals, global organizations, and official government publications. In order to discover recurring themes and patterns connected to microfinance, SME development, and SDGs, the author has rigorously analyzed and integrated the data and insights offered in various sources. The presented thoughts and policy suggestions are built upon the findings of this literature research.

In order to demonstrate the practical ramifications of microfinance programs, the author has primarily critically engaged with the body of literature, looking at different opinions and perspectives in addition to providing a focus on how the SMEs can be mapped with achieving SDGs. Furthermore, the author accepts that formulating opinions is inherently subjective because it takes into account our personal prejudices and experiences. This approach places a strong emphasis on source transparency, following accepted citation conventions and assuring accurate portrayal of the literature. The author aims to give readers a well-informed perspective on how microfinance can spur SME growth, community revitalization, and the achievement of the SDGs through this methodical approach, offering practical policy implications for decision-makers and stakeholders engaged in sustainable development projects.

Microfinance as a Catalyst for SDG Achievement and Entrepreneurship

A potent tool for fostering entrepreneurship and advancing the SDGs, microfinance involves the provision of modest loans and financial services to people and small enterprises with little access to traditional banks. Here are some ways that microfinance can support business and advance certain SDGs:

- Poverty Reduction (SDG 1): Microfinance primarily targets those with low incomes. Microfinance helps people create or grow their enterprises, which generates income and lowers poverty, supporting SDG 1s goal to end all forms of poverty.
- Decent Work and Economic Growth (SDG 8): Microfinance helps small enterprises and prospects for self-employment grow, which are important sources of employment, particularly in emerging nations. Microfinance's promotion of entrepreneurship directly advances SDG 8's objectives of full and productive employment for all, sustained, inclusive, and sustainable economic growth.
- Gender Equality (SDG 5): Microfinance particularly benefits women, who are frequently excluded from traditional financing. Microfinance institutions (MFIs) address gender inequities and advance SDG 5's aim of attaining gender equality and empowering women and girls through providing financial services to women entrepreneurs.
- Quality Education (SDG 4): Microfinance frequently incorporates components that help increase capacity, like training in financial literacy and business management. By improving entrepreneurs' knowledge and abilities and helping them to run their companies more successfully, these programs support SDG 4.
- Affordable and Clean Energy (SDG 7): By giving business owners in the field of renewable energy the funding necessary to make investments in sustainable energy solutions, microfinance can support their efforts. This is in line with SDG 7's goal of ensuring that everyone has access to affordable, dependable, sustainable, and modern energy.
- Responsible Consumption and Production (SDG 12): By assisting businesses that place a high priority on responsible consumption and production, microfinance may promote sustainable business practices. This covers enterprises that promote eco-friendly products, recycle resources, or decrease waste.
- Partnerships for the Goals (SDG 17): MFIs can work with authorities, nongovernmental organizations, and other stakeholders in order to create an

environment that is conducive to entrepreneurship. These collaborations can facilitate the coordination of microfinance initiatives with national development plans and the broader SDG agenda.

- Reduction in Inequality (SDG 10): By granting financial access to neglected and underprivileged communities, microfinance can help to reduce economic inequality by enabling individuals who had previously been kept out of financial services to engage in economic activity.
- Good Health and Well-Being (SDG 3): By assisting business owners in healthcare-related endeavors like pharmacies or clinics, microfinance can help SDG 3 achieve its objective of guaranteeing healthy lifestyles and fostering well-being for all.

Particularly among marginalized and economically underprivileged communities, microfinance is an essential instrument for fostering entrepreneurship. It encourages economic growth, creates job possibilities, and gives people the freedom to start and build their own businesses. Furthermore, through addressing poverty, inequality, gender inequities, and promoting sustainable business practices, microfinance can directly help to achieve numerous SDGs. As a result, it is essential to moving forward with the global sustainable development agenda.

How Microfinance Can Act as a Catalyst of Promoting Growth

Microfinance programs have the ability to significantly influence the economic development of emerging economies in several ways (Arora, 2023; Arora & Singh, 2016; Barguellil & Bettayeb, 2020; Ehigiamusoe, 2008; Nega & Schneider, 2014; Samineni & Ramesh, 2020). Through microfinance programs, a provision of small loans and financial services are made available to individual as well as small businesses who do not have access to traditional banking services, as they belong to low-income categories and lack collaterals to offer. Through this access, they can invest in their companies, buy goods or equipment, and expand their operations thanks to this access to cash, which eventually boosts their earnings and promotes economic growth. The access to capital can have ripple effects. Microfinance promotes entrepreneurial activities by assisting and providing aspiring entrepreneurs with necessary funds in order to start new ventures or expand existing businesses (Bruton et al., 2015; Sriram & Mersha, 2010). When new enterprises are created, it promotes newer jobs and employment opportunities, thereby reducing unemployment rates and promoting economic growth. Microfinance aids in lifting individuals out of deep poverty by giving them access to financial resources. Having access to finance allows people and households to invest in income-generating ventures, which can raise living standards and lower poverty rates. It is regarded as an effective tool of poverty removal.

Another dimension of microfinance is empowering women (Addai, 2017; Arora & Singh, 2018a, 2018b; Hunt, 2002). Women are disproportionately affected by financial exclusion in many emerging economies; thus, microfinance initiatives frequently focus on them. When women have access to finance, they may invest in small companies, health care, and education, which not only gives them economic power but also strengthens their position in family and community decision-making. Many emerging economies face a challenge of financial inclusion of deprived sections of the society. Through providing microfinance credit facilities, this problem is dealt with to a great extent (Abel, 2020; Mushtaq & Bruneau, 2019; Zulkhibri, 2016). In addition to provision of credit, microfinance firms frequently provide financial services like insurance, remittances, and savings accounts. These services encourage financial inclusion by assisting individuals in better money management and risk mitigation. The ripple effect of rural development extends to rural upliftment in many dimensions. A sizable share of the population lives in rural areas in many emerging economies. By giving farmers and agricultural businesses the money they need to invest in better farming practices, technology, and infrastructure, microfinance may play a crucial role in rural development by raising agricultural productivity and income levels. The concept of community building is easily achieved by microfinance activities. Self-help groups and cooperatives can provide a sense of community and mutual support among borrowers, and microfinance frequently encourages their creation (Arora & Singh, 2018c). These organizations may serve as platforms for knowledge exchange and communal problem-solving in the community. A wide variety of small enterprises, including those in agriculture, retail, services, and handicrafts, is supported through microfinance. This diversification can increase the economy's resistance to shocks and promote overall stability. The infrastructural development is promoted by financial support to the many sections of the society. Businesses help to build the community's infrastructure as they expand and make money. For instance, better utilities, transportation, and roads may be required to accommodate growing enterprises, which will be advantageous to the entire neighborhood. Microfinance has the ability to accelerate economic growth in developing nations, but in order to fully realize this potential, it is crucial to ensure responsible lending methods, client protection, and efficient financial education. Furthermore, regulatory oversight and assistance for MFIs can contribute to the development of a setting that supports long-term economic expansion.

Microfinance: A Catalyst for Sustainable Practices and Ventures Through SMEs

The COVID-19 pandemic has shown how urgent it is for all facets of society to adopt sustainable methods. SMEs are crucial in this regard since they may set the example by embracing environmentally friendly practices and fostering a more sustainable future. In order to encourage sustainable actions through SMEs, microfinance, which entails giving small loans and other financial services to people and small enterprises, can be a potent trigger. Following are the ways by which microfinance can promote sustainability.

- *Capital access for sustainability initiatives*

Giving SMEs the funds they need to invest in environmentally friendly products and services is one of the main ways microfinance can advance sustainability. It is difficult to apply sustainable strategies when many small enterprises lack access to conventional forms of finance. Microfinance organizations can close this gap by providing accessible, inexpensive loans that are specifically designed to promote green activities. This money can be invested in things like trash reduction, renewable energy sources, and energy-efficient machinery.

- *Training and capacity building*

Microfinance organizations frequently offer more than simply cash assistance. They typically provide their clients with training and capacity-building programs. These programs can concentrate on teaching SMEs about ethical business conduct in the context of sustainability. MFIs enable SMEs to adopt and implement eco-friendly measures successfully by disseminating knowledge and skills relevant to sustainability.

- *Risk reduction*

Initiatives for sustainability frequently have up-front expenditures and risks. The risks involved with these investments can be reduced with the aid of microfinance. MFIs lessen the financial load on SMEs by providing flexible repayment terms and affordable interest rates, enabling them to embrace sustainability without worrying about going bankrupt or becoming insolvent.

- *Fostering green start-ups*

Microfinance can be extremely important in fostering green start-ups and creative, sustainable businesses. Finding the initial funding they require to start their enterprises is difficult for many environmentally concerned business owners. The financial support needed to make these concepts a reality can be obtained from microfinance organizations. By doing this, they encourage economic growth in addition to sustainable business.

- *Inclusive growth and the eradication of poverty*

Sustainable businesses frequently have a significant social component, such as providing employment opportunities for underserved populations or tackling urgent environmental problems. These businesses can be the focus of microfinance, which will encourage inclusive growth and the reduction of poverty. Microfinance organizations help to accomplish a number of SDGs, including SDG 1 (No Poverty) and SDG 8 (Decent Work and Economic Growth), by assisting companies that place a high priority on sustainability.

- *Accountability and monitoring*

Institutions that offer microfinance can also help to monitor and guarantee that the money is used for good causes. They can add environmental and social performance metrics to their lending standards, which will motivate SMEs to continue working toward their sustainability objectives and hold them responsible for their deeds.

- *Using best practices again*

Microfinance-supported SMEs that have successfully implemented sustainability programs might serve as models for other businesses. These success stories can encourage other SMEs to embrace environmentally friendly practices and show that sustainability can have positive effects on both the environment and the economy.

Through SMEs, microfinance has the potential to be an effective catalyst for sustainable practices, endeavors, and policies. MFIs can enable small enterprises to take the lead in promoting a more sustainable future by giving them access to money, providing training and capacity-building opportunities, and supporting green start-ups. This benefits not only the environment but also economic development, the eradication of poverty, and the accomplishment of numerous SDGs. Utilizing the potential of microfinance to advance sustainability is more important than ever as the globe faces escalating sustainability issues.

The Crucial Role of SMEs in Addressing Pandemic-Related Challenges and Their Contribution Toward SDGs

The COVID-19 pandemic unconfined never-before-seen challenges that had an influence on everyday life of individuals, economics, and health. SMEs, frequently regarded to as the building blocks of economies, are vital for minimizing and resolving the complex problems brought on by the pandemic. In growing economies, SMEs play a vital and varied role. These businesses, which are frequently distinguished by their smaller workforces and revenue when compared to larger firms, support the economic and social growth of emerging economies in a number of ways. SMEs play a significant role in the generation of jobs in developing nations (Fiseha & Oyelana, 2015; Marinho & Costa Melo, 2022; Taiwo & Falohun, 2016). They can employ a sizable fraction of the workforce because they are often more labor-intensive than larger businesses. In areas with high rates of underemployment or unemployment, this is essential to focus on the promotion of SMEs. This holds a great deal of relevance for emerging economies also. SMEs have a great ability to generate revenue for different stakeholders. SMEs offer chances for local communities and business owners to make money (Hyder & Lussier, 2016). They enable people to launch and expand their own businesses, which can improve economic independence and lower poverty rates (Alharbi et al., 2015). SMEs frequently act as hubs for entrepreneurship and innovation (Brunswicker & Van de Vrande, 2014; Vrgovic et al., 2012). They encourage innovation and creativity because they are more adaptable and can change with the market more quickly. New products, services, and business models may result from this. This could play a very important role in the emerging economies as they need higher pace of industrialization and higher degree of employment. By fostering economic activity in remote or underdeveloped areas, SMEs can significantly contribute to the balanced regional development (Fernández-Serrano & Romero, 2013; Kowo et al., 2019; Mannar, 2019). They can aid in eliminating gaps between urban and rural areas by spreading economic gains more fairly across a nation or region. There are various connotations for SMEs in growing nations in relation to supply chain integrations also. Locally and worldwide, SMEs might join the supply networks of larger enterprises. By enhancing both SMEs' and larger enterprises' competitiveness, this integration can promote economic growth. SME production of goods and services for foreign markets might increase a nation's export potential. In order to reduce trade imbalances (Knight, 2001; Osano, 2019), they might also engage in import substitution by producing goods that were previously imported.

SMEs are more likely than large enterprises to implement sustainable practices (Gadenne et al., 2009). They frequently leave less of an environmental footprint and can help emerging economies achieve their goals for sustainable development. The following are the ways in which SMEs can contribute to addressing these challenges:

Economic Resilience Achieving SDG 9

SMEs have a reputation for being adaptable and flexible. They exhibited their ability to quickly pivot during the epidemic by changing their business strategies and producing necessary products like personal protection equipment (PPE) and hand sanitizers. The ability to adapt is essential for economic resilience. Several SDGs of the United Nations can be aligned with the idea of economic resilience exhibited by SMEs throughout the epidemic. One pertinent SDG that supports this notion is "SDG 9: Infrastructure, Industry, and Innovation". Target 9.3 of SDG 9 in particularly is very important in this direction, which highlights on the need of improving small-scale industrial and other businesses' access to financial services, especially affordable loans, and their inclusion into value chains and markets, particularly in emerging nations. Here is how SDG 9 and the economic toughness displayed by SMEs during the pandemic are related:

- Flexibility and adaptability, which are essential elements of SDG 9, are demonstrated by SMEs' capacity to quickly pivot and modify their business models throughout the epidemic. For SMEs to integrate into value chains and adapt to shifting market needs, they must be adaptable.
- During the pandemic, SMEs who switched their manufacturing to necessities like PPE and hand sanitizers helped to meet pressing needs for public health.

This fits with SDG 9's emphasis on improving infrastructure and industry to meet social requirements.

- Target 9.3 places a focus on expanding small businesses' access to financial services, especially finance that is affordable which highlights the significance of microcredit. Financial resilience, a key component of this SDG objective, is frequently displayed by SMEs as economic resilience.

Employment Generation Achieving SDG 8

In many nations, SMEs are one of the largest employers. By assisting these companies, we may maintain and even boost employment levels while limiting the negative economic effects of the pandemic. The idea of creating jobs by helping SMEs is in line with a number of SDGs set forward by the United Nations. One of the main SDGs with a strong connection to this idea is: Decent Work and Economic Growth (SDG 8). Target 8.5 of SDG 8 in particular is very important which states that "By 2030, all women and men will have full and productive employment, along with a fair standard of living, including equal pay for equal-value work for young people and those with disabilities." SME development promotes employment in line with SDG 8. In many nations, SMEs are important sources of employment, employing a sizable fraction of the labor force. The achievement of full and productive employment, as defined in Target 8.5, is aided by supporting these companies. The pandemic's economic issues made it crucial to maintain current positions while also developing new ones. Supporting SMEs will enable us to protect and increase job possibilities, which is a crucial component of Target 8.5.

Target 8.5 is focused on ensuring that everyone has access to quality employment, particularly women, young people, and people with impairments. SMEs frequently provide employment options for a variety of individuals, promoting inclusion in the labor market. Fair remuneration procedures are crucial, as seen by Target 8.5's mention of the objective of equal pay for work of comparable worth. Supporting SMEs can encourage equitable wage distribution and work practices. In essence, SDG 8's main goal of supporting decent work and economic growth is well aligned with the support provided to SMEs in creating jobs. It highlights the need of quality employment possibilities in addition to quantity, which is essential for sustainable growth.

Innovation and Adaptability Achieving SDG 9

SMEs frequently outperform larger companies in terms of innovation and adaptability. By inventing contactless payment options or improving e-commerce systems, they can quickly respond to new demands and meet immediate requirements. Numerous SDGs of the United Nations are aligned with SMEs' exceptional capacity for innovation and agility, notably in responding quickly to new demands and resolving developing requirements. SMEs can be innovation hubs since they are frequently unencumbered by complicated bureaucratic procedures. Their capacity to act quickly in response to new requirements, like creating contactless payment options or expanding e-commerce systems during the epidemic, directly supports innovation, a crucial element of SDG 9. SMEs help to increase the technological capabilities of industrial sectors by embracing technological breakthroughs and modifying their operations to meet changing needs. This is in line with SDG 9's larger objective of modernizing infrastructure and technology. Innovation and technology improvements are particularly beneficial for SMEs in emerging nations. In line with SDG 9's emphasis on inclusive industrialization, encouraging innovation in various industries aids in closing technology gaps and fosters economic growth. The agility and inventiveness displayed by SMEs closely match SDG 9's objective of promoting infrastructure, industry, and innovation. Particularly in developing nations, SMEs are essential for advancing industrial capacities, advancing technical advancement, and promoting economic growth.

Focus on Local Supply Chains Achieving SDG 9

Global supply chains were made vulnerable by the pandemic. By encouraging local production and sourcing, SMEs can help supply networks remain resilient by lowering reliance on out-of-region sources. Several SDGs of the United Nations can be aligned with the idea of economic resilience exhibited by SMEs throughout the epidemic. One pertinent SDG that supports this notion is SDG 9, i.e., "Infrastructure, Industry, and Innovation." Target 9.3 of SDG 9 in particular is very important in this regard which focuses on "Increase the access of small-scale industrial and other enterprises, in particular in developing countries, to financial services, including affordable credit, and their integration into value chains and markets." SDG 9 places a strong emphasis on innovation and adaptation, and SMEs' capacity to quickly change directions and modify their business models during the epidemic exemplifies these values. For SMEs to integrate into value chains and adapt to shifting market needs, they must be adaptable. Infrastructural investments are crucial to promote local production and sourcing. This is consistent with SDG 9's focus on creating resilient and sustainable infrastructure that supports economic growth and well-being. Infrastructure access that is both affordable and equitable is emphasized by SDG 9. Localizing production, particularly in underserved or rural areas, can support equal access to economic opportunities and resources. In line with more general sustainability objectives, encouraging local production can also benefit the environment by lowering the carbon footprint associated with long-distance travel.

In conclusion, promoting local production and sourcing by SMEs helps supply networks be resilient and sustainable, which are essential elements of SDG 9. This is in line with the objective of creating resilient infrastructure that is high quality, dependable, sustainable, and supportive of economic growth.

Community Engagement and Community Development Via SMEs Focusing on Achieving Multiple SDGs

SMEs have a strong presence in local communities. They can take the helm of neighborhood-based projects like helping vulnerable communities or participating in an active role in neighborhood immunization drives. By actively engaging with and supporting their local communities, SMEs may contribute to the accomplishment of numerous SDGs and play a vital role in community development. Here are a few ways that SMEs can make a difference:

- Employment and Decent Work (SDG 8): SMEs frequently play a significant role in local economies as employers. They immediately support the achievement of SDG 8's objectives of sustained, inclusive, and sustainable economic growth, full and productive employment, and decent work for all by generating employment opportunities and paying decent wages.
- Poverty Reduction (SDG 1): By offering steady job and income-generating possibilities, SMEs may assist in bringing people out of poverty. This is consistent with SDG 1's mission to eradicate all types of poverty.
- Quality Education (SDG 4): SMEs can promote education by providing their staff members with training and development opportunities. They can also participate in community education programs that support lifelong learning and equal access to quality education, as stated in SDG 4. Gender Equality (SDG 5): SMEs may advance gender equality by ensuring equal compensation for equal labor and providing opportunities that are open to both men and women. This is in line with SDG 5's goal of attaining gender equality and giving all women and girls more authority.
- Healthcare and Well-being (SDG 3): SMEs' support of local healthcare programs might come in the form of health insurance, health awareness campaigns, and participation in regional immunization drives. These initiatives support SDG 3's objective of ensuring healthy lifestyles and fostering well-being for all people.
- Sustainable Cities and Communities (SDG 11): In accordance with SDG 11, SMEs can participate in community development initiatives, infrastructure enhancements, and urban regeneration initiatives.
- Climate Action (SDG 13): SMEs can implement eco-friendly practices, lessen their carbon footprint, and take part in regional environmental conservation programs, all of which will help SDG 13 achieve its goal of preventing climate change.
- Partnerships for the Goals (SDG 17): SMEs can work with regional authorities, nonprofit groups, and other stakeholders to create partnerships that tackle diverse issues related to community development. This is consistent with SDG 17's focus on encouraging partnerships to realize the SDGs.
- SMEs are well-positioned to play a significant role in community development and contribute to the accomplishment of the SDGs because of their close relationships to local communities. SMEs may contribute to the development of more wealthy, equitable, and sustainable communities through encouraging

decent work, combating poverty, advancing health care and education, and adopting sustainable practices.

What Policy Implications Need a Thrust in Order to Promote Microfinance as a Catalyst of Growth

A comprehensive set of policies and efforts are needed to promote microfinance as a driver for growth, with a special focus on SMEs. Here are a few policy ramifications that can aid in fostering an atmosphere favorable to the growth of SME and microfinance sectors:

- *Framework for regulation and supervision*

To ensure consumer safety, financial stability, and transparency, governments should focus on establishing a clear regulatory framework for MFIs. Further, a thrust should be there to create efficient monitoring systems to keep an eye on MFI operations and legal compliance. The policymakers should encourage a balanced regulatory approach that takes into account the special requirements and characteristics of microfinance.

- *Financial access and inclusion*

To ensure that underserved populations, particularly those in rural and remote locations, have access to microfinance services through implementing policies to improve financial inclusion, the policymakers should focus on starting various schemes and programs for the vulnerable sections of the society. In order to reach unbanked and underbanked communities, the governments should promote the growth of branch networks and digital financial services.

- *Capacity development*

To improve financial literacy and management abilities, fund training and capacity-building programs for microfinance practitioners, business owners, and borrowers are must. Although these programs are conducted especially in developing nations at different levels, but their timely evaluation and impact assessment is necessary to understand their strengths and weaknesses. The policymakers should encourage initiatives for information sharing and technical support to improve the capacities of the microfinance industry.

- *Risk reduction and tools for credit scoring and evaluation*

In order to encourage financial institutions to lend to microfinance consumers and SMEs, the policymakers should establish risk-sharing mechanisms like credit guarantee schemes. They should further focus on the creation of credit information systems to aid in better risk evaluation and microloan pricing.

- *Differential collaterals*

To increase access to financing for SMEs lacking traditional collateral, the governments as well as regulatory bodies should investigate and promote alternative kinds of collateral such as group guarantees, social collateral, or movable asset-based loans.

- *Public–private alliances*

In order to maximize resources and expertise for advancing microfinance and SME development, the governments as well as regulatory bodies should encourage cooperation between governments, financial institutions, development organizations, and nongovernmental organizations (NGOs).

- *Ecosystem development for SMEs*

By lowering administrative obstacles to business registration and operation, the governments should create an ecosystem that is supportive of SMEs. They should focus on making it easier for SMEs to access markets, information, and technology to boost their competitiveness.

- *Sustainable finance*

By offering rewards for eco-friendly and socially conscious lending practices, the governments should promote the incorporation of environmental and social factors into microfinance operations.

To fully realize the promise of microfinance as an economic driver, particularly for SMEs, a comprehensive approach to microfinance promotion is required, one that includes legislative, financial, capacity-building, and support measures. To ensure that these policy implications are as effective as possible in promoting equitable and sustainable economic development, they should be customized to the unique requirements and context of each nation or region.

Conclusion

Depending on the particular needs and obstacles of each situation, the precise tactics and actions involved in rebuilding communities can differ significantly. To develop a thorough and long-lasting plan for reform, it typically needs cooperation between government agencies, nonprofit organizations, community leaders, and citizens. The ultimate objective is to build flourishing, resilient, and powerful communities that can face new challenges. Microfinance can act as a driver for building SMEs which in turn can solve various issues raised by pandemic.

References

Arora, M., & Singh, S. (2018a). Microfinance, women empowerment, and transformational leadership: A study of Himachal Pradesh. *International Journal on Leadership, 6*(2), 23.

Arora, M., & Singh, S. (2018b). Impact assessment of self-help group bank linkage programme on women empowerment in the state of Himachal Pradesh, India. *Amity Journal of Management Research, 3*(1), 66–80.

Arora, M., & Singh, S. (2018c). The impact of SHG bank linkage programme on the members of self help groups: An empirical investigation in the state of Himachal Pradesh. *Sumedha Journal of Management, 7*(1), 34–46.

Abel, B. B. (2020). Financial inclusion in Burundi: The use of microfinance services in semi-urban areas. *Journal of Economic Development, 45*(3), 101–116.

Addai, B. (2017). Women empowerment through microfinance: Empirical evidence from Ghana. *Journal of Finance and Accounting, 5*(1), 1–11.

Alharbi, A., Kanu, A. M., & Mamman, A. (2015). *Small and medium-sized enterprises (SMEs) and poverty reduction in Africa: Strategic management perspective.* Cambridge Scholars Publishing.

Arora, M. (2023). The holistic metamorphosis of rural lives through microfinance: A perspective. In *Transforming economies through microfinance in developing nations* (pp. 114–130). IGI Global.

Arora, M., & Singh, S. (2016). Disbursement of credit under the SGSY scheme: A comparison of SHGs' Swarozgaris and individual Swarozgaris. *Indian Journal of Finance, 10*(11), 54–63.

Banga, K., & te Velde, D. W. (2020). COVID-19 and disruption of the digital economy; evidence from low and middle-income countries. *Digital Pathways at Oxford Paper Series, 7.*

Barguellil, A., & Bettayeb, L. (2020). The impact of microfinance on economic development: The case of Tunisia. *International Journal of Economics and Finance, 12*(4), 1–43.

Brem, A., Viardot, E., & Nylund, P. A. (2021). Implications of the coronavirus (COVID-19) outbreak for innovation: Which technologies will improve our lives? *Technological Forecasting and Social Change, 163*, 120451.

Brodeur, A., Gray, D., Islam, A., & Bhuiyan, S. (2021). A literature review of the economics of COVID-19. *Journal of Economic Surveys, 35*(4), 1007–1044.

Brunswicker, S., & Van de Vrande, V. (2014). Exploring open innovation in small and medium-sized enterprises. *New Frontiers in Open Innovation, 1*, 135–156.

Bruton, G., Khavul, S., Siegel, D., & Wright, M. (2015). New financial alternatives in seeding entrepreneurship: Microfinance, crowdfunding, and peer–to–peer innovations. *Entrepreneurship Theory and Practice, 39*(1), 9–26.

Cheng, T., Zhao, Y., & Zhao, C. (2022). Exploring the spatio-temporal evolution of economic resilience in Chinese cities during the COVID-19 crisis. *Sustainable Cities and Society, 84*, 103997.

Datta, P., & Nwankpa, J. K. (2021). Digital transformation and the COVID-19 crisis continuity planning. *Journal of Information Technology Teaching Cases, 11*(2), 81–89.

Ehigiamusoe, G. (2008). The role of microfinance institutions in the economic development of Nigeria. *Publication of the Central Bank of Nigeria, 32*(1), 17.

Fernández-Serrano, J., & Romero, I. (2013). Entrepreneurial quality and regional development: Characterizing SME sectors in low income areas. *Papers in Regional Science, 92*(3), 495–513.

Fiseha, G. G., & Oyelana, A. A. (2015). An assessment of the roles of small and medium enterprises (SMEs) in the local economic development (LED) in South Africa. *Journal of Economics, 6*(3), 280–290.

Gadenne, D. L., Kennedy, J., & McKeiver, C. (2009). An empirical study of environmental awareness and practices in SMEs. *Journal of Business Ethics, 84*, 45–63.

Hunt, J. (2002). Reflections on microfinance and women's empowerment. *Women, Gender and Development in the Pacific: Key Issues, 13*.

Hyder, S., & Lussier, R. N. (2016). Why businesses succeed or fail: A study on small businesses in Pakistan. *Journal of Entrepreneurship in Emerging Economies, 8*(1), 82–100.

Ibn-Mohammed, T., Mustapha, K. B., Godsell, J., Adamu, Z., Babatunde, K. A., Akintade, D. D., ... Koh, S. C. L. (2021). A critical analysis of the impacts of COVID-19 on the global economy and ecosystems and opportunities for circular economy strategies. *Resources, Conservation and Recycling, 164*, 105169.

Jackson, J. K., Weiss, M. A., Schwarzenberg, A. B., Nelson, R. M., Sutter, K. M., & Sutherland, M. D. (2020). *Global economic effects of COVID-19.* Congressional Research Service. https://apps.dtic.mil/sti/pdfs/AD1152929.pdf. Accessed on November 10, 2021.

Knight, G. A. (2001). Entrepreneurship and strategy in the international SME. *Journal of International Management, 7*(3), 155–171.

Kowo, S. A., Adenuga, O. A. O., & Sabitu, O. O. (2019). The role of SMEs development on poverty alleviation in Nigeria. *Insights into Regional Development, 1*(3), 214–226.

Kumar, S., Maheshwari, V., Prabhu, J., Prasanna, M., Jayalakshmi, P., Suganya, P., & Jothikumar, R. (2020). Social economic impact of COVID-19 outbreak in India. *International Journal of Pervasive Computing and Communications, 16*(4), 309–319.

Laborde, D., Martin, W., & Vos, R. (2021). Impacts of COVID-19 on global poverty, food security, and diets: Insights from global model scenario analysis. *Agricultural Economics, 52*(3), 375–390.

Lund, S., Madgavkar, A., Mischke, J., & Remes, J. (2021). *What's next for consumers, workers, and companies in the post-COVID-19 recovery.* McKinsey & Company.

Mannar, B. R. (2019). Medium, small and micro enterprises: The Indian perspective. *Journal of Alternative Perspectives in the Social Sciences, 9*(4), 710–728.

Marinho, B. F. D., & Costa Melo, I. (2022). Fostering innovative SMEs in a developing country: The ALI program experience. *Sustainability, 14*(20), 13344.

Mukarram, M. (2020). Impact of COVID-19 on the UN sustainable development goals (SDGs). *Strategic Analysis, 44*(3), 253–258.

Mushtaq, R., & Bruneau, C. (2019). Microfinance, financial inclusion and ICT: Implications for poverty and inequality. *Technology in Society, 59*, 101154.

Nega, B., & Schneider, G. (2014). Social entrepreneurship, microfinance, and economic development in Africa. *Journal of Economic Issues, 48*(2), 367–376.

Osano, H. M. (2019). Global expansion of SMEs: Role of global market strategy for Kenyan SMEs. *Journal of Innovation and Entrepreneurship, 8*(1), 13.

Plzáková, L., & Smeral, E. (2022). Impact of the COVID-19 crisis on European tourism. *Tourism Economics, 28*(1), 91–109.

Radu, L. D., & Vodă, A. I. (2023). Accelerating the digital transformation of smart cities in COVID-19 pandemic context. In *Smart cities and digital transformation: Empowering communities, limitless innovation, sustainable development and the next generation* (pp. 13–33). Emerald Publishing Limited.

Rasul, G., Nepal, A. K., Hussain, A., Maharjan, A., Joshi, S., Lama, A., . . . Sharma, E. (2021). Socio-economic implications of COVID-19 pandemic in south Asia: Emerging risks and growing challenges. *Frontiers in sociology*, *6*, 629693.

Roshana, M., Kaldeen, M., & Banu, A. R. (2020). Impact of COVID-19 outbreak on Sri Lankan economy. *Journal of Critical Reviews*, *7*(14), 2124–2133.

Samineni, S., & Ramesh, K. (2020). Measuring the impact of microfinance on economic enhancement of women: Analysis with special reference to India. *Global Business Review*. 0972150920923108.

Shafi, M., Liu, J., & Ren, W. (2020). Impact of COVID-19 pandemic on micro, small, and medium-sized enterprises operating in Pakistan. *Research in Globalization*, *2*, 100018.

Shao, D., Mwangakala, H., Ishengoma, F., Mongi, H., Mambile, C., & Chali, F. (2023). Sustenance of the digital transformations induced by the COVID-19 pandemic response: Lessons from Tanzanian public sector. *Global Knowledge, Memory and Communication*, *72*(6/7), 700–713.

Sidhu, G. S., Rai, J. S., Khaira, K. S., & Kaur, S. (2020). The impact of COVID-19 pandemic on different sectors of the Indian economy: A descriptive study. *International Journal of Economics and Financial Issues*, *10*(5), 113–120.

Sriram, V., & Mersha, T. (2010). Stimulating entrepreneurship in Africa. *World Journal of Entrepreneurship, Management and Sustainable Development*, *6*(4), 257–272.

Taiwo, J. N., & Falohun, T. O. (2016). SMEs financing and its effects on Nigerian economic growth. *European Journal of Business, Economics and Accountancy*, *4*(4).

Vrgovic, P., Vidicki, P., Glassman, B., & Walton, A. (2012). Open innovation for SMEs in developing countries–An intermediated communication network model for collaboration beyond obstacles. *Innovation*, *14*(3), 290–302.

Yeganeh, H. (2021). Emerging social and business trends associated with the Covid-19 pandemic. *Critical Perspectives on International Business*, *17*(2), 188–209.

Yu, Z., Razzaq, A., Rehman, A., Shah, A., Jameel, K., & Mor, R. S. (2021). Disruption in global supply chain and socio-economic shocks: A lesson from COVID-19 for sustainable production and consumption. *Operations Management Research*, 1–16.

Zulkhibri, M. (2016). Financial inclusion, financial inclusion policy and Islamic finance. *Macroeconomics and Finance in Emerging Market Economies*, *9*(3), 303–320.

Chapter 6

The Significance of the Relationship Between Novel Coronavirus (COVID-19) and Smart Transportation System Applications for Tourism Activities

Betül Yılmazer[a], Ömer Saraç[a], Hüseyin Pamukçu[b] and Orhan Batman[a]

[a]Sakarya University of Applied Sciences, Turkey
[b]University of Afyon Kocatepe, Turkey

Abstract

Social/physical distancing rules that resulted in the novel coronavirus (COVID-19) have caused restrictions on national and international transportation. Since tourism activities are an industry based on transportation and travel, they have been affected negatively because of COVID-19. It has become necessary to create a contactless environment by leveraging technology to mitigate these negative impacts. smart transportation system (STS) applications have played a crucial role in enabling contact-free travel in providing the continuation of tourism activities in a controlled manner by utilizing information and communication technologies. Therefore, in this study, it was tried to determine whether STS applications are functional in ensuring the contactless transportation required in COVID-19 and in the face of possible future outbreaks. In this study, COVID-19 and STS terms are tried to be defined, and the importance of these two concepts in terms of tourism activities has been discussed considering their cause–effect relationship in line with the purpose of the research. STS applications have been determined to be the most appropriate approach in terms of carrying out controlled tourism activities in accordance with the social/physical distancing rules arising from COVID-19. According to the findings of the research, STS provides an opportunity for people to use contactless payments and purchase tickets online with smart phones. Additively, by controlling passengers'

Strategic Tourism Planning for Communities, 81–93
Copyright © 2024 Betül Yılmazer, Ömer Saraç, Hüseyin Pamukçu and Orhan Batman
Published under exclusive licence by Emerald Publishing Limited
doi:10.1108/978-1-83549-015-020241007

luggage through mobile applications and reducing the time spent waiting in the lobby, thereby minimizing prolonged interpersonal contact.

Keywords: COVID-19; smart applications; smart transportation systems; transportation and travel; tourism

Introduction

Radical changes in technology after the Industrial Revolution have been crucial in the development of the tourism industry, which serves as a significant source of income for countries. These technological developments cause an increase in people's well-being and the emergence of leisure time as a concept. On the other hand, innovations in the transportation sector have made traveling from one place to another easier, faster, and more affordable, and leading to a rise in tourism activities. Before the Industrial Revolution, traveling was mostly for religious, trade, health, war, and migration reasons to meet people's indispensable needs (Ataman, 2001, p. 43). In today's conditions, factors such as the fast-paced and stressful nature of globalization have prompted people to want to travel and carry out tourism activities in order to be discharged and renew themselves. In fact, tourism has evolved into an industry embraced by nearly a third of the world's population and is increasing its market share day by day (Kiper et al., 2020, p. 528).

Even though tourism is no longer a luxury and turns out to be an indispensable need with the significant changes brought by globalization to human life (Saraç, 2020), the tourism market remains sensitive and fragile (Thompson, 2011, p. 693). For this reason, natural disasters, terrorist attacks, internal conflicts, crises, economic instability, political issues, and epidemic diseases occurring worldwide have the potential to redirect demand and negatively impact tourism activities (Ghaderi et al., 2012, p. 81). Among these events, epidemics have the most profound influence on global tourism. As opposed to other events that occur worldwide, epidemics have the ability to spread and affect areas beyond their origin. Likewise, an epidemic, which has the feature of contagion transmitted through the respiratory tract, facilitates the rapid and easy spread of viruses between communities through global travel (Kiper et al., 2020, p. 529). In such a situation, individuals concerned about their health tend to abstain from engaging in tourism activities. On the other hand, governmental authorities responsible for public health have taken precautions at both regional and global levels. These are the measures, such as closing borders globally, changing travel plans, and canceling bookings, that have an adverse impact on tourism (Saraç, 2020, pp. 120–122). Accordingly, it can be stated that tourism possesses a dual nature: it both influences epidemics and is affected by them, as seen in Fig. 6.1 (Kiper et al., 2020, p. 529).

In recent times, a new epidemic transmitted through the respiratory tract has emerged, profoundly impacting global transportation and travel activities. This epidemic, known as the novel coronavirus (COVID-19), originated in the Wuhan

Epidemic   Tourism
            Activities

Fig. 6.1.   Interaction of Epidemic and Tourism Activities. *Source:*
Kiper et al. (2020, p. 529).

province of China in December 2019 and rapidly gained pandemic status in numerous European countries. This epidemic, which causes severe damage to human health and negatively affects tourism activities, has been described by the World Health Organization (WHO) as the most important epidemic of the last 50 years (WHO, 2022a). Despite the emergence of various epidemics such as bird flu, Severe Acute Respiratory Syndrome (SARS), Ebola, and swine flu in the last century, COVID-19 has proven to be much more impactful due to its high and rapid contagion characteristics (Kiper et al., 2020, p. 534). In addition, the devastation left by COVID-19 on the economy is much higher than the damage caused by other epidemics (BBC News Türkçe, 2020; Collaway, 2020).

One of the industries that the epidemic has had a significant economic impact on is tourism. Tourism is based on traveling from one place to another. Since tourism involves travel from one place to another, the interaction of tourists with infected individuals during their journeys (Min et al., 2010, p. 2129), as well as the gathering of infected tourists with the local population at their destination, can contribute to the spread of the pandemic; hence, travel restrictions have been imposed worldwide (Çetin & Goktepe, 2020, pp. 88–91). Similarly, controlling the impact of the epidemic requires the establishment of social and physical distancing measures between individuals. At the present time, although the captured success of vaccine studies for the COVID-19 pandemic has made the outbreak manageable in many countries, the epidemic is not over yet (WHO, 2022b), and people continue to observe social/physical distancing rules, which have become a habit for them (Sarac et al., 2022). Consequently, it is crucial to leverage technology to its fullest extent in order to maintain vigilance regarding the epidemic and ensure that the tourism industry adopts a proactive stance in the face of future outbreaks.

Smart applications hold an important place in creating a contact-free travel environment with developing technology (Sarac et al., 2022). One example of such applications is the smart transportation system (STS). STS, which was created with the use of information and communication technologies, can be used in transportation systems by integrating into existing transportation networks (Tufan, 2014, p. 2). STS enables contactless communication in transportation systems, which is crucial during the COVID-19 pandemic, through the utilization of electronic sensors and internet-based systems. At the present time, STS applications are used and continue to be developed in many countries. Hi-pass in South Korea (ESCAP, 2017), ETC in Japan (Hayakawa, 2013), and Telepass in Italy (MIT, 2014) can be given as examples of these applications. With these applications, motorists traveling on highways can make electronic toll payments using their cards without interacting with toll booth attendants (Saraç, 2021). In the same way, transportation cards used in many cities, such as Oyster Card in England (Oyster Cards, 2022) and Istanbul Card used in Istanbul (İstanbulkart-Belbim, 2022), provide a contactless environment that does not require contacting the officials for the road fee, and they are used by loading money in advance. Numerous studies are underway for contactless transportation, including research on driverless vehicles (Tektaş et al., 2019a, p. 4), driverless subways (Metro Istanbul, 2022), and parking guidance systems (C40 Cities Siemens, 2014) that utilize electronic signboards to locate available parking spaces (Saraç, 2021).

The fact that smart applications enable a contact-free experience paves the way for the tourism industry to effectively respond to the global problem of epidemics. Previous epidemics that occurred in the last century have highlighted the inadequacy of traditional approaches followed in the tourism industry. Therefore, it is essential to take precautions to ensure that tourism is managed in a controlled and healthy manner in the face of potential future outbreaks (Sürme, 2020). Among these precautions, the implementation of STS applications holds significant importance. STS applications play a crucial role in creating a contactless environment, particularly in the context of maintaining social/physical distance necessitated by COVID-19. They are especially valuable for ensuring that tourism activities, which heavily rely on transportation and travel, can proceed in a controlled manner during epidemic periods. This study aims to examine the functionality of STS applications in facilitating contactless transportation and their potential effectiveness in addressing future outbreaks.

Novel Coronavirus (COVID-19)

The COVID-19 pandemic first emerged in the province of Wuhan, China, in December 2019. This pandemic originated in the seafood and animal market in the region and quickly spread among humans, causing significant global impacts. A summary of the pandemic's impact can be seen in Table 6.1 (Sağlık Bakanlığı, 2022). Common symptoms of COVID-19 include fever, cough, and difficulty in breathing. It is important to note that COVID-19 belongs to a large family of coronaviruses that can cause various serious disorders in animals and humans, such as Middle East Respiratory Syndrome (MERS) and SARS. The disease primarily spreads through the inhalation of droplets that are released when infected individuals cough. Additionally, touching surfaces contaminated with these droplets and then touching the eyes, nose, or mouth without proper hand hygiene can also lead to infection (Sağlık Bakanlığı, 2022).

Table 6.1. Coronavirus Data in Detail.

No	Country	Deaths	Death Rate[a]	Total Cases
1	United States	966,557	2,945	79,194,425
2	Brazil	657,495	3,115	29,637,814
3	India	516,510	378	43,009,390
4	Russia	357,634	3,477	17,356,036
5	Mexico	322,072	2,525	5,633,928
6	Peru	211,865	6,517	3,541,397
7	United Kingdom	163,511	2,447	20,093,762
8	Italy	157,785	2,617	13,861,743
9	Indonesia	153,738	568	5,962,483
10	Iran	139,610	1,684	7,141,033
11	Colombia	139,452	2,770	6,081,131
12	France	137,831	2,055	23,477,062
13	Argentina	127,494	2,837	9,007,753
14	Germany	126,933	1,527	18,809,998
15	Poland	114,218	3,008	5,891,140
16	Ukraine	112,459	2,534	5,040,518
17	Spain	101,703	2,160	11,324,637
18	South Africa	99,881	1,706	3,704,218
19	Turkey	97,267	1,166	14,693,917
20	Romania	64,685	3,342	2,816,039

Source: BBC News Türkçe (2022).
[a]Deaths per 100,000 people.

Even though mortality rates for the COVID-19 epidemic are relatively low compared to other epidemics, the rate of propagation velocity is quite high (Li et al., 2020, p. 1205). For this reason, because of being a regional pandemic, COVID-19 was declared as a global outbreak (pandemic) by the WHO on March 11, 2020 (McCartney, 2020). During the COVID-19 epidemic, taking some precautions to reduce the rate of propagation velocity of infection, the number of deaths and cases has become necessary. In this scope, many social activities have been temporarily limited by implementing mandatory social isolation. While curfews have been imposed in some areas, settlements, where the spread of the virus is very high, have been declared quarantine zones. International flights and transportation systems have been suspended (Atay, 2020, p. 168). Precautions such as maintaining a physical distance of 1.5 meters and reducing contact with surfaces have been started to be taken to prohibit the transmission of the disease through social/physical distancing (Sağlık Bakanlığı, 2022). With the development of vaccines, the epidemic has become more manageable; nevertheless, the failure to prevent the spread of the virus leads to the continuation of social/physical distancing. Following the crisis, maintaining social distancing has been ingrained in the subconscious of the people during the normalization process, and it is expected that people will not abandon these precautions even after the end of the epidemic, choosing to lead contactless lives in many aspects (Sarac et al., 2022).

COVID-19, Tourism, and Transportation Relationships

The COVID-19 pandemic that emerged in China has been expanded to other countries through international human mobility. To be able to keep the epidemic under control, many countries have implemented travel restrictions, and they have strictly imposed these restrictions (Saraç, 2020, p. 120). There has been a significant contraction in the activity level of many sectors observed worldwide due to travel restrictions. One of these sectors is tourism. According to the COVID-19 report prepared by the Tourism Organization (UNTWO), in the first year of the epidemic, it was observed that the number of international tourists decreased by 98% due to travel restrictions and strict pandemic conditions, and the tourism sector worldwide contracted by 73% due to the pandemic. In other words, 7 out of 10 people were unable to travel during this period. As a result of the decline in travel, 64% of loss in tourism revenues occurred. With the decrease in the influence of the pandemic and successful vaccination practices, there was a 4% increase in the number of international tourists in 2021 compared to 2020. However, it can be observed that this number is 72% lower than the number of visitors prior to the 2019 pandemic. Also, Europe and the United States of America have made further progress in the year 2021 compared to the year 2020. However, both regions remained below 63% of their prepandemic levels (UNWTO, 2022). Likewise, tourism revenues in Turkey increased by 103% in 2021 compared to the previous year, but they are still 71% below the prepandemic period levels (TUIK, 2022). For this reason, it can be stated that the rate of tourism recovery worldwide is slow and uneven. The primary reason for this is the travel restrictions imposed due to social/physical distancing rules.

Interprovincial travel restrictions that were brought at the national and international levels have affected expenditures on tourism negatively. Similarly, the precautions taken by the governments regarding social/physical distancing and hygiene rules result in the closure of hotels, meeting rooms, cultural activities, and recreational areas, and they also result in the implementation of strict measures in transportation (Hoque et al., 2020). In spite of this, normalization efforts are progressing rapidly. In parallel with normalization, it is expected that tourism activities will also increase. Likewise, tourism is a whole of social relationships based on a translocation basis. The fact that tourism is an activity that is based on social relationships implies that tourism will persist as long as human life exists. As a matter of fact, in the study of Turgut and Saraç (2022), even though the

COVID-19 epidemic is considered to be one of the most serious crises of the 21st century, it is expected that tourism will continue to thrive after this pandemic.

According to the opinions of the UNWTO experts, it is expected that tourism will return to prepandemic levels by 2024 and in the subsequent years (UNWTO, 2022). Based on this inference, it can be concluded that the COVID-19 pandemic has significantly impacted the global tourism market for a period of five years. The most important reason for this is that the virus poses a threat to travel and transportation, which are the fundamental pillars of tourism. While tourism activities have been affected by previous epidemics, the extensive spread of COVID-19 has resulted in a prolonged negative impact on the tourism sector for a period of five years. Furthermore, the COVID-19 pandemic has highlighted the need for radical structural changes in the tourism industry. One of the key areas requiring such transformative changes is undoubtedly travel and transportation.

Travel and transportation systems in tourism are service activities that enable tourists to travel safely and quickly from their respective regions to tourist attractions. The movement of displacement necessary for tourism can only be achieved through transportation. Therefore, any efforts to enhance transportation infrastructure directly contribute to the advancement of the tourism sector (Albalate & Fageda, 2016, p. 174; Yangve & Li, 2020, p. 1975). In tourism, as transportation services are made with one of the railway, highway, airway, and seaway systems, cooperation among them is also essential for swift transportation to the intended destination (Doğaner, 2012, p. 1). At the present time, the fact that transportation systems serve as a bridge between production and consumption is crucial not only for the development of tourism but also for overall economic progress. For this reason, advancements in travel and transportation systems have positioned tourism as an integral part of the global economy.

The development of transportation systems and tourism worldwide has given rise to new destinations, and this has led to an increase in the number of tourists over time. However, this surge in tourist numbers has posed certain challenges for transportation systems, including infrastructure issues, traffic congestion, high costs, and lengthy travel times. In parallel with these reasons, technological advancements have been pursued to enhance transportation systems. One such initiative is the implementation of STS applications. These applications have been developed out of necessity and are being adopted and further refined in many countries globally. At present time, where nearly every traveler possesses a smartphone and has easy access to the internet, the widespread use of STS applications has become inevitable. These applications aim to minimize physical contact and ensure the continuity of tourism activities. Especially during the pandemic, tourists have shown a preference for STS applications that can reduce reliance on conventional transportation methods, prioritize tourist health, and minimize interpersonal contact.

STS Applications

Indicators such as population growth, urbanization, and economic development have necessitated smart solutions to address the challenges in the transportation sector. One of these solutions is STS applications. STS, which utilizes information and communication technologies, emerged in the transportation field during the 1960s for the purpose of shortening travel time, ensuring energy efficiency, and improving traffic safety (Tektaş & Tektaş, 2019b, p. 193). Between the years 1970 and 1980, plate reading systems and radars that were used for speed detection are considered as early stages of STS applications. In the following years, STS application studies were initiated to address traffic issues and develop rapid transit systems and the Global Positioning System (GPS). Besides, the utilization of speed stabilizer systems in vehicles and navigation technologies commenced during this period. Since 1990, electronic fare collection systems, smart buses, and speed tracking applications have been implemented. In the year 1994, mobile applications such as Bluetooth, 3G, and Wi-Fi emerged, improving upon existing systems within the realm of STS and making daily life more convenient. The widespread adoption of wireless network usage (Wi-Fi) in the 2000s, driverless vehicle applications, transportation information systems, and traffic information service technologies gained widespread usage (Saraç, 2021).

Relation of STS Applications to COVID-19

With the rapid advancement of technology, STS has become extremely important and functional on national and international platforms, particularly during the ongoing pandemic. Especially during the pandemic period, the importance of STS has gradually increased. Likewise, STS plays a crucial role in ensuring transportation is carried out in a contactless and safe manner, taking into account social/physical distancing measures. After the pandemic period, especially, it would be more accurate to view STS as not just an innovative transportation technology but also as a new way of life and culture (Meriç, 2018, p. 34). STS applications have significantly contributed to the smooth operation of highways, seaways, and airlines during the pandemic by reducing the risk of infection and limiting interpersonal interactions.

The vast majority of countries in the world have been using STS applications for years. Delta Airlines, based in the United States, allows passengers to manage their luggage using the Delta mobile app and minimizing the time passengers spend in the luggage waiting room and reducing prolonged contact between individuals (Yalçınkaya et al., 2018, p. 96). Carnival Cruise, a world-renowned company, also enables guests to enter their rooms without any direct contact using the smart bands they have designed, to track their current location in real time, and pay with a credit card connection through these wristbands (Barnes, 2017). Through the use of "Hi-pass" applications in South Korea, transactions are efficiently carried out without physical contact by eliminating cash transactions at the ticket office (Kim et al., 2014). Within the scope of STS applications for railway transportation, train tickets can be purchased by phone, and passengers can report any issues or concerns they encounter on the train to the relevant personnel without direct contact (Yalçınkaya et al., 2018). In addition, Turkish Airlines provides a "Kiosk Check-in" option to expedite and streamline the travel process, minimize contact, and alleviate queuing. With this application, passengers can make their own check-in transactions and purchase their tickets. At the same time, they have their boarding passes approved by leaving their luggage in the automatic luggage system (Turkish Airlines, 2022).

In a study conducted by Darsena et al. (2020), the implementation of a new application called Safe and Reliable Public Transportation System (SALUTARY) that can be evaluated within the scope of STS was planned. SALUTARY is an android-based application that provides online ticket purchasing, vehicle access control, crowd-sensitive route planning, and additional transportation services against excessive demand. This application allows crowd analysis and detection at bus stops through the utilization of Bluetooth and infrared sensors.

Individuals who monitor crowd situations with the help of this application can be inclined to alternative transportation routes, or they choose to travel during off-peak hours. Similarly, passengers can obtain information about capacity at stations, and they can have a more contact-free journey based on the provided information through mobile transportation applications (Darsena et al., 2020).

STS needs to be improved so that it can respond to changes that happen. Autonomous vehicle technologies, which have emerged in recent history, are a crucial component of the STS and continue to advance in their development. The pandemic plays a critical role in the spread of these autonomous systems. The most striking ones from these autonomous systems in traveling and transportation are driverless vehicles. The innovations brought about by the pandemic have facilitated access to driverless vehicles. Likewise, the delivery of COVID-19 test results has been carried out with autonomous vehicles in Florida. Similarly, autonomous vehicles such as Nuro have been delivering medications to homes in Texas. Also, in Wuhan province, where the origin of the virus emerged, autonomous vehicles have been used to deliver medical supplies and food, minimizing interpersonal contact (Oakey et al., 2022, p. 3). In this process, utilizing autonomous vehicles in this process not only reduces people's exposure to the virus but also helps protect healthcare workers. In the same manner, the implementation of the Smart Parking app in various parts of the world plays a vital role in maintaining social distancing measures by determining whether there is an empty space in the parking lot with the use of magnetic sensors (Gupta et al., 2021, p. 3).

Conclusion

Transportation systems can cause the rapid spread of epidemics if adequate precautions are not taken depending on the experienced social interaction. For this reason, travel and transportation are among the sectors that are most affected by the COVID-19. Additionally, travel and transportation are the first steps in the realization of tourism activities. Smart applications can be regarded as an alternative solution against social/physical distancing rules that arise during the pandemic process and hinder the sustainability of tourism activities. One of these applications in travel and transportation is STS, and it is very important for tourism to take a firm stance in the face of epidemics.

Even though STS applications have not been developed for the purpose of protecting social/physical distance between people, they effectively mitigate the risk of infection during a pandemic by facilitating contactless journeys. STS provides individuals with a seamless and contact-free transportation experience for individuals from the beginning to the end. The features such as contactless card payments on public transportation, the opportunity to buy tickets online, and self-boarding options on airplanes greatly resist the possible physical contact. Henceforth, the utilization and advancement of STS, in conjunction with the implementation of precautionary measures, become increasingly important in preparing for future crises that may arise.

Research on STS applications has gained momentum during the epidemic. However, these studies are concentrated in certain regions and countries. It is anticipated that countries implementing these systems will be better prepared for future crises and will experience minimal negative impacts. In the light of these evaluations, it can be stated that STS applications will become a crucial element in urban and international competitiveness in the coming years.

Recommendations

It is required that governments and stakeholders in the tourism industry should work in cooperation to determine regional plans, policies, and strategies. Likewise, the applications to be carried out for STS ensuring controlled and healthy management of tourism. The negative influences of current epidemics and possible crises that may happen in the future on tourism demand are obvious. The spread of STS applications around the world will take time. Accordingly, recommendations to mitigate the impact of crises on tourism demand and strengthen its resilience can be outlined as follows:

- STS applications should be improved in order to safely manage mass activities that may pose a risk factor for epidemics in the long term.
- Studies should be carried out to increase the use of information/communication technologies, especially robotics and automation systems in tourism, travel, and transportation.
- Adequate training programs should be established to meet the demand for skilled personnel who can effectively operate and utilize the developed STS applications.
- The contact between the people should be regulated to keep it at the minimum level with the innovations that will be implemented in the transportation systems.
- Long-term studies should be conducted on the sustainability of public transport.
- Hygiene standards should be adapted to the changing requirements after the COVID-19 pandemic, emphasizing the importance of social and physical distancing practices at every stage of tourism.
- Tourism policies should be planned in order to meet the safety and health needs of the tourists.

References

Albalate, D., & Fageda, X. (2016). High speed rail and tourism: Empirical evidence from Spain. *Transportation Research Part A, 85,* 174–185.

Ataman, G. (2001). *İşletme Yönetimi: Temel Kavramlar & Yeni Yaklaşımlar.* Türkmen Kitabevi.

Atay, L. (2020). Covid-19 Salgını ve Turizme Etkileri. *Seyahat ve Otel İşletmeciliği Dergisi, 17*(1), 168–172.

Barnes, B. (2017). *Coming to carnival cruises: A wearable medallion that records your every whim.* https://www.nytimes.com/2017/01/04/business/media/coming-to-carnival-cruises-a-wearable-medallion-that-records-your-every-whim.html. Erişim Tarihi: March 18, 2022.

BBC News Türkçe. (2020). https://www.bbc.com/turkce/haberler-dunya-51719684. 15 Nisan 2020 tarihinde.

BBC News Türkçe. (2022). *Covid: WHO'nun koronavirüsü 'pandemi' ilan etmesinin birinci yılında ülkelerde son durum ne?* https://www.bbc.com/turkce/haberler-dunya-51719684. Erişim Tarihi: March 18, 2022.

C40 Cities Siemens (C40). (2014). *City climate leadership awards.* PR Newswire.

Çetin, G., & Göktepe, S. (2020). *COVID-19 Pandemisinin Ekonomik, Toplumsal ve Siyasal Etkileri* (pp. 87–97). Istanbul Universty Press.

Collaway, E. (2020). https://www.nature.com/articles/d41586-020-00758-2. 18 Mart 2020 tarihinde.

Darsena, D., Gelli, G., Iudice, I., & Verde, F. (2020). *Safe and Reliable Public Transportation Systems (SALUTARY) in the COVID-19 pandemic.* arXiv preprint arXiv:2009.12619.

Doğaner, S. (2012). Türkiye Ulaşım Sistemleri Turizm ve Çevre İlişkileri. *Coğrafya Dergisi, 6,* 1–25.

ESCAP. (2017). *Development of model intelligent transport systems deployments for the Asian highway network* (pp. 21–25, 85–95, 98–99). Economic and Social Commission for Asia and the Pacific.

Ghaderi, Z., Som, A. P. M., & Henderson, J. C. (2012). Tourism crises and Island destinations: Experiences in Penang, Malaysia. *Tourism Management Perspectives, 2*(3), 79–84.

Gupta, D., Bhatt, S., Gupta, M., & Tosun, A. S. (2021). Future smart connected communities to fight covid-19 outbreak. *Internet of Things, 13,* 1–26.

Hayakawa, K. (2013). *Japan: Intelligente Transport Systemen in de logistiek.* Embassy of the Kingdom of The Netherlands. https://www.rvo.nl/sites/default/files/2013/10/Intelligent%20Transport%20Systems%20(ITS)_logistics.pdf. Erişim tarihi: March 19, 2021.

Hoque, A., Shikha, F. A., Hasanat, M. W., Arif, I., & Hamid, A. B. A. (2020). The effect of coronavirus (COVID-19) in the tourism industry in China. *Asian Journal of Multidisciplinary Studies, 3*(1), 52–58.

İstanbulkart-Belbim. (2022). https://www.belbim.istanbul/urunler-hizmetler-istanbulkart. Erişim Tarihi: March 18, 2022.

Kim, D. I., Kim, J. C., & Joo, Y. I. (2014, July 31). Development of the EM wave absorber for improving the performance of Hi-Pass system in ITS. *Journal of the Korea Institute of Information and Communication Engineering.* Korea Institute of Information and Communication Engineering (Nurimedia). https://doi.org/10.6109/jkiice.2014.18.7.1505

Kiper, V. O., Saraç, Ö., Çolak, O., & Batman, O. (2020). Covid-19 Salgınıyla Oluşan Krizlerin Turizm Faaliyetleri Üzerindeki Etkilerinin Turizm Akademisyenleri Tarafından Değerlendirilmesi. *Balıkesir Üniversitesi Sosyal Bilimler Enstitüsü Dergisi, 23*(43), 527–551.

Li, Q., Guan, X., Wu, P., Wang, X., Zhou, L., Tong, Y., & Wong, J. Y. (2020). Early transmission dynamics in Wuhan, China, of novel coronavirus–Infected pneumonia. *New England Journal of Medicine, 382,* 1199–1207.

McCartney, G. (2020). The impact of the coronavirus outbreak on Macao, from tourism lockdown to tourism recovery. *Current Issues in Tourism,* 1–10.

Meriç, E. B. (2018). Akıllı Ulaşım Sistemleri (AUS) ve Kalkınma Ajansları. *Akıllı Ulaşım Sistemleri ve Uygulamaları Dergisi, 1*(2), 33–55.

Metro Istanbul. (2022). https://www.metro.istanbul/haber/detay/avrupa-yakasinin-ilk-surucusuz-metrosu-acildi. Erişim Tarihi: March 18, 2022.

Min, J. C., Kung, H. H., & Liu, H. H. (2010). Interventions affecting air transport passenger demand in Taiwan. *African Journal of Business Management, 4*(10), 2121–2131.

MIT. (2014). *Piano di Azione Nazionale sui sistemi di Trasporto ITS, Ministro delle Infrastrutture e dei Trasporti.* https://www.mit.gov.it/mit/site.php?p=cm&o=vd&id=1394. Erişim Tarihi: March 19, 2021.

Oakey, A., Grote, M., Royall, P. G., & Cherrett, T. (2022). Enabling safe and sustainable medical deliveries by connected autonomous freight vehicles operating within dangerous goods regulations, *Sustainability, 14*(2), 930.

Oyster Card. (2022). https://oyster.tfl.gov.uk/oyster/entry.do. Erişim Tarihi: March 18, 2022.

Sağlık Bakanlığı, T. C. (2022). Covid-19 nedir? https://covid19.saglik.gov.tr/TR-66300/covid-19-nedir-.html. Erişim Tarihi: March 18, 2022.

Sarac, O., Kiper, O., & Batman, O. (2022). The significance of smart hotels in the novel coronavirus (covid-19) pandemic process. In C. Catenazzo (Ed.), *Challenges and opportunities for transportation services in the post-COVID-19 era.* IGI Global.

Saraç, Ö. (2020). Yeni koronavirüs (COVID-19) pandemi sürecinin sürdürülebilir turizm üzerindeki muhtemel etkileri. In C. F. S. Eyelve Gün (Ed.), *COVID-19 döneminde iktisadi, idari ve sosyal bilimler çalışmaları* (pp. 115–141). Iksad Publishing.

Saraç, Ö. (2021). Akıllı ulaşım sistemi uygulamaları ve turizm. In A. Ülkü (Ed.), *Dijital dönüşüm ve turizm* (pp. 191–215). Nobel Publishing.

Sürme, M. (2020). *Turizm ve Kovid-19.* İksad Yayınevi.

Tektaş, M., Közkurt, C., & Demir, B. (2019a). Bandırmanın Ulaşım Geleceğine Dair Çözüm Önerileri. 3. Uluslararası Bölgesel Kalkınma ve Üniversitelerin Rolü Sempozyumu. IRDARUS'19, November, Bandırma – Balıkesir, Turkey.

Tektaş, M., & Tektaş, N. (2019b). Akıllı ulaşım sistemleri (AUS) uygulamalarının sektörlere göre dağılımı. *Akıllı Ulaşım Sistemleri ve Uygulamaları Dergisi, 2*(1), 1–10.

Tektaş, N., & Tektaş, M. (2019a). Dünyada Akıllı Ulaşım Sistemlerinin Gelecek Hedefleri Japonya Örneğinin İncelenmesi. *Paradoks Ekonomi Sosyoloji ve Politika Dergisi, 15*(2), 189–210.

Thompson, A. (2011). Terrorism and tourism in developed versus developing countries. *Tourism Economics, 17*(3), 693–700.

Tufan, H. (2014). *Akilli Ulaşim Sistemleri Uygulamalari ve Türkiye için bir AUS Mimarisi Önerisi. Ulaştırma ve Haberleşme Uzmanlığı Tezi, TC Ulaştırma Denizcilik ve Haberleşme Bakanlığı.*

Turgut, N., & Saraç, Ö. (2022). Effects of coronavirus (Covid-19) on camp and caravan tourism demand. *4th International Family, Youth and Child Friendly Tourism Management Congress*, 1–3 June 2022.

Turkish Airlines. (2022). Check-in. https://www.turkishairlines.com/tr-int/bilgi-edin/check-in/. Erişim Tarihi: March 21, 2022.

Türkiye İstatistik Kurumu (TUIK). *Turizm İstatistikleri.* https://data.tuik.gov.tr/Bulten/Index?p=Turizm-Istatistikleri-IV.Ceyrek:-Ekim-Aralik-ve-Yillik,-2021-45785. Erişim Tarihi: March 18, 2022.

WHO. (2022a). *Pandemic (H1N1) 2009 in the European region.* http://www.euro.who.int/influenza/ah1n1. 22 Mart 2022 tarihinde.

World Health Organization. (2022b). *Coronavirus disease (COVID-19) pandemic.* https://www.who.int/emergencies/diseases/novel-coronavirus-2019. Erişim Tarihi: March 21, 2022.

World Tourism Organization (UNWTO). (2022). *Tourism grows %4 in 2021 but remains far below pre-pandemic levels.* https://www.unwto.org/news/tourism-grows-4-in-2021-but-remains-far-below-pre-pandemic-levels. Erişim Tarihi: March 18, 2022.

Yalçınkaya, P., Atay, L., & Karakaş, E. (2018). Akıllı Turizm Uygulamaları. *Gastroia: Journal of Gastronomy and Travel Research*, 2(2), 85–103.

Yangve, Z., & Li, T. (2020). Does high-speed rail boost urban tourism economy in China? *Current Issues in Tourism*, 23(16), 1973–1989.

Chapter 7

Collective Nuance of Culture and Tourism in the 21st Century: A Case Study of Neighbourhood Museum in Delhi

Sarah Chauhan and Nusrat Yasmeen

Jamia Millia Islamia, India

Abstract

Travel aimed in experiencing the arts, heritage, and activities that authentically depict the stories and people of the past and present is referred to as cultural and heritage tourism. This has gathered a lot of attention in the last 10 years. In order to protect their valuable history, developing countries require assistance from the international community. Cultural heritage tourism is a significant economic development tool and one of the best components of the tourism sector.

In the 21st century, in terms of museums and showcasing culture, there has been a significant commotion toward the role of people or community, rather than the morality of objectification of knowledge in a close-ended glass case. This concept can be traced back to "New Museology," emerging since the 1970s, where a section of like-minded museologists believed that museums are for the people and of the people. It is important to include the "voices of the community" as a whole, therein, becoming a broad parlance of social culture (MacDonald, 2006).

Community participation is a process where people are facilitated by themselves and their responsiveness to their own traditions and culture. Henceforth, this chapter is an approach toward a case study of an emerging concept in Delhi – A Neighbourhood Museum in Shadi Khampur area, where the locality is prevalent since the 12th century. Other locals preside over the predating of Partition in the 17th century, when their ancestors settled from Lahore since then.

Keywords: Culture; tourism; museums; heritage; community; neighborhood

Strategic Tourism Planning for Communities, 95–104
Copyright © 2024 Sarah Chauhan and Nusrat Yasmeen
Published under exclusive licence by Emerald Publishing Limited
doi:10.1108/978-1-83549-015-020241009

Introduction

The collective nuance of culture and tourism in the 21st century is a concept that emphasizes the need to bridge the divide between cultural heritage and sustainable tourism.

The collective nuance of culture and tourism in the 21st century is an essential concept that defines the relationship between local heritage and tourism. The principle of this concept is based on the idea that heritage and tourism are interdependent and can influence each other positively or negatively. The preservation and promotion of cultural heritage can attract tourists, while tourism can provide economic benefits to cultural heritage sites. The principle also emphasizes the importance of sustainable tourism that preserves cultural heritage for future generations.

The case study of the Neighbourhood Museum in Delhi is a practical application of the collective nuance of culture and tourism in the 21st century. The museum is a unique cultural heritage site that showcases the rich history and cultural diversity of Delhi's neighborhoods. The museum has incorporated tourism as a means of promoting cultural heritage and generating economic benefits for the local community. The museum also promotes sustainable tourism by preserving the cultural heritage of the neighborhood and creating awareness about the need for its conservation.

The success of the Neighbourhood Museum in Delhi is an excellent example of how the collective nuance of culture and tourism can benefit both the cultural heritage and tourism industries. It acknowledges the importance of preserving cultural heritage and making it accessible to visitors. Tourism can be a powerful tool for economic development and cultural exchange if it is effectively managed, according to this principle. This requires a collaborative approach between stakeholders in the tourism and cultural heritage sector.

The Neighbourhood Museum in Delhi is an example of the implementation of the collective nuance of culture and tourism in the 21st century. The museum is a community-based initiative that seeks to preserve and promote the cultural heritage of the surrounding area while also providing a distinctive tourism experience. The museum features exhibits and interactive displays that highlight the history, art, and traditions. In addition, it provides guided excursions and cultural activities, such as theater classes and dance performances, that enable guests to interact with the local community. The Neighbourhood Museum in Delhi demonstrates the potential for a viable tourism industry that is beneficial to both the local community and visitors by integrating cultural heritage and tourism.

The sense of culture and tourism in terms of museums, these days is the visitor no longer intermediates between "tour" and "baggage," facilities at the airport or travel services; the visitor is more concerned about the destinations and significant local attractions to venerate and explore the places with their own concerns and priorities which connected tourism and museums in this context.

The level of tourism had expanded where every continent and state is revealing their culture and marketing themselves through advertisements and well-known celebrities. Every country is promoting itself for the sake of being "stunning and promising the exploration of their own art and aesthetics." Here, museums play a very adamant role to be emancipated in a more complete reality or virtual possibility or both at the same time – turning a destination into fascination for the visitor.

The historicity of the museum is a very contemporary prodigy in the worldly context. It dates back since the inception of the British and the Louvre Museum as the first public museums. Historically, it goes back to the classical times, to the Ptolemaic *mouseion* at Alexandria, considered to be an institute for scholars and learned men (Vergo, 1989). The primary collections of the initial museums were antiquities, animal remains, fossils, art, and quite valuable minerals – which were conceived as rare and precious to be collected by "those who could afford them" – the rich and the affluent. In addition, the place to attain "knowledge" in terms of cultural display and heritage vulnerability since the dawn of 18th century, museums are sharing a number of common principles among various disciplines across different ontologies. The basic ontology of tourism in terms of cultural and museological meaning is that tourism in itself is a platform to showcase what the museum is all about. On the other hand, a museum tends to venerate the possibilities for a visitor to conjure the process of "visiting" and "traveling" that place for better emulation of what the local culture is all about. Museums being a part of the heritage sector signifies the place of its establishment a turn it into a "Destination for tourism" (Gimblett, 1998).

The essence of "New Museology," a concept precluded in the 1990s, is that museums are not immune to certain social, economic, or other cohesions but are seen as structures with a role: neither being static or movable. The mobility might end, and museums are now targeted toward instinctual discussions about "how" and "why" and that who might benefit from the same. Museums are available to provide quite "authentic" experience by using objects as media and curatorial form of interpretation: to educate and entertain the masses (Prentice, 2007). The current issue in this regard is of suppliers which can be posted by many historic centers and the way of interpretation since the last decade. It is quite difficult though due to the adaptation discourse: where museums required to bring novel ideas and combine them with the minds of the best curatorial practices and also to maintain the basic museum ethics. Today's strategy to employ new museums requires integration, not incorporation (Prentice, 2007).

In India, museums appear to be the result of the British rulers' deliberate intention to unearth, classify, catalog, and show India's artifactual past to themselves, rather than philanthropy. Museums are likewise a complicated component of the tale of Western growth since the sixteenth century, despite the fact that they are now a part of the cultural infrastructure of most emerging nations. Both museums and tourism have an essential domestic aspect in the public cultural contexts of countries like India because they give methods for national communities to conceive their own heterogeneity and reflect on their different cultural practices and histories. Without a reasonably sophisticated media infrastructure, both institutions in Urban India would be difficult to imagine (Appadurai & Breckenridge, 2004).

In terms of the concept of "Neighbourhood Museum," this idea was first recognized in the Anacostia Museum in the 1960s in the United States by S. Dillon Ripley. He states:

> People from the Neighbourhoods tend to stay and were not mobile. Such were called as "disadvantaged," and will never go to a museum ever. Agreeing with sociologists, such people might feel very awkward, badly dressed or not going at all. If the above portrays the truth, then we should bring the museum to them. They deserve the museum to be seen.

In terms of cultural evolution since the late 20th century, much valuable course has been set up for human participation and their concerns – from the past to the present and also how will they evolve in the future through the integration of digital advancement. The museums invariably were inspired by "New Museology" where the purpose of the museums changed and evolved from more object-oriented culture and people-centered attitude and their significance from past to the future (Hauenschild, 1988). In terms of community, this idea represented the social conditions of the people and the relationship with the museum in a broad sense.

The significance of the community museum is the role of two entities into one – first, the museum in terms of its wholesome experience to every visitor outside the community and, secondly, the engagement of the community in the development of the museum and its exhibition process moderated by its curator(s) and the team to conceptualize the meaning of "Neighbourhood Museum." It is more of a collective process, driven by the force of "cultural accumulation and participation." As Crooke states, the term "community" is more of a displaced term where the terms like "audience" and "public" have been used interchangeably. The aspect of community participation is centered on policies of the society, the development of the idiosyncratic community and the evolution of the local history and heritage in the mid of the actual community, through the experiences and renderings of the people (Crooke, 2006).

The formation of community and museums revolve around certain considerations such as – participation, representation, people and the social intervention of the museum in this field. The concept of community is interlinked with other social studies such as anthropology, sociology, cultural studies and heritage, history and public issues, and more. In the longer run, the community with the fixation literature turns into community studies – where the sensation of identity formation, the corelation between different contexts and the echo or belief about the level of belongingness of the people is highlighted. Other aspect is from museum side of view – where the role of exhibition and documentation is more of a pragmatic approach – to build museums at the local level, to engage the people and make the community – both in the museum and outside, aware about the multiethnic solidarity of the culture.

The museum arena is not untouched with the term community. The "community" is labeled as a rare rendering mainly related to policy building and participation of the people, where it is more of display of indigenous culture to the visitor but not beyond that. But firstly, the term community has a lot of meanings, associations and terminologies in every discipline (Crooke, 2006).

Riger and Lavrakas (1981), attributed community with two distinctive factors known as social bonding and behavioral rootedness. They are quite similar anecdotes. The factor of social bondness measures the level of neighbor identification, the level of accumulation in the neighborhood and the knowingness of the children to the respondent. Behavioral rootedness refers to the number of years prevalent to the person, physical placement of the home – being owned or rented and the level of future residency in the area.

Ahlbrandt (1979) highlight the idea of community as an "important role in the making of a neighborhood with the content of satisfaction." They argued that the people who were the most satisfied saw the neighborhood as small and were quite judicious with the level of activities the neighborhood provides to the community. Here, one can see that the role of the community is quite oblivion and connected with the sense of community in terms of "social fabrication" – to strengthen communication at the personal level.

Both the definitions link community with neighborhood with the level of interaction and understanding with each other, where one talks about the physical characteristic, the other emphasis on the social front; but both the areas are quite interconnected at the collective level of coherent relationships and is required for every cultural enthusiast to be considered in terms of museums and tourism at the local level. For some, it might be very inappropriate research as they see community in a "thin" line (Crooke, 2006), where it is only drawn upon the paper as rural or urban, village-based or city-based community.

However, the frequent assumption about the role of community is to have a place or an area to be established, to have social interaction with people and indulging with the leap of shared interests such as common friendship, family history or background, common place of employment, same religion or ethnic background. Such considerations tend to arise debates about how one feels to be a part of that "neighborhood" specifically and how can nostalgia and collective identity play a significant role in the community.

In India, the fact that the country has always been excellent is evidenced by its long-term ownership of a high culture. One or a few interrelated strands are used to create a high national culture from which the dominant, representative or mainstream culture was chosen among the plethora of regional cultures. Typically, applicants from the "Mainstream" culture are linked with a certain ethnic group which dominates at the moment.

In terms of tourism, the concept of cultural tourism has gained significant importance in recent times. Daniel Boorstin, a social historian, was one of the first to comment on the concept of authenticity in the tourism environment. Boorstin (1961) claimed that individuals go away from home seeking pleasure and excitement, regardless of whether the areas they visit or the sensations they have are legitimate. Tourists are seeking originality but are deceived into witnessing artificial landscapes and false settings produced by the tourist industry apparatus to gain from tourists' naivety. And they are unwilling look past the facade; most tourists are pleased with manufactured, insincere locations and goods (MacCannell, 1973).

The pieces confirm a wide range of varied interpretations of genuineness, implying that the idea is more than just realism or that not all locations and things are legitimate to everybody. Many researchers have examined various forms and levels of validity, but (Carol J. Steiner, 2006) The Studio Safdar Trust (Trust, 2017), present one of the most thorough overviews. The authenticity of historical items, events, places, and settings can be accessed from three philosophical viewpoints: verisimilitude, structuralism, and postmodernism.

The sense of verisimilitude depicts the fact the tourism accounts for regional reality and not for "dismissed trivia." In relation to the neighborhood, it should be in relation to the people living in the area where their memories, myths, and dreams should be represented via exhibitions in the same area in the form of their material items, logo or name of the museum, or even the interviews or information they provide about their identity or existence in the area. It can be in lure of "place representation," where it is reused or re-accumulated by the residents into a museum.

Structuralism is a sense of theory which the tourism scholars can use. It examines the role of society and how certain organizations influence people and their behavior. In majority, structuralism has been associated with Marxism which is significantly known in research. Accordingly, Marx was interested about the concept of "capitalist" society and how the relationship of the people influence the way of production. Britton (1991) states in his research about structuralism and would like the academia to consider tourism as an entrepreneurial hub with the main aim of wealth creation. This notion suggests about the level of exterior factors affecting tourism at the local level. For instance, when the international community tends to cycle in the state of misery and chaos, it might lead to a state of fluctuation of the tourism locally also. Also, structuralism can foster the prediction of tourist behavior.

Acknowledging the importance of capitalist production for a tourism company can assist to explain many of its decisions, such as site selection, staff interactions, and host community conflicts. Third, a structuralism Marxist approach can assist a researcher in examining how attitudes and behaviors fluctuate among people with varying relationships to the means of production. A researcher can actually determine how the attitude of the person toward tourism can differ based upon being the owner of the enterprise or a wage earner who is working in the same environment.

From a post structuralism perspective, what is more considerate is the role of space to indulge in social activities. Space is a phenomenon which is recreated, produced, and contested according to Foucault (1984). Similarly, the hermeneutic perspective argues that the space is formulated in accordance to the individual performing the representation in relation to the space itself, like actors in theater. James Duncan (1993) has observed that tourism spaces, when regarded as spaces of leisure, places of cultural engagement, gendered spaces, spaces of production and consumption, and spaces of economic development, can be better analyzed with the understanding that the meanings of these spaces for the various individuals who use them vary and are also influenced by power relations or legitimacy.

Curators of museums, heritage site interpreters, employees, archaeologists, and many historians despise the notion that legitimacy can be subjective. Things and places are intrinsically genuine to them because of their own features. For many, their role is to use scientific and archival data to substantiate the objective past. Curators, for the most part, frame and interpret what they perceive to be true about the places they are responsible for. Traveling to a transnational homeland or attending an ethnic festival or visiting a museum in a new nation can evoke sentiments of sincerity and nostalgia.

The premise that there are numerous parties involved in the legacy – with varied opinions on authenticity and nostalgia – falls under the category of constructivism. Every social group such as government entities, tour guides, cultural brokers, etc., have different perspectives and tend to contribute invariably in their own manner to create such experiences.

Another factor that contributes toward the originality is the role of heritage locations and cultural integrity. The sense of accuracy in relying the tale and preservation of the built environment are critical. One assumption is that indigenous past is related to indigenous people and the ethnicity of the place that dwells in the local culture – the handicrafts that originates from a native place, embodies the cultural characteristics of the place. Accordingly, museums, antiquuities, and historic places ought to reflect the local character, history, and factual accuracy to the greatest extent possible. A well-documented history of the reign based on such archival and empirical evidence is essential.

Neighbourhood Museum – Shadi Khampur

We are witnessing the time of change where museums are seeking to enhance their civic responsibilities, the places in which they are dwelling, and their mission to engage with the audiences, as a direct act of "prioritizing" themselves. It depends upon the number of local communities the museums are collated with. In this span of time where museums are more widely regular and trying to be visible, trustworthy, and becoming more digitally empowered, this is a very improving stance for museums to come up with the possibility to entice with the community. It might nurture the museums to be more partner-oriented, where initially, the museums are seen as "single entities" where they act as autonomous institutions to admire and collect cultural objects for display. It might also boost the lacunae of the community and will make them aware about of all the other possibilities of a museum as a valuable asset for their local culture.[1]

---

[1]These are extracts from the Shadi Khampur Neighbourhood Museum's 2012–2013 show.The exhibition, a collaboration between Jana Natya Manch and Ambedkar University's Centre for Community Knowledge, brought to light complex and layered histories of our city through intriguing tales, ordinary items, visual prints, artefacts, recordings, and inciting stories from this West Delhi colony that arose from a slew of events in the past and continues to evolve.

With this collective effort, this chapter seeks to highlight one of the first neighborhood museums in West Delhi, at Shadi Khampur. This neighborhood, which is six kilometers away from the central Connaught place, with the Pusa Institute in the vanity toward south, is made of four independent localities namely Shadipur, Khampur, and New Ranjit Nagar. It gives a vivacious picture of a "mini-India" (Trust, 2017). Many languages and dialects can be heard; many communities and social groups are visible. Some of the settlements are very distinct and divided into clusters based on religion and caste. Most of the communities have diverse culture and live in a mixed populace since the last two decades and have migrated from different areas of Delhi and from the entire country.

The entire neighborhood has a notorious culture – humming with vitality. From small to medium businesses spanning across the neighborhood such as – shops saloons, clinics, workshops, godowns and also universal property agents. And one cannot forget the availability of the rickshaw walas who are ferrying people from one place to another while navigating midst the small lanes and by-lanes experientially.

Talking about the legacy of the area, some believe their ancestry dates from the reign of Rajput monarch of Prithvi Raj Chauhan from the 12th century. Khampur is said to have been originated in the early 17th century. Some claim that the early settlers were from Lahore area of present-day Pakistan. Some claim to have come from Rajasthan and Haryana. Additionally, some people also claim to settle since the time of Shah Jahan, when Shajanabad was established. The first rights of the land were unofficial. Afterward, the British formalized the properties in the names of the locals in 1908.

The area was mostly woodland and bushy in the early 20th century. In what is known as Pusa, Khampur, and Shadipur, the early village sprang up around the most fruitful fields. The landholdings of the families that used to work on their land were typically small to medium in range. Cattle were also owned by the majority of the family. Jats, Rajputs, and the Yadava clans as well as Brahmins also lived in the area.

The older population worked on the property and received rent from service workers. If one tends to trace around the Partition period, there was an increase in the educational and employment level. In Khampur, there was a primary school, and surrounding private schools recruited children from the villages. Also, a lot of local business was started by the people who were also not from that area; they settled afterward.

Surojit Sarkar and Sudhanva Deshpande planned and curated the exhibition.[2]

The Shadi Khampur Neighbourhood Museum is a one-of-a-kind display of ordinary things from one of the city's oldest neighborhoods. The exhibition brings rich and nuanced histories of our city to life through engaging narratives, everyday objects, photographic prints, artefacts, audio playback, and video

---

[2]Associate Professor, Centre for Community Knowledge, Ambedkar University, New Delhi.

recordings, thanks to collaboration between Jana Natya Manch and Ambedkar University's Centre for Community Knowledge. Over three dozen local inhabitants, of various ages, genders, and walks of life, contributed stories to the exhibition using pen and paper, cameras, recorders, and mobile phones.

He went on to say that the purpose of the exercise is to unearth stories of ordinary people that are relevant to life in a community.

"History is about more than kings, queens, lords, and wealth. History is made by the people as well. Their stories, on the other hand, rarely make it into books or recordings. We have no information about the inhabitants of Delhi or their way of life. This neighbourhood museum, or pop-up museum is an attempt to record and display the histories, perspectives, and voices of inhabitants in the neighbourhood" (www.hindustantimes.com/delhi/neighbourhood-museums-to-tell-stories-of-delhi-s-communities/story, 2016). It was a temporary effort by the community and the curators to make a community-based museum in the neighborhood in the year 2012.

Conclusion

The legacy of museums – since the dawn of the first museum of the world, with the relevance of one of the most novel pedagogies- Museology is still an emerging concept in relation to its allied sub-disciplines such as Culture and Tourism. Culture represents the ideology to forward the legacy of values and traditions, while tourism represents the effectiveness of the culture through the notions of the people involved to promote the same. One includes the prowess of the people behind the curtain; the other gives it a majestic outlook – to be explored at the extreme conditions. And in the middle lies the glue to adore both the ideologies – the museums – a place conceived to reflect education and activities delivered by the people. But, one thing is for sure – all these definitely require people to be involved: whether visible such as visitors or not visible such as organizers (Hooper-Greenhill, 1999).

In this scenario, it is the community who strongly jostled into the process of participation – to promote their culture and gave an impetus toward local tourism by salvaging a community neighborhood museum for the very first time in the vanity of the capital city – Delhi, witnessing a lot of stories and experiences of their lives through their voices. The museum has been founded by the community itself and catering to their own demands. The community tends to debate and valorize the local issues, conduct research, and exhibit their story quite staunchly. In this manner, the community tends to advocate the legacy of communal interpretation, and the local operations constitute variety of programs and initiatives accordingly.

It gives a new opportunity to the ongoing community projects, the community museum is a methodology which reinforces the collective subject; it is a medium through which a neighborhood can react on its own memory and wise. Not only is participation required but also decision-making. The community decides to construct a site to conserve its memory and heritage, which will run the museum, what aspects of its heritage will it address, and how to display this legacy during this process. It also specifies the initiatives the museum will carry out on a daily basis.

In the realm of the 21st century, the community museums play an essential role and can act as important institutes in the global context where the global communities may come together and resonate for their rights and maintain their uniqueness – by strengthening their communal identity. In the near future, this concept might serve as a weapon for the dispraised indigenous communities, ethnic groups, and other minor communities who are not able to fight for their respect and dignity in the society. It might act as a tool to showcase their feelings and expressions about their history and local culture. But, the significance of the museum can be fundamentally altered if this process of shared decision is lacking within the community on nonparticipatory basis.

References

Ahlbrandt, R. S. (1979). *A new public policy for neighborhood preservation.* (No Title). Praeger.

Appadurai, A., & Breckenridge, C. A. (2004). Museums are good to think: Heritage on view in India, *Grasping the world* (p. 14). Routledge.

Boorstin, D. (1961). *The image: A guide to pseudo events in America.*

Britton, S. (1991). Tourism, capital, and place: Towards a critical geography of tourism. *Environment and Planning D: Society and Space, 9*(4), 451–478.

Carol J. Steiner, Y. R. (2006). Understanding existential authenticity. *Annals of Tourism Research.* https://doi.org/10.1016/j.annals.2005.08.002

Crooke, E. (2006). Museums and community. In S. Macdonald (Ed.), *A companion to museum studies* (p. 592). Blackwel Publishingl.

Foucault, M. (1984). Dream, imagination and existence. *Review of Existential Psychology & Psychiatry,* 29–78.

Gimblett, B. K. (1998). *Destination culture tourism, museums, and heritage.* University of California Press.

Hauenschild, A. (1988). *Claims and reality of new museology: Case studies in Canada, the United States and Mexico.*

Hooper-Greenhill, E. (1999). *The educational role of the museum.* Psychology Press.

James Duncan, D. L. (1993). Representing the place of culture. In *Place/Culture/ Representation* (p. 21). Routledge.

MacCannell, D. (1973). Staged authenticity: Arrangements of social space in tourist settings. *American Journal of Sociology,* 589–603.

MacDonald, S. (2006). *A companion to museum studies.*

Prentice, R. (2007). *Experiential cultural tourism: Museums and the marketing of the new romanticism of evoked authenticity.* Museum Management and Curatorship.

Riger, S., & Lavrakas, P. J. (1981). Community ties: Patterns of attachment and social interaction in urban neighborhoods. *American Journal of Community Psychology,* 55.

Trust, T. S. (2017). https://www.studiosafdar.org/shadi-khampur

Vergo, P. (1989). In P. Vergo, & P. Vergo (Eds.), *The new Museology.* Bath Press.

Chapter 8

Using "Drama Gong" as a Communication Channel *on* Implementation of Pro-Poor Tourism in Pemuteran Village, Bali Province, Indonesia

I Made Sarjana and I Gde Pitana

Udayana University, Indonesia

Abstract

Pro-poor tourism (PPT) can be a strategy for sustainable tourism realization. The strategy puts local people as the subject of tourism development processes from planning, executing, controlling, and also evaluating. It means local people, including poor people, are empowered to increase their income because their daily activities are connected to the tourism sector. Tourism development in Pemuteran Village can be recorded as a good example of successful PPT implementation in Bali Province, Indonesia. In the 1990s, a Balinese socio-entrepreneur came to the north Bali Islands, introducing the tourism business as a new source of family income for poor people. To change poor people's perception that tourism can provide a positive impact on the village, it faced a difficult challenge. Therefore, the socio-entrepreneur approached poor people with such a special touch that he modified drama gong (a traditional art performance in Bali) and Hindu ritual ceremonies in the temple as development communication channels. This is a good strategy to encourage poor people's participation in tourism development so that Pemuteran Village is known as a popular tourist destination in Bali. Tourism activities provide better income to local people because residents of Pemuteran Villa can get jobs or manage businesses in the tourism sector. Therefore, this research discusses the transformation process of Pemuteran Village from a poor village to a favorite maritime tourism destination. In fact, both of this process and progress had been inspired and supported by the Balinese socio-entrepreneur in order to lead poor people shifting their mindset and behavior to engage in tourism development.

Strategic Tourism Planning for Communities, 105–119
Copyright © 2024 I Made Sarjana and I Gde Pitana
Published under exclusive licence by Emerald Publishing Limited
doi:10.1108/978-1-83549-015-020241010

Keywords: Drama gong; development communication channel; pro-poor tourism; transformation; socio-entrepreneur

Introduction

In March 2021, the number of poor people in Bali Province, Indonesia, increased to 201.97 thousand from 196.92 thousand in September 2020. The poverty rate in Bali is on average 4.45%; in rural areas, it is about 5.52%, and in urban areas, it is about 4.12% (BPS, 2021). These conditions are caused by tourism activities that have been stopped because of COVID-19. There are many inhabitants in Bali who lost their jobs and businesses, so they do not have a good family income without the tourism business. It means the tourism sector is the backbone of economic development in Bali.

For decades, tourism has been identified as having many positive impacts on any region of the world, so it can be utilized as a tool for poverty alleviation and reducing the gap in people's incomes who have occupations in different sectors of economic development. The term "pro-poor tourism" (PPT) has been implemented to spread tourism benefits for poor people in Indonesia, including Bali Province. In some villages or areas, tourism activities were introduced as a good solution to catalyze the income inclination of poor people. Thus, PPT is not an easy task because it requires some activities to connect development agents and poor people, including empowerment of poor people and development communication as two main significant components involved.

As Purbantara and Mujianto (2019) described, empowerment is a process to facilitate poor people working together and reaching communal goals with the identification of the target, collection of resources, and socialization of action or a development program in order to revitalize community power in the development process. Thus, the socialization of the development program can be realized by using development communication channels. There are some reasons why development communication is needed to help poor people participate in the development process. Firstly, to increase the quality of life of poor people, we need a development program. Secondly, to realize a development program, it requires people's acceptance. Thirdly, development ideas, progress, and its benefits must be informed to society, and then people must be willing to participate in a successful development program (Schramm in Nasution, 1998). Finally, it can be said that empowerment activities and development communication have a close relationship.

Pemuteran Village, Buleleng Regency, could be the most popular best practice to figure out poverty alleviation in Bali. Up until the late 1980s, the village was noted as a poor village. Most residents in Pemuteran worked as farmers or fishermen with an unstable and small income. There were many ways to involve Pemuteran villagers in tourism developments. One of them occurred during the arrival of a businessman from Denpasar who was careful to help local people optimizing local resource for increasing local people welfare. Because of his typical attitude, the businessman had been called as socio-entrepreneur. The socio-entrepreneur had big contribution to develop Pemuteran Village as tourism destination because, in the early 1990s, villagers never expected their village to have tourist attractions. Mostly, villagers in Pemuteran Village got income from agricultural sector or their livelihood were in farming activities. Farmers usually have lack of knowledge on how to manage their resource as tourism attractions; they have no idea that tourism could provide additional income for farming families. Therefore, the socio-entrepreneur came and offered the idea to develop Pemuteran Village as a tourist destination; local people thought it was a joke. In fact, when the socio-entrepreneur bought a square of land in the coastal area of Pemuteran Village, many people said, "You can develop anything on my land freely!" The study is about how to communicate with rural people to empower them for tourism development participation. Data for this research were gathered based on testimony from Pemuteran residents who said they had real experience in the tourism development process. A socio-entrepreneur, who was the owner of Taman Sari Vila in Pemuteran Village, was recognized as a key person who has worked hard to elevate poor people's tourism awareness in Pemuteran Village. Pemuteran Village can be briefly described in Fig. 8.1.

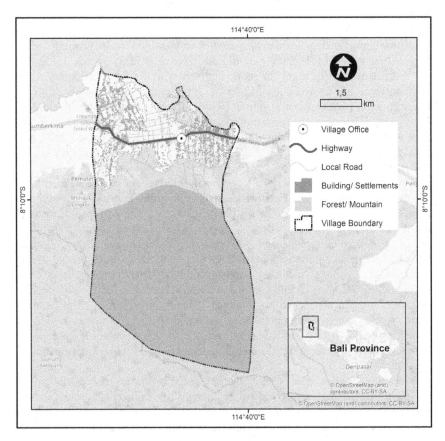

Fig. 8.1.   The Map of Pemuteran Village.

Fig. 8.1 shows that Pemuteran Village is located in Grokgak Sub-District, Buleleng Regency, Bali Province, Indonesia. The village has borders such as the sea in the north, Banyupoh Village in the east, protected forests in the south, and Sumberkima Village in the west. The area of Pemuteran Village is around 33.03 square kilometers, and the village has huge tourism potential for tourist attractions such as beaches, temples, local culture, and hills. The village is near Pulaki Temple and Menjangan Islands in the west of Bali (Pinuji et al., 2019; Pitana et al., 2013; Setiawan, 2015). Moreover, Pitana et al. (2013) described that snorkeling and diving are two kinds of tourism activities that are popular in Pemuteran Village. Moreover, the accessibility of Pemuteran Village is really good; so many tourists can travel to Pemuteran Village easily. The road is wide enough, and the quality of the road is not bad for any kind of tourism transportation vehicle, so that tourists can reach Pemuteran Village by bus, car, or motorcycle. As a tourism destination, Pemuteran Village is relatively clean and comfortable for tourists because amenities and ancillaries have been well developed.

The Balinese socio-entrepreneur had a vital role in motivating and leading local people to develop Pemuteran Village as a tourism destination. In the 1990s, he started to identify tourism potential, and he also communicated with local people about his idea of transforming the village into a place for recreational activities. Unfortunately, local people did not understand the idea properly. Many local people rejected it because they did not have clear ideas on how to develop the tourism sector. In many in-depth interviews, as tourism businessman, the socio-entrepreneur figured out that tourism development is not just about how to create tourism packages but also how to develop tourism awareness in the local community. Therefore, the socio-entrepreneur said tourism development requires hard work and takes a long time. As a result, the socio-entrepreneur's endurance in supporting and motivating local people influenced collaboration among stakeholders in the village for the tourism development sector.

According to Bikse et al. (2015), a "social entrepreneur can be defined as an entrepreneur operating his enterprise not only focusing on reaching maximum economic benefits but also dedicating the benefits to helping poor people or social problem-solving." In other words, a person who can give solutions to social problems with an entrepreneurial spirit (Barendsen & Gardener, 2004). Connectivity between social entrepreneurs and PPT is really close. Poor people usually face complex problems that they can't solve alone. Social entrepreneurs could help the poor. As Mtapuri and Giampiccoli (2019) described, PPT has the goal of providing tourism benefits to poor people. Tourism benefits can be provided in some aspects, such as economics, social, and environmental aspects. In economic terms, tourism will be a new source of income for poor people. If poor people have a good family income, they can maintain social and environmental problems properly.

Moreover, Ashley et al. (2000) figured out that the tourism sector can be projected as a strategy for poverty alleviation. When tourists visit tourism destinations, there will be new markets for local products (goods and services). To realize it, the community must change their mindset about tourism's contribution to socioeconomic aspects and apply PPT concepts properly so that PPT shows evidence of poverty alleviation (Bowden, 2005). By seeing his track record on tourism development in Pemuteran Village, it is clear that Interviewee #1 can be recognized as a social entrepreneur. Interviewee #1 applies a development strategy to involve poor people in tourism activities.

Cultural Approach to Development Communication in the Tourism Sector

Indonesia is known as a country with huge cultural diversity because more than 250 ethnicities live in the archipelago. Each ethnicity has a unique language, which can influence the effectiveness of the development communication process. This condition caused complexity in the development process in Indonesia. According to Iskandar (2004), a cultural approach must be adapted to communication activities. He stated that mutual understanding of cultural backgrounds drives an effective communication process to support development progress and conflict resolution. In fact, a cultural approach to communication can minimize misunderstandings of differentiation in communication goals, ethnocentrism, distrust, stereotypes, etc.

Some scholars or researchers formulated the definition of development communication. Nasution (1998) defined development communication as the efforts of development initiators to persuade communities by introducing ideas and skills that are useful for communities' participation in the development process. Moreover, development communication is related to initiators' activities in delivering technology innovation to their audiences in order to ascertain the motivation for change in society by creating a modern atmosphere (Rogers, 1986). In short, development communication is utilized to develop awareness through innovation, which is introduced to help people reach a better life.

In other words, development communication is about communication activities supporting the development process. It requires the initiator and communities to engage in effective communication. Effective development communication means the initiator can deliver messages easily, and the message can be understood completely by the communicants or communities as the object of development. For this reason, communicators should have good communication skills. The skills are not only about how they can use their communication abilities effectively but also how they manage resources properly.

Hedebro (1979) (in Nasution, 1998) figured out that development communication has three approaches: the development of a nation, the role of mass media in national development, and alteration in the local community or rural areas. Additionally, development communication could be implemented in the development sector in any country. For example, in Indonesia, development communication is needed to support programs or projects in many sectors like religion, agriculture, education, energy, and the tourism sector.

Indonesia has many stories about development communication activities in the tourism sector. The transformation of Pemuteran Village from a poor village to a tourist village can be a success story that is often talked about in formal or nonformal discussions. Pemuteran is a village in the northwest area of Bali Island. It is around 55 kilometers to the west of Singaraja City or 30 kilometers to the east of Gilimanuk Harbor. Pemuteran village has an area of about 33.03 kilometers square with boundaries such as Banyupoh Village (east) and Sumberkima Village (west). Pemuteran Village has been divided into nine banjar (a division in a smaller area of a village in Bali is called a banjar), such as Banjar Kembang Sari, Banjar Pala Sari, Banjar Loka Segara, Banjar Yeh Panes, Banjar Sendang Lapang, Banjar Pengumbahan, Banjar Sari Mekar, Banjar Sumber Wangi, and Banjar Sendang Pasir (Pitana et al., 2013; Setiawan, 2015). The village has many tourism potentials, such as nature, culture, and man-made. Originally, tourism potential had been identified by Interviewee #1 because, before he arrived in the late 1980s, Pemuteran Village was the only coastal area without tourism activities.

Interviewee #1 had been recognized as a local champion for tourism development in Pemuteran Village. The recognition is coming from local community leaders and also tourism development experts in Bali at the national and international levels. The role of the local champion can be the most important in rural tourism development because they have the initiative to lead poor people to change their knowledge, attitude, and skills in tourism development (Simanungkalit et al., 2017).

"Drama Gong" as a Traditional Communication Channel

Using traditional media to disseminate innovation to rural people is frequently done in the agriculture sector. In Bali, traditional media have been mentioned related to art performance activities like wayang, bondres, arja, or drama gong. According to Purnami (2012), drama gong is a Balinese art performance that is created through the integration of modern (western) theater and Balinese traditional theater. Drama gong has special characters such as actors and actresses using the Balinese language and gong kebyar (a kind of Balinese traditional music). Moreover, drama gong was created in the 1960s, and it became the most popular art performance in Bali between the 1970s and 1990s. Drama gong gained popularity because it can be used as entertainment and educational media for Balinese people (Putra, 2008; Sugita, 2020).

In addition, Sugita (2020) figured out that the drama gong has a function in the development process in Bali for delivering social critique. Some topics are usually covered in drama gong performances, such as health, agriculture, the environment, socio-politics, and tourism. Sugita (2020) described deeply the message in the tourism sector that is usually provided to encourage the bargaining position of Balinese society on the development process. Ideally, Balinese people must act as subjects in the tourism business environment in Bali. Unfortunately, many Balinese get tourism jobs at a low level, so they do not get good economic benefits from the tourism sector.

Social critiques about the gap between ideal and reality and the role of Balinese people in actuating in the tourism sector could be properly responded to by a drama gong viewer. It is because social critique has been delivered softly, so rulers, decision-makers, and other stakeholders do not get irritated when they receive it. The critique is usually packaged with a joke, and it makes the audience happy. Thus, the participants gradually understood and adopted the message to change their mind, attitude, and behavior.

There are some aspects that could be considered in changing society. Mardikanto (2010) figured out that an empowerment program should pay attention to some efforts, like (1) consensus building, (2) human empowerment, (3) capacity building, and (3) transmission of culture. In practice, Interviewee #1 utilized development communication to inspire Pemuteran villagers. The villagers had been invited to a consensus building that they joined for a religious ceremony in a Hindu temple. The ritual ceremony aimed to build trust between Interviewee #1, as an agent of change, and community members so that their relationship would be without falsehood.

The socio-entrepreneur introduced the tourism business as a source of additional income for the villagers' families. Unfortunately, he has realized that raising local tourism awareness is not easy. It took time and patience because people without proper tourism knowledge would not believe quickly that tourism could bring some benefits to their lives. Moreover, tourism development needs local people's participation, so to catalyze people's understanding of tourism, effective tools are needed. Therefore, he engaged drama gong artists to socialize tourism development requirements and processes.

Fig. 8.2 shows that drama gong is a popular folk art in Bali, especially in the 1970s and 2000s. At that time, the drama gong performance was eagerly awaited by Balinese society, including residents of Pemuteran Village. The high enthusiasm of the community for watching the drama gong can be seen as an opportunity by the socio-entrepreneur to socialize the tourism development program in Pemuteran. In this context, drama gong has been capitalized on as a traditional Balinese communication channel for the development of the tourism sector. He did it because he knew that he must approach rural people with the same position level and language. The most important thing is that the massage must provide a joyful situation.

> The actors and actresses of drama gong have the proficiency to modify serious to funny atmospheres. "Consequently, I engaged drama gong actors and actresses in the socialization of my idea to build Pemuteran Village as a tourism destination," Interviewee #1 said in a personal communication.

The socio-entrepreneur has worked hard to socialize the idea of identifying and managing tourism potential in Pemuteran Village because he was an outsider who could act as an agent of change. It needed a lot of effort. Komarudin (2014) noted that to act as an agent of change, someone must have some competencies, such as (a) understanding the social system, (b) being able to talk in the same language as the community, (c) he could be able to identify society's needs and aspirations, and (d) he must be well known by most of society's members.

Fig. 8.2.   An Illustration of Drama Gong Performance. *Source:*
Sarjana's personal collection.

Why does the socio-entrepreneur pay drama gong to communicate with local people extensively? Because he understood that at that time, drama gong was the most popular Balinese traditional art performance. Drama gong has been performed related to holding religious ceremonies or toward holidays in Bali, and Pemuteran villagers were similar to other communities in Bali in that they needed entertainment activities in their spare time. In addition, drama gong will deliver messages effectively on creating tourism awareness because drama gong artists have competencies in packaging and delivering messages with the right choice of words to local people in order to talk in an equal-level language to rural people.

Drama gong artists had a job to communicate the message about tourism development properly to poor people. They should provide information related to any benefits of tourism activities, like economic, sociocultural, and environmental benefits. On the contrary, tourism development needs the positive role of villagers, so villagers must elevate their tourism knowledge. The first priority of tourism is learning that rural people must adapt a tourism awareness value called "sapta pesona" or the seven elements of creating a tourism destination. The elements are cleanliness (bersih), neatness (tertib), safety (aman), coolness (sejuk), beauty (keindahan), friendliness (ramah tamah), and memorials (kenangan). For sapta pesona to be implemented, local people should transform their behavior to manage the natural and cultural resources well. For example, local people should keep their environment clean and conserve the forest, coastal, and marine areas.

A popular drama gong artist, Nyoman Subrata/Petruk (Fig. 8.3), said he often performed in Pemuteran Village. "Drama gong is a Balinese art performance, and it can be utilized to deliver innovation or information to society," (I Nyoman Subrata or Petruk interview, October 16, 2023). In this performance, Petruk delivered a message about the important role of coral reef conservation as a tourist attraction. He also said that the same message had been delivered during his performances in the 1970s and 2000s.

The Balinese socio-entrepreneur followed up the consensus building with human empowerment. He educated rural people with some methods, like small discussions, to make them more familiar with the idea. Fortunately, he met some local community leaders, and they promised to work together on delivering the message to community members. A local leader who had a position as secretary of the Pemuteran Village government described how he and other community

Fig. 8.3.   A Drama Gong Artist I Nyoman Subrata (Petruk). *Source:* Sarjana's and Dolo's personal collection.

leaders were enthusiastic about supporting tourism development in their village. "For us, the Balinese socio-entrepreneur is like a representative of God to help the residents of Pemuteran find out and manage the tourism potential in this village. Without the big idea of the Balinese socio-entrepreneur to build the village as a tourism destination, it would be possible for this village to still be recognized as a poor village," said a man around 60 years old.

Moreover, the former local leader told the story that Balinese socio-entrepreneur was a patient person who accompanied Pemuteran residents. As he is known, Balinese socio-entrepreneur built his enterprise in Pemuteran Village which is called "Taman Sari Villa" and shared the economic benefits of the enterprise, mostly to improve the quality of the environment. For example, Interviewee #1 inspired the local people to fix and improve some temples, both physically and through ritual ceremonies. The Balinese socio-entrepreneur also created and sponsored an institution that was dedicated to managing coral reef conservation. The institution was named "Yayasan Karang Lestari," which in English means Conservation of Coral Reefs Foundation. According to Pitana et al. (2013), Yayasan Karang Lestari was launched in 1990. The foundation had the function of raising local people's awareness of tourism and cultural transformation.

To be able to apply a cultural transformation, the Balinese socio-entrepreneur worked hard to increase the capacity of the local people. In the beginning of the 1990s, Pemuteran residents mostly thought that education was not a priority in their lives, so the highest educational background of people was in junior high school. The Balinese socio-entrepreneur said a low level of education has not supported the effort to develop tourist destinations. Therefore, local people were motivated to continue their studies in senior high school and university. A young man who manages a villa in Pemuteran illustrated that he got the inspiration to study at university because of the Balinese socio-entrepreneur's motivation. His father and the Balinese socio-entrepreneur were close friends, so when he and his father met the Balinese socio-entrepreneur, he always received suggestions from the Balinese socio-entrepreneur that he must have high spirits when studying in school. "Actually, Mr. the Balinese socio-entrepreneur had adopted children that work in his enterprise, and they got a chance to continue the study at no cost because the money for the tuition fee had been paid by the Balinese socio-entrepreneur," said the man, who is a member of the tourism organization board in Pemuteran. Moreover, to gain the goodwill of local people in tourism business activities, Interviewee #1 invited local people to on-site visits to some popular tourist destinations in the south of Bali, such as Ubud, Sanur, and Nusa Dua. The Balinese socio-entrepreneur persuaded local people that they would get an improved quality of life as an impact of tourism development, like people staying in Ubud, Sanur, or Nusa Dua.

It is logical that capacity building is a basic condition for the transmission of culture in the community because it requires mutual understanding between local champions and community members about the innovation or culture that is transmitted. Mutual understanding could be arranged if the capacities of local champions and community members shared similarities. Therefore, the Balinese socio-entrepreneur achieved success in transmission culture in Pemuteran Village.

How to keep the environment of Pemuteran clean could be the most important value transmitted to local people. The Balinese socio-entrepreneur has done it for a long time. He started it in 1990, and local people adopted it gradually. Local people implemented the value as their habit in the 2000s, or it took around 10 years. After clean living habits were applied, beautiful scenery occurred both in the beach areas and in the mountains around Pemuteran Village. Furthermore, clean living habits have been combined with coral reef conservation efforts, making Pemuteran Village an ecotourism destination. Many tourists came to visit Pemuteran Village. Besides providing economic benefits, tourists also teach or work together with local people to keep the environment clean.

In brief, using drama gong as a traditional communication channel in development communication in the tourism sector for transforming Pemuteran Village is successful. The results of transformation can be seen in some of the results of a research report about ecotourism in Pemuteran. According to Dwiyasa and Citra (2017), most local people in Pemuteran Village have a good educational background. Pemuteran residents also have good participation in planning, implementing, monitoring, and evaluating ecotourism development in their village. Moreover, Suwena and Arismayanti (2016) concluded that the tourism sector has been recognized as a source of family income for rural people in Pemuteran. Therefore, green tourism can be utilized as a strategy for empowering poor people, in which Pemuteran residents must increase their capacities in information technology and entrepreneurship. That evidence showed that development communication can catalyze the welfare of community members.

Impact of Development Communication in Pemuteran Village

Today, Pemuteran Village is well known as one of the most popular tourist destinations in the Buleleng Regency. It showed that the transformation of Pemuteran Village had been successful. The transformation started in the 1980s. At that time, the Balinese socio-entrepreneur found out that people in Pemuteran Village had many limitations. Farmers worked on marginal land and used limited water for irrigating the land because water is available for farming activities in the rainy season. People also had narrow jobs and business opportunities, so rural people got family income only by feeding cattle and fishing. Fishermen usually catch fish with unfriendly environmental technology like fish bombing. Fish bombing damaged coral reefs and then decreased the quantity of fish in the sea around Pemuteran Village. Encouraging local people to improve their environmental quality could be the key factor driving tourism activities in Pemuteran Village right now.

The improvement of the quality of the environment started with coral reef conservation. The decision had been arranged by the Balinese socio-entrepreneur with local people because they really understood that coral reefs are a proper place for fish. By implementing biorock technology for coral reef restoration in

2000, Pemuteran residents changed their behavior toward consuming natural resources. Pemuteran residents had stopped exploiting or spoiling the coral reefs, and they had turned their minds to conserving them. In fact, they created "pecalang laut," or "bodyguard of the sea," in which young men of Pemuteran supervise sea areas in order to protect coral reefs from bombing fish activities. Because of successful coral reef conservation, Pemuteran Village got many rewards at the international and national levels. In 2002, Pemuteran Village got the Konas Award from Kementerian Kelautan dan Perikanan Republik Indonesia, the Asianta Award and Piala Kalpataru (2015), the TOBO Award (2007), the PATA Gold Award (2008), the Tri Hita Karana Award (2011), and the Equator Prize Award from UNDP (2012) (Pitana et al., 2013).

Because of the many publications related to accepting environmental rewards from Pemuteran residents, it provides other benefits for the village. Pemuteran village has been known as a place for coral reef restoration around the world. It is a free promotion for Pemuteran as an ecological tourism (ecotourism) destination. As evidence, tourists' arrival in Pemuteran has increased from time to time. The rise of visitors numbers was recorded by Badan Pusat Statistik/BPS Kabupaten Buleleng (Buleleng Regency Central Bureau of Statistics) that in 2015, 24,858 tourists arrived in Pemuteran village (1,723 domestic tourists and 23,135 international tourists); in 2017, it increased to 27,018 persons (2,007 domestic tourists and 25,011 international tourists). The last time before Pandemic COVID-19, in 2019, the total number of tourists arriving in Pemuteran Village was 31,755 (3,255 domestic tourists and 28,500 international tourists) (BPS, 2016, 2018, 2020).

Moreover, the progress of tourism development in Pemuteran Village has already provided many business and job opportunities. In 2015, 17 hotels were operated in Pemuteran, and two years later, it increased to 44 hotels. Those hotels hired 633 employees (in 2015) and 1,158 employees (in 2017). The inclination toward job opportunities in two years was around 83.0% (BPS, 2016, 2018, 2020).

The inclination of tourists' arrival and job opportunities showed that Pemuteran Village had been recognized as a popular ecotourism destination in Bali. It has many tourist attractions, such as nature tourism, spiritual tourism, and cultural tourism. Pitana et al. (2013) described many tourism activities related to coral reef conservation, such as diving and snorkeling. There are four locations for diving and snorkeling: the Bio Rock Coral Project, Remple Reef/Gondol Reef, Nights Diving in the Bio Rock Coral Project, and Menjangan Island.

In 2022, more tourism activities will be offered in Pemuteran Village. Tourists can do something special as a memorable tourism experience. Tourism activities in Pemuteran include seeing Pemuteran beach, visiting Menjangan Island, involving turtle projects, exploring Biorock Pemuteran, trekking around Table Stone Hill, visiting Pandya Art Gallery, diving, relaxing in a spa, snorkeling, and culinary (www.tripadvisor.com; www.indonesia.travel).

Tourism development in Indonesia must be applied in four dimensions: tourism destination, tourism marketing, tourism industry, and tourism institution (UU No. 10 Tahun 2009). Besides the destination development described above, Pemuteran villagers also pay attention to other dimensions of tourism development. The tourism industry and marketing aspects have been well developed because local people can see them as opportunities for their participation in tourism. Most people in Pemuteran build and manage the tourism industry, such as accommodation, transportation, dive learning centers, and restaurants.

To get customers for each tourism enterprise, marketing strategies are created and applied continually. Tourism marketing has been managed by each tourism enterprise through collaboration among stakeholders. Digital marketing is a popular strategy for tourism marketing in Pemuteran Village. It can be seen that almost all management in the tourism industry puts their tourism product information on websites and social media. Moreover, traditional marketing strategies are also utilized, and the Pemuteran government has collaborated with other stakeholders to create events and other promotion methods. The Pemuteran Festival has been held annually, and it is recognized as the most effective marketing strategy because many tourists come to attend the festival.

Badan Pengelola Pariwisata Desa (BP2D) Desa Pemuteran, or Rural Tourism Management Board, was created based on local regulation No. 15/VII/DPP/SK/ 2011. It was launched on July 29, 2011. The board had tasks to manage the economic benefits of tourism activities in Pemuteran, maintain the cleanliness of Pemuteran Village, educate and empower Pemuteran's young generation, and create zones in Pemuteran areas. BP2D has been created to support sustainable tourism, and every program of BP2D focuses on reaching an advantaged economy, a solid community, and a sustainable environment (Pitana et al., 2013).

Conclusion

It can be seen that tourism development in Pemuteran Village is an implementation of PPT. Originally, the Balinese socio-entrepreneur wanted to transform the village into a tourism destination because he wanted to help local people have a higher income and diversify their source of income. Therefore, the Balinese socio-entrepreneur educates and empowers local people in the tourism sector, and he utilized drama gong as a communication channel to introduce tourism knowledge to local people. This strategy worked effectively in that most people in Pemuteran had tourism awareness, and they agreed and supported the tourism development process. Finally, the Balinese socio-entrepreneur receives many rewards from some institutions because of his big effort in developing sustainable tourism in Pemuteran, and local people have good respect for him. As a recommendation on developing PPT, one must find a local champion or socio-entrepreneur and apply the development communication strategy properly.

References

Ashley, C., Boyd, C., & Goodwin, H. (2000). Pro-poor tourism: Putting poverty at the heart tourism agenda. *Natural Resource Perspectives, 51.*

Barendsen, L., & Gardener, H. (2004, Fall). Is the social entrepreneur a new type of leader? *Leader to Leader, 2004*(34), 43–50.

Bikse, V., Rivza, B., & Riemere, I. (2015). He social entrepreneur as a promoter of social advancement. *Procedia - Social and Behavioral Sciences, 185*(2015), 469–478.

Bowden, J. (2005). Pro-poor tourism and the Chinese experience. *Asia Pacific Journal of Tourism Research, 10*(4), 379–398.

BPS. (2016). *Kecamatan Gerokgak Dalam Angka 2015*. Badan Pusat Statistik Kabupaten Buleleng.

BPS. (2018). *Kecamatan Gerokgak Dalam Angka 2017*. Badan Pusat Statistik Kabupaten Buleleng.

BPS. (2020). *Kecamatan Gerokgak Dalam Angka2019*. Badan Pusat Statistik Kabupaten Buleleng.

BPS. (2021). *Tingkat Kemiskinan Bali Tahun 2020*. Badan Pusat Statistik Provinsi Bali.

Dwiyasa, I. B. P., & Citra, I. P. A. (2017). *Partisipasi Masyarakat Lokal Dalam Pengembangan Ekowisata Di Desa Pemuteran.* https://ejournal.undiksha.ac.id

Iskandar, D. (2004). Identitas Budaya Dalam Komunikasi Antar-Budaya: Kasus Etnik Madura dan Etnik Dayak. *Jurnal Masyarakat dan Budaya, 6*(2), 119–133.

Mardikanto, T. (2010). *Komunikasi Pembangunan*. Universitas Sebelas Maret.

Mtapuri, O., & Giampiccoli, A. (2019). Tourism, community-based tourism and ecotourism: A definitional problematic. *South African Geographical Journal, 101*(1), 22–35.

Nasution, Z. (1998). *Komunikasi Pembangunan: Pengenalan Teori dan Penerapannya (Edisi Revisi)*. PT RajaGrefindo Persada.

Pinuji, S., Savitri, A. I., Noormasari, M., Wijaya, D., & dan Kurniawan, A. (2019). Efektivitas Data Spasial Peta Rupa Bumi Indonesia (RBI) dan open street map dalam Pengambilan Keputusan Menggunakan Inasafe (effectiveness of Indonesian Earth map (Rbi) and Openstreet map Spatial Data in decision making using Inasafe). *Jurnal Dialog Penanggulangan Bencana, 10*(1), 22–29. https://perpustakaan.bnpb.go.id/jurnal/index.php/JDPB/article/view/128/98

Pitana, I. G., Diarta, I. K. S., & Sarjana, I. M. (2013). *Ekonomi Wisata Hijau Dalam Pariwisata*. Pusat Penelitian dan Pengembangan Kebijakan Kepariwisataan, Badan Pengembangan Sumber Daya Kementerian Pariwisata dan Ekonomi Kreatif.

Purbantara, A., & Mujianto. (2019). *Modul KKN Tematik Desa Membangun Pemberdayaan Masyarakat Desa*. Kementerian Desa, Pembangunan Daerah Tertinggal dan Transmigrasi Republik Indonesia.

Purnami, I. A. (2012). Implikatur Percakapan dalam Naskah Drama Gong Gusti Ayu Klatir Karya A.A. Wiyat S.Ardhi. *Jurnal Pendidikan Bahasa, 1*(1).

Putra, I. N. D. (2008). Modern performing arts as a reflection of changing balinese identity. *Indonesia and the Malay World, 36*(104), 87–114.

Rogers, E. M. (1986). *Communication technology: The new media in society*. The Free Press.

Setiawan, I. B. D. (2015). *Identifikasi Potensi Wisata Beserta 4a (Attraction, Amenity, Accessibility, Ancilliary) Di Dusun Sumber Wangi, Desa Pemuteran, Kecamatan Gerokgak, Kabupaten Buleleng, Bali*. Laporan Penelitian. Fakultas Pariwisata Universitas Udayana. Denpasarrepositori.unud.ac.id/protected/storage/upload/penelitianSimdos/

Simanungkalit, V., Sari, D. A., Teguh, F., Ristanto. H., Permanasari, I. K., Sambodo, L., Widodo, S., Masyhud, Wahyuni, S., Hermantoro, H., Hartati, C., & Vitriani, D. (2017). *Buku Panduan Pengembangan Desa Wisata Hijau.* Asisten Deputi Urusan Ketenagalistrikan dan Aneka Usaha Kementerian Koperasi dan UKM Republik Indonesia, Jakarta.

Sugita, I. W. (2020). Drama Gong sebagai Media Pendidikan dan Kritik Sosial. *Jurnal Kajian Bali, 10*(No. 2), 557–578.

Suwena, I. K., & Arismayanti, N. K. (2016). *Pengembangan Pariwisata Hijau Sebagai Upaya Pemberdayaan Masyarakat di Desa Pemuteran Kabupaten Buleleng Bali.* Seminar Nasional Sains dan Teknologi (Senastek) diselenggarakan Lembaga Penelitian dan Pengabdian kepada Masyarakat (LPPM) Universitas Udayana di Denpasar 15–16 Desember 2016.

Chapter 9

Sustainable Tourism in India: An Integrative Approach for Economic Development and Poverty Alleviation

Parag S. Shukla and Sofia Devi Shamurailatpam

The Maharaja Sayajirao University of Baroda, India

Abstract

In recent decades, the concept of pro-poor tourism has emerged as one of the integral mechanisms that benefit the poor and the underprivileged sections of society. Eradication of poverty is a top priority of human development that is mentioned in the United Nations (UN) Millennium Development Goals (MDGs). Given the expansion of the tourism industry at present in India, the sustainability of this sector is significant, particularly in the rural and remote areas for the facilitation of income-generating opportunities to these vulnerable sections of society at large. The present research study aims to find out the various factors that determine the growth and expansion of the Indian tourism industry and to evaluate how such factors correlate with the alleviation of poverty in India. A panel regression is fitted to find out the nexus between the growth and expansion of the tourism industry in India and its impact on poverty alleviation standards. The selected dimensions, viz. number of tourists visited, per capita income at the state level, index of poverty as measured by headcount ratio, inequality index measured by GINI coefficient, economic specific variables such as literacy rate and infant mortality rate, and state of instability in states measured as by frequency of incidence of crimes in the region are being employed in the study. The estimated model reveals that the effects of tourism development have significant and bountiful outcomes in reducing poverty in India during the study period 2005–2018, as indicated by the estimated coefficient value of (-0.0655), controlling for the selected economic and state/region-specific variables.

Strategic Tourism Planning for Communities, 121–141
Copyright © 2024 Parag S. Shukla and Sofia Devi Shamurailatpam
Published under exclusive licence by Emerald Publishing Limited
doi:10.1108/978-1-83549-015-020241011

Keywords: Pro-poor; sustainable tourism; poverty alleviation; employment; integrative approach

Introduction

Over the period, significant measures are being taken up by the government and regulatory bodies to fight against the poverty and unemployment issues, given the underlying targets oriented by sustainable development goals. There is a dire need for policy initiatives by the ruling government and attitudinal predisposition for inclusive growth with the underlying concept of sustainability to bring maximum economic welfare, taking account of the poor and marginalized sections of society are gaining traction. The concept of poverty is multidimensional in nature, driven by economic, sociopolitical, and cultural factors which require an integrative framework that represents a holistic and conceptual understanding (World Bank, 2000). Sustainable economic development demands investing in the poor so far as social and economic infrastructures is concerned to augment the productive capacity of the aggregate economy by that means reducing inequality in the distribution of income and wealth be justified across space of demographic dividend in India. It is, therefore, intensely focusing on poverty and its eradication programs that have been continued as one of the major policy goals by nations, taking note of the abysmal cost of poor on allocation of resources in the economy. Pro-poor tourism (PPT) is a holistic tourism concept aimed at poverty alleviation in the periphery of selected tourism hubs through interventions pertaining to the economic, social, and cultural aspects of the area. Tourism is better placed than many sectors to address the needs of the poor. Because tourism is consumed at the point of intervention, even low-skilled workers in remote areas can become tourism exporters. Tourism is a diverse and labor-intensive industry and provides a wide range of employment opportunities. Tourism's capacity to generate employment is particularly important in labor intensive economies, given the overall low level of education and skills among local populations. As an industry where entry barriers can be low or easily lowered, tourism creates opportunities for small entrepreneurs and allows poor people to establish new activities or formalize existing micro-ventures. Taxes and levies on tourism income can be used by governments for poverty reduction purposes. Tourism requires relatively less investment (it uses readily available natural and cultural attractions) than other industries, and the requisite infrastructure and superstructure can benefit both tourists and local populations.

Tourism is also one of the few sectors with a wide range of upstream and downstream effects on other economic activities, due to its large and diversified supply chain. Finally, tourism provides an opportunity to support traditional lifestyles and maintain traditional architectural and building styles. A comprehensive picture of global trends in poverty is reported for low and middle income groups of South Asian countries (Table 9.1). The report of the United Nations Development Programme (UNDP) shows that still 1.3 billion people, i.e., 22% live in multidimensional poverty and maximum portion of these lives in

Table 9.1. Multidimensional Poverty Index (MPI) in Developing Countries.

Countries	Multidimensional Poverty Index (MPI)	Population Vulnerable to Multidimensional Poverty (%)	Population Living Below Income Poverty Line (%) National Poverty Line	PPP $1.90 a Day
Afghanistan	0.272	18.1	54.5	–
Bangladesh	0.104	18.2	24.3	14.8
Bhutan	0.175	17.7	8.2	1.5
India	0.123	19.3	21.9	21.2
Maldives	0.003	4.8	8.2	0.0
Nepal	0.148	22.4	25.2	15.0
Pakistan	0.198	12.9	24.3	3.9
Sri Lanka	0.011	14.3	4.1	0.8
South Asia	*0.132*	*18.4*	*22.9*	*18.2*
Sub-Saharan Africa	0.299	17.9	43.4	45.7
Developing countries	0.108	15.2	20.7	14.7

Source: Multidimensional Poverty Index 2020, UNDP.

sub-Saharan Africa (558 million) and South Asian countries (530 million). Looking about the percentages of population which are vulnerable to multidimensional poverty, South Asia is having the highest share of 18.4%, within which Nepal recorded 22.4% of such endangered population group. However, among the developing countries, sub-Saharan African countries have huge percentage of population living below income poverty line when compared to South Asian countries. A microscopic look on the contribution of deprivation to overall Multidimensional Poverty Index (MPI) in terms of three inter-related dimensions, namely health, education, and standard of living, revealed that standard of living condition contributes 44.5%, followed by education of 29.6% and 25.8% in health deprivation (Multidimensional Poverty Index 2020, UNDP).

The key objective is to investigate that is tourism industry a source of economic progression in developing countries? The United Nations and World Tourism Organization highlighted the potentiality of tourism in reducing the extent of poverty – the Sustainable Tourism as an effective tool for Eliminating Poverty (STEP) programs under the support of UNCTAD. Recently, the UNDP and the United Nations World Tourism Organization (UNWTO) have moved together during the International Year for Sustainable Tourism for Development to assure and bring forward sustainable development through 2030 and beyond (UNWTO, 2020). From the perspectives of poverty in rural areas, the endowed natural resources have strong association with the tourism sector and hence development in tourism has significant poverty-reduction strategies which are often referred to as PPT. PPT means an approach which aims to increase the net benefits for the poor and marginalized income groups from the source of tourism industry. The main thrust behind the PPT strategy is to generate economic opportunities for poor who will help in reducing the extent of poverty through opportunities in terms of economic gains and livelihood benefits. Though the PPT opens a route toward development in tourism industry, the PPT implementations in different regions of different countries produce varied results, a few are lifted out of income poverty while others face with income gaps, including access of the poor to market, commercial viability, policy framework, skills gap, managing costs, expectations, product quality and price, and physical location to mention the major factors. Therefore, in order to promote the PPT model, it requires incorporating the poor and concerns at each level of planning and strategy being taken up to alleviate the bottom-of-pyramid communities. As tourism industry is gradually growing; it can be a significant contributor to economic growth, particularly the rural sector as by nature of activity; it is labor-intensive which is a suitable dominant aspect in service delivery in tourism. However, experts are of the view that the expansion is at the cost of the society in terms of environmental damage owing to its highly fluctuating business determined by the geopolitical conditions across the countries, as well as vulnerable to national and international transactions of shifts in exchange rates, which calls for a new form of risk and difficult to stabilize immediately and under control. Though economic theory indicates the direct linkages between tourism development and poverty reduction due to the diffusion effect, there are arguments against such establishment due to limited studies on the extant literature, forming a grey area of research to delve out for arriving at a concrete theoretical validation and meaningful implications.

The interconnectedness between development in tourism industry and poverty reduction and the way to sustainable economic development is expressed with the help of the conceptual framework as depicted in Fig. 9.1. There are three different aspects of multidimensional poverty – health, education and standard of living, the economies with poor valued of MDI are characterized by low per capita income, slow economic growth, lack of skills and knowledge of the laborers and consequently low productivity, thereby a source of high rate of unemployment, though structural unemployment is preceded in the structure of developing economies. The fundamental premise of this research study is that tourism is associated with certain positive externalities and advantages to the inhabitants around in the form of employment generation, income earnings of the poor, and promotion of local goods, conservation, and monitoring of environmental resources.

The other factors are containment in global warming and preservation of cultural heritage. There are associated negative externalities generated from the expansion of tourism industry which is in terms of inequality in the distribution of income and employment sources/opportunities confined to a particular

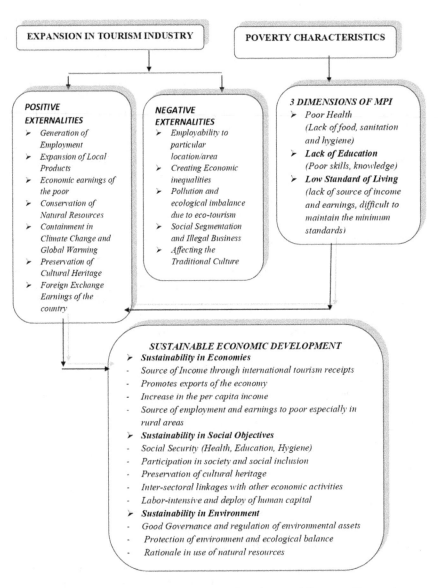

Fig. 9.1.   The Linkages Between Tourism and Poverty Toward Sustainable Economic Development: A Framework. *Source:* Prepared by authors.

geographical location for supporting means of livelihood from such industry, related to increase in pollution and threatening to environmental assets when object of ecotourism targets, illegal entry of drugs and prostitution, other social contravenes. Besides the negative externalities of expansion of tourism sector in the economy, the economic benefits derived from this source is valuable, specifically benefitting the poor and underprivileged groups who are directly connected with natural assets, predominantly dependent on primary activities for livelihood. In this connection, Fig. 9.1 reveals the positive linkages between expansions in tourism sector and brings to reduction in poverty through economic benefits, thereby lifting the poor out of the poverty to an extent that is a significant contribution to the sustainable economic development in the economy.

Rationale of the Research Study

The present study attempts to evaluate the impact assessment of the linkages between tourism industry and poverty with the basic theoretical idea that the unemployed poor masses can be absorbed in the tourism industry, particularly in rural areas which has the capacity to absorb surplus labor and generate economic values by provision of employment opportunities. The rationale of present study is established based on the proposition that tourism has had significant effects across the globe from time to time and can effectively work as a tool to alleviate poverty, particularly in rural areas, where most of the tourist sites, scenic beauty, natures are highly associated. Though academic views on the nexus between development in tourism sectors and poverty reduction have however varied views across time and space, tourism sector is keyed out as a potential source of employment opportunities and earnings from foreign exchange, particularly in developing and emerging market economies. Sustainable Tourism is an effective tool for Eliminating Poverty (ST-EP) to alleviate poverty and hunger among the sustainable development goals. It is fascinating to determine the nexus between tourism sector development and poverty in a developing country like India, given its diversity in different aspects – languages, regions, culture and ethnicity, and geopolitical stability context (UNWTO).

A Brief Review of Literature on Poverty and Tourism

This section gives a brief review of literature on the issue of poverty and the development of tourism industry across time and space. Extant literature in the field established a positive association between tourism industry and reduction in poverty and that tourism industry has potential in poverty reduction, particularly for rural residents (Ashley et al., 2001, pp. 1–64; Ashley & Roe, 2002; Binns & Nel, 2002; Rodriguez, 2019; Sharpley, 2002); despite the emergence of such significant views, there remains skepticism about this ideology, with the view that it costs to the physical environment in the form of destruction of natural resources, addition to pollution, loss of cultural identity, etc., and discussed several conceptual as well as substantive criticisms on the issue (Burns, 1996; Harrison, 2008; Kamuaro, 1996). Akrong (2019) highlighted the impact assessment of PPT and opined that product development among others is one of the means for tourism to become an avenue for the source of economic and noneconomic opportunities for local residents. This product development calls for elements necessary for tourism development at destinations and are developed so that it becomes a source to deliver benefits for local residents. Though the income from small enterprises by locals through participation in tourism may be small, it can be a critical buffer (Singh, 2012). Accordingly, the study highlighted three main ways that tourism can impact on vulnerable people – direct effects on poor through provision of jobs and small tourism enterprises; secondary effects like earnings form supply chain industries; and dynamic effects on economy such as entrepreneurship, infrastructure development, skill development, and preservation of the natural environment. Besides, there are barriers to tourism development in the form of poor human capital, gender constraints, lack of micro credit, lack of product planning process, inadequate access to market, and lack of proactive government support for involvement by the poor, etc., and among others, empowerment can be a tool for poverty reduction through local tourism development.

From a tourism development perspective, destination competitiveness, local participation, and destination sustainability are three independent themes to address in anti-poverty tourism development programs (Zhao & Ritchie, 2007). Regionalism and associated price discrimination toward nonlocal tourist agents is another aspect of tourism which has been a serious concern so far as inter-regional transactions and national development. Zhang (2009) established an integrative framework and comprehensive assessment to analyze the determinants of a region's international inbound tourism and various factors of international tourism receipts. The study found that development level, openness, tourism resources, tourism facilities, and tourism organization are all positively associated to a region's international tourism receipts. Further, it added that spatial effects are highly significant, stating that an increase in one region's international inbound tourism benefits its neighbors and the regions with which it has spatial connections in terms of tourists. On impact assessment of community tourism on regional development, a case study of Mt. Kenya region found that this form of community tourism stabilizes the livelihoods of rural households, contributing to community welfare, and reduces the vulnerability of families (Steinicke & Neuburger, 2012). However, the study further added that even though such community-based tourism helps to alleviate poverty, it has limited impulses; the equitable welfare for households and the community depends on the respective organizations' internal participatory and demographic structures to initiate sustainable regional development. Sub-Saharan countries possess nature-based assets to attract huge number of tourists each year, and the international tourists' arrival in the region has grown up significantly, more than the world average according to UNWTO reports. With nature-based tourism around Kibale National Park in western Uganda as a case study, impact assessment of regional development of tourism sector on the distribution of employment on the local livelihoods revealed that urbanized settings have larger employment accommodation and wider spatial space than the influence in rural areas, where the extent of poverty is much higher; hence, understanding spatial differences of the distribution of tourism benefits is important for better informed policies in poverty alleviation (Adiyia et al., 2014). Developing countries are endowed with natural assets, which resources can be allocated for earnings of the economy and despite the economic significance of such countries to tourism; there is distinct dearth in studies so far as the tourism-poverty nexus is concerned. Very recent study on tourism poverty nexus of BRICS group of nations points out the heterogeneity of the influence of tourism on poverty, whereby receipts from travel subsector and exports dimensions of tourism contribute to poverty alleviation in the long run, but receipts from hospitality and accommodation were found only to influence poverty in the short run (Garidzirai & Matiza, 2020). Notwithstanding different views on the linkages between tourism sector development and the poverty reduction and specific outcomes experienced by countries across time and space, probably a concrete clue and decision be arrived after empirical research studies and the nature of relationship established as an outcome of review of literature.

Tourism and Poverty in India

An overview of the trends and progress of tourism industry with special reference to India is discussed; the average poverty rates and poverty line in rural and urban areas are discussed in the following section.

Trends and Progress of Tourism Industry

India's economic growth structure is strongly influenced by service-led growth hypotheses, as validated by its contribution to gross value added growth of around 55%, with a year-on-year growth rate of 6.9% during the period 2019–2020. The increasing role of services sector in the economic activity is also obvious from the performance of its key subsectors in aggregate economic growth. In our present study, focus is on tourism sector and its role in economic development through reduction of poverty. In India, the tourism industry witnessed a significant growth during the last decades, with high growth in the number of foreign tourist arrivals (FTAs) and earnings from foreign exchange, though there was slight deceleration in tourist arrivals during 2018–2019 onward. The number FTAs and foreign exchange earnings (FEEs) during 2000–2018 are depicted in Table 9.2.

Based on data from the Bureau of Immigration, India ranked 22nd in the world with respect to international tourist arrivals in 2018, accounting for 1.24% of world's international tourist arrivals as against 26th position in 2016. And the FEEs through the arrival of tourist have a positive growth rate of 15.4% in 2017, though decelerated in the subsequent period to 9.6% in 2018 (India Tourism Statistics, 2019, Ministry of Tourism, Government of India).

Table 9.2. Foreign Tourist Arrivals (FTAs) and Foreign Exchange Earnings (FEEs) in India During 2000–2018.

Year	No. of FTAs (in Millions)	% Change Over Previous Year	Rank of India[a]	Amount of FEEs (Rs. Crore)	% Change Over Previous Year
2000	2.65	–	50th	15,626	–
2001	2.54	−4.2	51st	15,083	−3.5
2002	2.38	−6.3	54th	15,064	−0.1
2003	2.73	14.7	51st	20,729	37.6
2004	3.46	26.7	44th	27,944	34.8
2005	3.92	13.3	43rd	33,123	18.5
2006	4.45	13.5	44th	39,025	17.8
2007	5.08	14.2	41st	44,362	13.7
2008	5.28	3.9	41st	51,294	15.6
2009	5.17	−2.1	41st	53,754	4.8
2010	5.78	11.8	42nd	66,172	23.1
2011	6.31	9.2	38th	83,036	25.5
2012	6.58	4.3	41st	95,607	15.1
2013	6.97	5.9	41st	107,563	12.5
2014	7.68	10.2	24th	120,367	11.9
2015	8.03	4.6	24th	134,844	12.0
2016	8.80	9.6	26th	154,146	14.3
2017	10.04	14.1	22nd	177,874	15.4
2018	10.56	5.2	22nd	194,881	9.6

Source: India Tourism Statistics (2019), Ministry of Tourism, Government of India.

[a](*Note:* Ranking of India in international tourist arrivals in the world).

The details of entry of foreign tourists in India with country of nationality are depicted in Table 9.3. The largest percentage share of tourists in India arrives from South Asia, accounting from 24.9% in 2016 to 29.4% in 2018; this is followed by Western European countries, whose share is 23.1% in 2016 to 21.3% in 2018. From the countries of nationality, the list of top 10 countries for FTAs in India during 2018 are – Bangladesh, the United States of America, the United Kingdom, Sri Lanka, Canada, Australia, Malaysia, China, Germany, and Russia Fed, respectively. The figures from the total number of arrivals of foreign tourists revealed that the annual growth rate is at 5.2% during 2017–18 against 14% annual growth rate during 2016–17 period, positive growth rates. Thus, over the period, the number of entries of foreign tourist is increased, improvement in the ranking of data of tourist entries in the world, adding more values to aggregate FEEs over the period.

Table 9.3. Nationality-Wise Foreign Tourist Arrivals in India, 2016–18.

Country of Nationality	Number of Arrivals			Percentage Share		
	2016	2017	2018	2016	2017	2018
North America	1,614,178	1,712,358	1,807,718	18.33	17.06	17.12
Central and South America	78,730	92,067	101,085	0.89	0.92	0.96
Western Europe	2,029,412	2,133,673	2,243,635	23.05	21.26	21.25
Eastern Europe	406,002	472,872	466,049	4.61	4.71	4.41
Africa	302,164	318,023	351,198	3.43	3.17	3.33
West Asia	451,842	457,760	449,548	5.13	4.56	4.26
South Asia	2,194,555	2,951,665	3,104,422	24.93	29.41	29.40
South East Asia	746,069	824,575	887,088	8.47	8.22	8.40
East Asia	617,563	663,295	724,568	7.01	6.61	6.86
Australasia	348,908	386,059	412,628	3.96	3.85	3.91
Not Classified elsewhere	14,988	23,456	10,037	0.17	0.23	0.10
Grand total	8,804,411	10,035,803	10,557,976	100.00	100.00	100.00

Source: India Tourism Statistics (2019), Ministry of Tourism, Government of India.

Poverty in India and Its Estimates

Over the decades, great initiatives were being taken up to minimize poverty in developing countries; taking the case of India, various schemes and programs were being implemented across different time and space to benefit the poor and underprivileged groups under the five-year plans, such as the Integrated Rural Development Programme (IRDP) in 1978 to the passing of the Mahatma Gandhi National Rural Employment Guarantee Act (MGNREGA), 2005, with its different adaptations and amendments. More than 273 million people in India were lifted out of poverty from 2005 to 2016, showing that India has recorded the largest country to experience during the period (Human Development Report, 2019). All such initiatives were launched with the expectations of significant impact in reducing the extent of poverty, which impact assessment requires from both micro and macro environments.

The term poverty in its simplest sense is a circumstance or state in which an individual or a household does not have enough financial resources to afford the basic needs for survival. In India, the extent of poverty is measured using different methodologies under different committees framed and reviewed across time and space, incorporating different dimensions in defining poverty over the period, say from the calorie norms to the expenditure on health and education to the additional components in basket of goods for household consumption. As before 2005, food security was the base to measure poor and the extent of poverty, defining the per capita expenditure for a person to consume enough calories and capacity to access necessities for survival. However, since 2005, the Tendulkar methodology is adopted, shifting from calorie anchor to a basket of goods along with the minimum expenditure required for survival, for a given standard of living. One of the special features of measuring poverty based on the definitions of poverty given under this committee is that it has shifted from Uniform Reference Period (URP) to Mixed Reference Method (MRP). Table 9.4 reveals the number and percentages below poverty line in both rural and urban areas as well as the aggregate picture for 2004–05, 2009–10, and 2011–12.

Poverty line in rural areas was Rs. 446.68 per capita per month and Rs. 578.80 per capita per month in urban areas in 2004–05; these has increased to Rs. 816 per capita per month in rural areas and to Rs. 1000 per capita per month in urban areas in 2011–12 (RBI, Handbook of Statistics on Indian Economy, 2018–19).

Though the percentage of poor has declined in both population group over the period, and combined average from 37.20% to 21.92% in 2004–05, in terms of the number of persons counted, the figure is still alarming of 269,783 1000 (27 crores persons) as on 2011–12 using the Tendulkar methodology. According to the latest committee of defining poverty line, the Rangarajan Committee, the indicators used are namely monthly expenditure of family of five, adding protein and fat in calorie expenditure estimation and also other accessories of living requirements in defining poor and poverty lines. This research study is based on the Tendulkar methodology of defining poverty line (RBI, Handbook of Statistics on Indian Economy, 2018–19).

Specification of Variables, Data, and Methodology

This section gives details of data and its sources, the justification of selection of variables, their theoretical expected signs, and main objectives of the present study.

Data and Theoretical Signs of the Variables

Data are compiled from various secondary sources namely – India Tourism Statistics of the Ministry of Tourism, *Handbook of Statistics on Indian States* and *Handbook of Statistics on Indian Economy of the Reserve Bank of India*, and reports of the Planning Commission for socioeconomic characteristics, Statistics of Crime in India of the Ministry of Home Affairs for the relevant years. Data pertaining to tourism and its attributes such as number of FTAs and amount of FEEs across states are compiled from the various publications of India Tourism Statistics. As mentioned above, reports of the Reserve Bank of India, data on poverty indices and per capita income, literacy rate at state levels, infant mortality rate are taken from these reports; so far as the inequality index (GINI coefficient), it is taken from the annual report of the Planning Commission (now NITI Aayog); data on number of cognizable crimes under the Indian Penal Code (IPC) and Special and Local Laws (SLL) across states are taken from the Crime in India reports published by the National Crime Records Bureau, Ministry of Home Affairs.

Details of variables with their theoretical expected signs are shown in Box 9.1. Poverty variable (POV) is measured by headcount ratio. The explanatory

Table 9.4. Number and Percentages of Population Below Poverty Line.

(Based on MRP Consumption)	Number of Persons (Thousands)			Percentage (%) of Persons			Poverty Line	
	Rural	Urban	All India (Combined)	Rural	Urban	All India (Combined)	Rural	Urban
2004–2005	325,810	81,410	407,220	42.00	25.50	37.20	446.68	578.80
2009–2010	278,210	76,470	354,680	33.80	20.90	29.80	672.80	859.60
2011–2012	216,658	53,125	269,783	25.70	13.70	21.92	816	1,000

Source: RBI: Handbook of Statistics on Indian Economy, 2018–19.

variables are number of FTAs (TOU), Inequality Index as measured by GINI coefficient (GINI), gross state per capita income as a measure of economic growth (SPCI), economic specific characteristic variables (ESV) which composed of literacy rate, infant mortality rate; and lastly state specific variable denoted by (SSE), measured by data on cognizable crimes under IPC and SLL in state concerned, thereby influencing the arrivals of tourists in the state based on stability of the region. For the purpose of this research study, 32 states and union territories (UTs) are taken in the study, selection of these states is based on the availability of data on each of the variables mentioned.

The explanatory variables that have theoretical positive associations with poverty variables are TOU, SPCI, LIT, and INFM, while the variables that have negative association are GINI and SSE. Given the positive role of tourism industry development on economic growth in terms of addition to net revenue earnings, job and employment opportunities to the locals and rural areas in tourism spot, etc., it is expected that number of poor and poverty measured in terms of number of headcount ratio will decrease as tourism sector intensifies. Literacy rate and infant mortality rate have positive association with poverty reduction, while crime rates in the region will bring down number of tourist arrivals that will be less in instable regions, probably increasing the extent of poverty.

Box 9.1.   Definition of Variables and Theoretical Expected Signs.

Variables	Proxy	Measurement/Meanings of Variable	Theoretically Expected Signs
Poverty alleviation	lnPOV	Poverty headcount ratio	
Tourists arrivals	lnTOU	Number of international tourists arrivals	+VE
Inequality index (GINI coefficient)	lnGINIR	Inequality in the distribution of wealth (GINI at rural sector is used in the model)	−VE
Economic growth	lnSPCI	State level per capita income	+VE
Other economic characteristics (ESV)	lnLIT	Literacy	+VE
	lnINFM	Infant mortality rate	+VE
Regional/ state-specific institutional variable	lnSSE	Incidence of crime in states	−VE

Source: Compiled by authors.

Objectives of the Study and Model Specification

In view of the associated linkages between development in tourism industry and poverty reduction, the following objectives are pertinent to measure.

- What is the nature of linkages between tourism development and poverty reduction?
- How tourism development connects to the reduction in poverty?
- At what rate of changes in tourism development will impact the reduction in poverty?
- What is the role of tourism as futuristic development strategy of pro-poor?

Accordingly, the following hypotheses are framed with expected theoretical economic signs.

Hypotheses:

H0. There are no linkages between tourism development and reduction in poverty.

H1. There are strong and positive linkages between tourism development and reduction in poverty.

To examine the nature of relationship between tourism development and poverty reduction, we follow the studies and models used by Adams (2004) and Folarin and Adeniyi (2019). Our model, however, slightly differs in terms of the determinants of socioeconomic variables taken, based on the prevailing interstate variation in such variables. Thus, the tourism-poverty linkages equation is expressed as follows:

$$ln(\text{POV})_{it} = \alpha_0 + \alpha_1 \ ln(\text{TOU})_{it} + \alpha_2 \ ln(\text{SPCI})_{it} + \alpha_3 \ ln(\text{GINIR})_{it} + \alpha_4 \ ln(\text{ESV})_{it} + \alpha_5 \ ln(\text{SSE})_{it} + \varepsilon_{it} \tag{1}$$

where,

POV is the measure of poverty, measured by poverty headcount ratio.

TOU is the measure of number of FTAs.

SPCI is the gross state per capita income.

GINIR is the measure of inequality in rural areas (reflecting the extent of income inequality in economy, whose values range from 0 to 1, with 0 signifies equality in the distribution of income and 1 implies absolute inequality in the distribution of income).

ECV is the economic-specific variables across different states (this includes literacy rate and infant mortality rate).

SSV is the state specific effect variables (cognizable crime rate is taken for stability position in state).

ln is the natural logarithm.
i is the cross-section.
t is the time period.
ε_{it} is the error term with its usual statistical properties of zero mean and constant variance σ^2.

The above model is estimated using random effects generalized least squares (GLS) regression for the time period from 2005 to 2018. In the following section, the results of the estimated coefficients and their theoretical significance about the establishment of relationship between tourism development and poverty reduction are explained in much detail.

Toward Assessment of Tourism-Poverty

The model as given in the previous section in Eq. (1) is estimated using the random effects GLS regression, after nonsuitability of adopting the fixed effects model statistically rejection of null hypothesis of Hausman test.

The null hypothesis is accepted based on this test, explaining the outcome that chi-square value of 6.70 with probability value (*p*-value = 0.3492), and theoretically, it is meaningful and significant to explain the poverty and tourism development nexus based on the economic, social, and region-specific factors that determine the nature of association between it.

The result for this test is not reported here, but given these underlying factors, we estimate the model using the fixed effects GLS regression, and the results are reported in Table 9.7. Table 9.5 gives the descriptive statistics of the variables. The values of the standard deviation reveal that no much variation is found for each of the variables from its mean values. And not much lapse is seen between the minimum and maximum values.

Results of the correlation matrix of the dependent variable and explanatory variables are reported in Table 9.6. The results indicated that tourism development is negatively correlated with the measure of poverty (−0.049), though statistically significant, meaning that tourism development might be poverty reducing strategy for different states and union territories in India. This is supported by positive correlation with tourism development with state-level per capita income (0.235). Further, poverty index is also influenced by literacy rate, with correlation coefficient of (−0.484), and state-specific variable with correlation coefficient of (0.304) and are statistically significant. A analysis of the nature of association between various strategies of poverty alleviation through the perspectives of tourism development, given the socioeconomic conditions in the region may be cleared by the results of regression Eq. (1).

Table 9.5. Descriptive Statistics of the Variables.

Variable	Mean	Standard Deviation	Minimum	Maximum	Observations
*ln*POV	3.00	0.82	−1.61	4.11	448
*ln*TOUR	11.36	2.47	5.61	15.62	448
*ln*SPCI	10.85	0.71	8.93	12.68	448
*ln*GINIR	−1.37	0.19	−1.86	−0.87	448
*ln*LIT	4.29	0.14	3.85	4.54	448
*ln*INFM	3.42	0.54	1.39	4.33	448
*ln*SSE	10.58	2.06	6.57	14.73	448

Table 9.6. The Results of Correlation Analysis.

Variables	*ln*POV	*ln*TOUR	*ln*SPCI	*ln*GINIR	*ln*LIT	*ln*INFM	*ln*SSE
*ln*POV	1.00						
*ln*TOUR	−0.049	1.00					
*ln*SPCI	−0.578*	0.235*	1.00				
*ln*GINIR	0.039	0.448*	0.151*	1.00			
*ln*LIT	−0.484*	0.055	0.719*	0.096*	1.00		
*ln*INFM	0.416*	0.047	−0.602*	0.122*	−0.667	1.00	
*ln*SSE	0.304*	0.695*	−0.171*	0.441*	−0.248*	0.386*	1.00

Notes: *, statistically significant at 5% level.

Table 9.7. Effects of Tourism on the Level of Poverty in India.

Variables	Estimated Coefficients	Standard Error	*t*-Values
Constant	11.446*	1.6609	7.22 (0.000)
*ln*TOUR	−0.0655*	0.0199	−3.30 (0.001)
*ln*SPCI	−0.4897*	0.0914	−7.12 (0.000)
*ln*GINIR	0.2850	0.1914	1.51 (0.131)
*ln*LIT	−0.7268*	0.3654	−2.10 (0.035)
*ln*INFM	−0.0750	0.0841	−0.90 (0.368)
*ln*SSE	0.1304*	0.0257	5.25 (0.000)
Overall R-square	0.3981		
Number of observations	448		
Wald chi-square	291.67 (p value = 0.000)		

Notes: *, statistically significant at 5% level; figures in the parentheses are the p-values.

The empirical results of the effects of tourism development on poverty are reported in Table 9.7. It involves measuring Eq. (1) using the random effects model for cross section of variables and states given the time period 2005–2018. The estimated regression model can be expressed as follows in Eq. (2):

$$\ln(\text{POV})_{it} = 11.45^* + (-0.066)^* \ln\text{TOUR}_{it} + (-0.490)^* \ln\text{SPCI}_{it} + (0.285) \ln\text{GINIR}_{it}$$
$$+ (-0.727)^* \ln\text{LIT}_{it} + (-0.075)\text{INFM}_{it} + (0.130)^* \ln\text{SSE}_{it} + \varepsilon_{it}$$

$$(2)$$

All the estimated coefficients of the model, except the inequality index (GINIR) and the economic specific variable namely, infant mortality rate (INFM), found to be not statistically significant. The estimated coefficient of tourism development indicator (TOUR) is found to be statistically significant with an estimated value of (-0.0655), the negative coefficient values indicating that tourism development might be a poverty reducing strategy for the states/UTs in India. Further, the estimated coefficients of the state per capita income is (-0.4897), stating that trickle-down effect of the distribution of wealth, thereby reducing poverty. This is also supported by the expected sign of estimated values of the inequality index, though it is not statistically significant. The estimated coefficient of the economic variable, literacy index, do support the theoretical establishment of high level of literacy and poverty reduction over the period. Lastly, the state-specific stability parameter measured by the state of crimes in the region produces an estimated coefficient of (0.1304) which is statistically significant, meaning that a high level of such incidence in the region retards growth and promote poverty and number of poor.

Key Discussions

Tourism is a powerful engine for socioeconomic development and an instrument to safeguard biodiversity and cultural heritage, especially in developing economies with population as a demographic dividend. The need of the hour is to harness sustainable tourism development strategy or sectoral policy that should consider the cross-sectoral dimensions of tourism and the need to integrate tourism development in the broader development agenda while building the country's competitive advantage. Differentiated approaches and contextualized solutions are needed.

Based on the review of literature, the authors in this present research deduce that tourism employs more women and young people than most industries, resulting in increased incomes, empowerment, and social inclusion. Any strategy for tourism development should be dynamic enough to adapt to changing circumstances and priorities in order to maximize poverty reduction impacts as supported by the findings of this research study. This study aims to offer policy implications for creating an institutional and legal framework that would ensure security, protection of tourists against any sort of cognizable crimes and instability in the region. It not only results into reduction in number of tourist arrivals but also fuels poverty, deteriorating the possible income earning opportunities of that particular region. The research study also envisages that better amenities for tourists can be made available through financing on infrastructures, ease of passing and entry, documentations, immigration policies, and special schemes. At the current scenario, we know that the entire world is hit by the COVID-19 pandemic, and it is worthwhile to mention its ill-effects for world's poorest countries. The World Tourism Organization (UNWTO) has stated that tourism is one of the most affected sectors from COVID-19, estimating that in 2020, global international tourist arrivals could decline between 20% and 30%, from an estimated growth forecast of 3%–4% in January 2020. This means a loss of US$30–50 billion in spending by international visitors. For some developing economies, tourism is likely the worst affected area. The world's 47 less developed countries (LDCs), home to 900 million and categorized as such by the United Nations based on their structural economic and social challenges and vulnerability to natural disasters, have few weapons to deal with the pandemic. They have not experienced a peak of the outbreak yet; however, as of May 5, 2020, more than 25,000 infections and around 650 deaths have been reported in 47 LDCs, of which around 11,000 infections and around 200 deaths have occurred in 14 Commonwealth LDCs (UNWTO, 2020). This study holds significance in light of the fact that the intensification of tourism sector in India is interconnected to overall economic growth and development, and the Indian economy will be able to usher into the new dawn of "Atmanirbharta" as envisaged by Hon'ble Prime Minister Narendra Modiji to make India a hub of tourism on the global footing with a mission of self-reliant India.

Limitations of the Research Study and Future Scope

Our results have significant contributions in the tourism-poverty nexus, and it possesses implications for policy framing in the context of a developing country like India with a large presence of rural poverty. The findings provided empirical evidence in support of PPT concept of United Nations and for bringing sustainability in the Indian economy. Our findings suggest that economic variables and regional/area-specific variables have an impact on the extent of poverty in India, though the efforts of the Government to promote Indian tourism are on in full swing. An analysis in the form of adding and incorporating other institutional variables like infrastructure, quality of amenities provided to tourists, policy about the tourists, corruption index, gender empowerment, political instability in the state, measures of poverty, severity of poor, and poverty gap are some of the other important variables which is not taken into account in the present study.

This may be a limitation to our present study, and hence, more meaningful insights can be produced if certain specifications of other parameters are incorporated in building the tourism-poverty nexus model.

Further, impact assessment of poverty alleviation strategies being taken up under region-specific programs launched by the government from time to time to lift poor in terms of unemployment, social security, incentives, farmers waive off schemes, funding and development of infrastructures in given sites, tourist area, and projects undertaken is also important in determining the extent of poverty in that particular region/state/union territories are other aspects which can be taken up by other researchers in future.

Conclusion

The PPT approach has emerged as a mechanism for tourism development, thereby influencing poverty reduction. This study examined the nature of relationship between tourism industry development and the reduction in poverty, with perspective to Indian economy. One of the reasons for studying the scenario of India is that the economy has transitioned from the agriculture sector to the services sector by passing the manufacturing sector, after certain level of growth. The contribution of services in GDP is increasing over the period, and among the components of services sector, the tourism sector is significant in terms of its potential role in providing job opportunities and income source to the locals, particularly in the rural India. In view of this, it is pertinent to measure the extent of tourism development and its association in reducing the degree or level of poverty across various states/UTs in India. Accordingly, we have evaluated the linkages between poverty and tourism with a priori assumption that the tourism industry development has a positive outcome in terms of poverty reduction by providing job opportunities and income earnings to the poor, particularly residing in the rural areas that has directly or indirectly connected to nature.

We estimated a model of tourism-poverty nexus for the time period from 2005 to 2018, incorporating economic specific, state specific variables, along with parameters of poverty and tourism development. Poverty is measured in terms of headcount ratio and tourism by the number of FTAs over the period. Indicators on inequality and per capita income across states and union territories of India are also taken in the explanatory variables. The economic-specific variables such as literacy rate and the infant mortality rates are taken and incidence of crimes to indicate the state of stability in the region. The estimated model reveals that tourism has an important role to play in reducing poverty, shown by the negative sign of the estimated value of (-0.0655), controlling for the various economic and state specific variables, the effects of tourism development have significant outcomes in reducing poverty. In other words, this study summarizes the diverse findings in tourism related poverty eradication programs that were undertaken by various pilot projects being launched at different levels of organizations including nongovernment, multilateral organizations, tourism associations, and other stakeholders that engaged in the promotion and implementation of PPT with reference to India. Literacy has a big role in reducing the extent of poverty, stability in the region, given the strong institutional and legal framework to reduce number of crimes and incidences are some the factors that can establish a quite positive association between the tourism sector development and poverty reduction in the country.

References

Adams, R. H. (2004). Economic growth, inequality and poverty: Estimating the growth elasticity of poverty. *World Development, 32*(12), 1989–2014.

Adiyia, B., Vanneste, D., Rompaey, A. V., & Ahebwa, W. M. (2014). Spatial analysis of tourism income distribution in the accommodation sector in western Uganda. *Tourism and Hospitality Research, 14*(1/2), 8–26.

Akrong, K. K. (2019). Pro-poor tourism: Critical perspective and implications for future research. *Journal of Tourism and Hospitality Management, 7*(1), 23–35.

Ashley, C., & Roe, D. (2002). Making tourism work for the poor: Strategies and challenges in southern Africa. *Development Southern Africa, 19*(1), 61–82.

Ashley, C., Roe, D., & Goodwin, H. (2001). *Pro-poor tourism strategies: Making tourism work for the poor – A review of experience.* Tourism Report No.1. Overseas Development Institute.

Binns, T., & Nel, E. (2002). Tourism as a local development strategy in South Africa. *The Geographical Journal, 168*(3), 235–247.

Burns, D. (1996). Attitudes toward tourism development. *Annals of Tourism Research, 23*(4), 935–938.

Folarin, O., & Adeniyi, O. (2019). Does tourism reduce poverty in Sub-Saharan African Countries? *Journal of Travel Research, 59*(1), 140–155. https://doi.org/10.1177/0047287518821736

Garidzirai, R., & Matiza, T. (2020). Exploring the tourism-poverty alleviation nexus in the brics group of nations. *Ekonom, 99*(1), 93–109.

Government of India. (2019). *India tourism statistics, 2019.* Ministry of Tourism, Government of India. http://tourism.gov.in/sites/default/files/Other/India%20Tourism%20Statistics%202019.pdf

Harrison, D. (2008). Pro-poor tourism: A critique. *Third World Quarterly, 29*(5), 851–868.

Human Development Report. (2019). *Beyond income, beyond averages, beyond today: Inequalities in human development in the 21st century.* UNDP. http://hdr.undp.org/sites/default/files/hdr2019.pdf

Human Development Report. (2020). *Charting pathways out of multidimensional poverty: Achieving the SDGs, the 2020 global multidimensional poverty index (MPI).* UNDP. http://hdr.undp.org/en/2020-MPI

Kamuaro, O. (1996). *Ecotourism: Suicide or development? Voices from Africa.* Sustainable Development, Issue no. 6 UN Non-governmental Liaison Service, Geneva.

Rodriguez, J. G. (2019). Tourism and poverty reduction in Mexico: An ARDL cointegration approach. *Sustainability, 11*(3), 1–10. www.mdpi.com/journal/sustainability

Sharpley, R. (2002). Rural tourism and the challenge of tourism diversification: The case of Cyprus. *Tourism Management, 23*(3), 233–244.

Singh, P. (2012). Pro poor tourism approach in India – Status and implication. *Research Scapes*, *I*(II), 1–10. https://www.semanticscholar.org/paper/Pro-Poor-Tourism-Approach-in-India-Status-and-Singh/f297944e702660141009a3d999477b c6a57dde12

Steinicke, E., & Neuburger, M. (2012). The impact of community-based afro-alpine tourism on regional development: A case study in the Mt Kenya region. *Mountain Research and Development*, *32*(4), 420–430.

UNWTO. (2020). *Tourism and the sustainable development goals- journey to 2030.* https://www.unwto.org/global/publication/tourism-and-sustainable-development-goals-journey-2030

World Bank. (2000). *Attacking poverty: World development report 2000/2001.* Oxford University Press.

Zhang, J. (2009). Spatial distribution of inbound tourism in China: Determinants and implications. *Tourism and Hospitality Research*, *9*(1), 32–49.

Zhao, W., & Ritchie, J. R. B. (2007). Tourism and poverty alleviation: An integrative research framework. In C. Michael Hall (Ed.), *Pro-poor tourism: Who benefits? Chapter II* (pp. 9–33). Channel View Publications.

Chapter 10

COVID-19 Impact on Tourism Industry: A Bibliometric Study

Azamat Maksüdünov and Kyialbek Dyikanov

Kyrgyz-Turkish Manas University, Kyrgyzstan

Abstract

The COVID-19 pandemic has had a profound impact on the world, particularly on the international travel and hospitality industry, which is highly sensitive to such disruptions. The global tourism industry has been severely impacted by the COVID-19 pandemic, leading to extensive discussions and examinations of the relationship between the virus and tourism in international tourism literature. Based on this premise, this chapter presents the results of a bibliometric study analyzing the COVID-19 literature in tourism. The study aims to identify current research areas and provide recommendations for future research. A total of 537 studies, comprising 477 articles and 60 other types, were included in the analysis. Analysis was conducted using R tools to identify and discuss the most pertinent sources, authors, affiliations, and countries. The most frequently cited countries and documents were also examined. The 537 studies that were examined in these discussions have developed various propositions. It is desirable for these propositions and other research findings to serve as a roadmap for potential research opportunities.

Keywords: COVID-19; tourism industry; international tourism literature; bibliometric study; COVID-19 literature

Introduction

The world is directly affected by various factors, including economic, sociocultural, demographic, political, and technological factors. These factors will result in subsequent changes in job performance across all industries. Such impacts may be specific to an industry or region. The pandemic, which is considered an

Strategic Tourism Planning for Communities, 143–162

Copyright © 2024 Azamat Maksüdünov and Kyialbek Dyikanov

Published under exclusive licence by Emerald Publishing Limited

doi:10.1108/978-1-83549-015-020241012

external factor, has the potential to bring about significant changes in the world. As noted by Wolfe et al. (2007), infectious diseases have been a leading cause of human mortality, morbidity, and social cognition, exerting significant selective forces on the human genome. These diseases have impacted various aspects of human life, including the economy, politics, society, and human attitudes toward nature. The transformative affects and potential of modern epidemics are not new, as they appear to only impact the developed world and generations who have not experienced or have forgotten the benefits of antibiotics and modern medicine. However, the most recent pandemic, COVID-19, has put the entire world in a challenging situation. On December 31, 2019, the China Country Office of the World Health Organization (WHO) reported cases of pneumonia with an unknown cause in the city of Wuhan, located in the Hubei province of China. Subsequently, a new and previously unidentified coronavirus was identified. This disease, initially referred to as 2019-nCoV, was later named COVID-19. It emerged in China and quickly spread to affect the entire world within a short period of three months (Budak & Korkmaz, 2020). According to information from the WHO information (2022), there have been over 545.2 million cases of COVID-19 and 6.3 million deaths worldwide.

While other factors may be partially controllable by broader social systems or individuals, pandemics are relatively uncontrollable when they strike suddenly. Given the globalized nature of tourism, it is particularly susceptible to changes in external factors. The tourism industry cooperates directly or indirectly with more than 50 sectors and contributes to varying degrees in the development of these sectors. Therefore, the significant value of tourism on a global scale cannot be ignored. The impact of the pandemic on the tourism sector is also unavoidable, regardless of region or nationality. In recent years, the literature has also framed the relationship between pandemics and tourism in terms of risk (Wen et al., 2020). This epidemic, which originated in China, has impacted the tourism industry as well as other sectors. People's travel and holiday plans have been completely canceled, and tourism industry, along with other supporting sectors, has come to a complete halt, as mentioned above. At the same time, due to the high transmission rate of the coronavirus (SARS-CoV-2), governments around the world have been left with no choice but to impose quarantines. The spread of the virus has seriously threatened lives, and measures such as the curfew have posed a critical risk to the livelihoods of the masses (Sharma & Mahendru, 2020). Undoubtedly, these challenges have impacted all stakeholders in the tourism industry. Due to travel bans and social distancing measures, there has been a decrease in tourists' travel desire and ability to travel, as mentioned above. This caused tourists to cancel their travel plans and tour reservations, which affected employment opportunities as well. This global issue has been researched by various disciplines, resulting in a surge of scientific publications on the subject. As of July 2022, there are 289,438 records on the Web of Science (WoS) related to COVID-19. In this context, the purpose of this chapter is to evaluate academic research on the impact of COVID-19 on global tourism. Specifically, the goal is to identify the most significant authors, institutions, academic papers, academic journals, and countries related to this topic.

Global COVID-19 at a Glance

In December 2019, a pneumonia outbreak with local features emerged in Wuhan, China. Due to the rapid spread of the disease, which was later identified as a new type of coronavirus (COVID-19), the WHO declared a pandemic (Li et al., 2020; Lu et al., 2020; Wang et al., 2020; World Health Organization, 2022). When examining the causes of epidemic spread throughout world history, attention is drawn to the acceleration of urbanization resulting from the industrial revolution. This revolution triggered the transition from an agricultural society to an industrial one, and rapid population growth followed. It is believed that various factors such as societal interconnectedness, globalization, and ecological degradation contribute to the emergence and spread of epidemics (Pongsiri et al., 2009). Based on this, the coronavirus (COVID-19) epidemic is a human tragedy that affects billions of people in this world. The epidemic, which has emerged as a global health crisis, causes millions of deaths worldwide (Table 10.1). The COVID-19 epidemic has absolutely affected the entire world not only in terms of public health but also economically and socially (Şahin, 2021). The COVID-19 pandemic, which initially presented as a health crisis, has compelled many countries to take urgent measures. In this regard, many measures have been taken to limit social mobility, such as social distancing, curfews, quarantine processes, and "stay-at-home" orders in many countries around the world (Donthu & Gustafsson, 2020; Oral & Sevinç, 2020). These measures also have an impact on economic activity, causing a decrease in both supply and demand. It is evident that numerous countries have implemented their economic emergency action plans.

Furthermore, when examining impact of economic development on the labor market, the International Labor Organization (ILO, 2020), has reported that the COVID-19 pandemic has resulted in significant consequences for employment. The International Labor Organization reports that global working hours are decreasing, impacting 2.7 billion employees or 81% of the world workforce. However, the pandemic has not affected every sector equally. While fields such as education, human health, social work, public administration, and defense are the least affected by the pandemic, sectors such as accommodation, food, food and beverage, real estate, and vehicle repair are foreseen as the most affected.

As mentioned above, the COVID-19 pandemic, which started to be felt all over the world at the beginning of March 2020, has had profound impact on numerous, including tourism, in almost every continent in the world. Tourism has experienced a trust problem in this period. In fact, unexpected situations and events that occur suddenly, such as a pandemic, can reduce trust in tourism destinations where they occur (Çeti & Ünlüören, 2019; Karakaş, 2020; Seyfi et al., 2020). The declining trust in the tourism sector has caused people not to participate in tourism, and countries have been affected by this situation in waves. Not

Table 10.1. Coronavirus (COVID-19) Global Situation.

Cases – Cumulative Total	Cases – Newly Reported in Last 7 Days	Deaths – Cumulative Total	Deaths –Newly Reported in Last 7 Days	Total Vaccine Doses Administered Per 100 Population	Persons Fully Vaccinated With Last Dose of Primary Series Per 100 Population	Persons Boosted Per 100 Population
545,226,550	4,957,783	6,334,728	9,410	153.77	61.1	24.7

Source: WHO (2022) (Available at: https://covid19.who.int/table, accessed on July 03, 2022).

every country has been affected by the COVID-19 pandemic at the same rate. However, there are almost no countries left that have not been affected by the pandemic. Firstly, economies depending on tourism have suffered serious damage. Most of them are from developing or underdeveloped countries. Economic, social, and psychological problems have emerged in the tourism industry, particularly in the accommodation sector, in various countries around the world (Gürsoyet al., 2021). Even in New Zealand, which is located in an isolated geography away from the land, damages due to COVID-19 have been recorded in the service sector (Hall, Prayag, et al., 2020).

The impact of COVID-19, which has become a global issue, defines the broad scope of the overall context that our thoughts on the subject should encompass. For this reason, we should examine global actions through a suitable framework to determine the direction and changes that are likely to trigger an epidemic. Appropriate analytical categorizations can shed light on the path to the answers we seek. Systems of meaning, including ideas about geopolitics, economics, and politics broadly defined to encompass the various layers of security, can show us in focusing our attention to understand the context of the major epidemic and the modes of transformation. The crises that have emerged in these three interconnected fields can be analyzed individually or as a whole, considering both horizontal and vertical dimensions for ease of analysis (Okur, 2020).

Global Tourism Industry During the COVID-19

Throughout human history, communicable diseases such as cholera, HIV, Ebola, H1N1, H5N1, SARS, MERS have posed significant challenges. It has been observed that these diseases can spread rapidly on a global scale due to increased tourism and mobility (Baker, 2015; Hollingsworth et al., 2007). In addition to epidemics, several significant events have impacted various industries on a global scale. These include the Indian Ocean tsunami in 2005, the Gulf of Mexico oil spill in 2010, the September 11 terrorist attack in 2001, and the global economic crisis that emerged in 2008–2009 (Gössling et al., 2020; Ritchie et al., 2014; Rossello et al., 2020). For example, it has been observed that the tourism, food, transportation, and entertainment industries were the most affected sectors in terms of employment loss following the spread of the SARS virus (Pine & McKercher, 2004). Changing consumer attitudes in the affected sectors plays an important role. For example, in the destinations where the SARS virus is spreading, it has been seen that consumers are in search of safer holidays due to the cancelation of their holiday reservations, the change in holiday and travel trends, and their concerns about public hygiene (Wen et al., 2005). The coronavirus (COVID-19) pandemic has had a significant impact on nearly every sector of society, including businesses. The hospitality and tourism industry has been severely impacted by the COVID-19 pandemic, with a vast majority of hospitality and tourism businesses facing significant financial difficulties due to the loss of demand caused by travel restrictions and national and local quarantines (Shin et al., 2021).

Although there have been numerous epidemics and events that have had a significant impact on the world, COVID-19 is different from other contagious disease because it poses a serious threat to human health and has created global demand shocks. When compared to major economic and political crises, climate events, and other epidemics, the impact of the COVID-19 epidemic can be seen as a turning point in world history. The pandemic has resulted in significant loss of life and widespread disruption of work and daily activities. Despite all efforts, it is evident that epidemic has had significant effects on many industries. This is due to the individual decisions made by people who have reviewed their lifestyles in response to the course of the epidemics, as well as the new habits they have adopted in line with the measures taken by their respective countries. The concerns and panic atmosphere in some countries also contributed to these effects. All the strict measures implemented in the early period of epidemic are also closely related to the tourism sector, which is one of sectors that provide the country with an important source of income. The listed precautionary practices caused a slowdown in production and consumption in economic terms, reservations were delayed or canceled due to the restriction of human mobility, workforce employment was negatively affected, so the tourism sector had to manage a crisis that it had not experienced before (Yang et al., 2020). Due to the crisis and travel bans imposed by countries, as well as closed borders or quarantine processes, international and domestic tourism has rapidly declined for weeks (Gössling et al., 2020). The United Nations World Tourism Organization (UNWTO) data reported that at the end of April 2020, 72% of international tourism in the world was stopped and destinations were closed (UNWTO, 2022). During the early stages of the COVID-19 epidemic, high levels of uncertainty regarding the timing of the outbreak, perceived risk, fear and panic created an atmosphere of crisis. As a result, it was inevitable that all industries would be affected. The tourism sector has coming to a standstill is also a result of the negative impacts experienced (Gössling et al., 2020). The most important data confirming this situation are expressed in the COVID-19 reports of the World Tourism Organization. In the September 2021 addendum to the aforementioned reports, it was stated that during the first seven months of 2021, the number of international tourist visitors decreased by 40% compared to 2020 levels and by 80% compared to the same period in 2019. Recent research has revealed that visitors are likely to avoid travel during the pandemic due to perceived health risk (Shin & Kang, 2020; Zheng et al., 2021). In particular, there have been reported cases of in-flight transmission during air travel, which may cause prospective travelers to be concerned about the potential for infection.

The number of international tourists arriving worldwide dropped sharply with the onset of the coronavirus (COVID-19) pandemic, with approximately 1 billion tourists (Fig. 10.1) lost in 2020 compared to 2019 (UNWTO, 2022). As depicted in Fig. 10.1, the number of international tourists in 2019 was 1,463.7 million, whereas in 2020, it significantly decreased to only 406.9 million. However, the UNWTO is endeavoring to substantiate identical statistics. Based on current trends, the UNWTO predicts a decrease of 70%–75% in international tourist arrivals for the entire year of 2020. This indicates that the international tourism

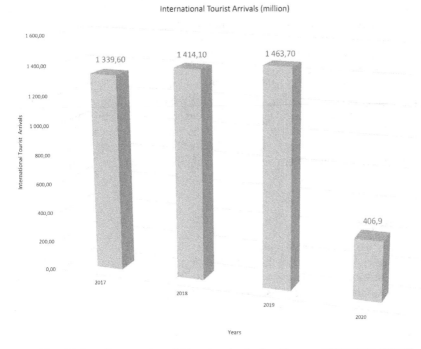

Fig. 10.1.   International Tourist Arrivals. *Source:* UNWTO (2022).

industry is rebounding to levels that were last observed three decades ago. The projected decrease in global tourist arrivals in 2020, there is an estimated loss of around 1.1 trillion USD in international tourism revenue (UNWTO, 2022).

It should be emphasized that the epidemic's effects on tourism sector are an issue that requires attention. Practices such as closing the borders, social distancing protocols to prevent the rapid spread of diseases in crowded areas, and restrictions on domestic travel may adversely affect summer tourism, especially. This problem will not only reflect the government's policies but also the psychological and social processes of individuals and households in behaving in crowded environments as they did before the pandemic (Aslan, 2020). According to research by Chua et al. (2020), the COVID-19 pandemic has had a significant impact on behavioral intentions globally, particularly in severely affected areas. To recover after the pandemic, it is necessary to conduct research studies that increase our understanding of the external and internal factors that significantly predict the tourist's future travel behavior. The removing of postpandemic restrictions is an integral part of the tourism recovery. Initially, this was at the local level, especially where new cases were no longer being recorded (Worthington, 2020). The resumption of tourism in most countries is expected to occur domestically and will likely involve promotion campaigns for domestic tourism to boost the economy and encourage people to travel within their own country or region. This will also help to maintain COVID-19 surveillance and safety measures. On the other hand, the impact of COVID-19 on the tourism industry and related sectors has promoted extensive research in the field of tourism. As academics shared their thoughts and comments, they began to produce a plethora of research studies backed by empirical data. The journals are also working on academic articles by developing special issues that address critical and emerging issues in tourism caused by the pandemic. Tourism professionals have adopted various theoretical lenses and methodological approaches to explore the multifaceted nature of COVID-19 and its complex implications for tourism research and industry (Sigala, 2020). This multidisciplinary approach allows for a more comprehensive understanding of the pandemic's impact on the tourism sector.

Methodology

This study uses bibliometric methods to evaluate the existing literature on COVID-19 impact on tourism industry. The primary data source is the WoS, and the data were downloaded from WoS on June 23, 2022. "COVID-19 Impact on Tourism Industry" was used as a keyword, and total 537 records were found. Distribution of these records demonstrated in the figure (Fig. 10.2), according to

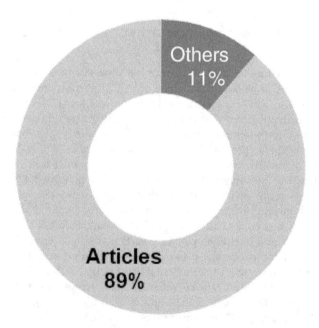

Fig. 10.2.   Published Documents Distribution.

documents type. According to the figure, 89% (477) of the total records are articles, while the remaining 11% (60) are comprised of other types, including 31 review articles, 20 proceedings papers, 6 editorial materials, 2 letters, and 1 book chapter.

Analyses were performed using R Studio to identify and discuss the most relevant sources, authors, affiliations, countries, document, and the most cited countries.

Findings

Outputs of academic research on this topic have mainly been published in tourism-related academic journals. Fig. 10.3 demonstrates the most relevant 25 sources, with Sustainability being the predominant journal, accounting for approximately 12% of the total papers. *Current Issues in Tourism* with 41 papers (8%) and *Worldwide Hospitality and Tourism Themes* with 20 papers (4%) are both addressing sustainability issues. All the other sources published fewer than 20 papers. In general, 299 out of 534 papers (56%) were published in these 25 journals. The average number of published papers is 12, a minimum of 5 and a maximum of 67. Academic papers on this topic have been presented in periodicals outside of the tourism field, such as *Sustainability, International Journal of Environmental Research, Frontiers in Psychology*, and *Scientific Papers –* Series Management, Economic and Engineering. This topic is presented in various academic journals because tourism is an interdisciplinary field. Academic papers on this topic are ongoing, and authors who are working in this field can focus on publishing their findings in relevant journals.

On the other hand, when we examine the local impact sources (h index), the ranking of academic journals has changed. According to the results, the *Sustainability* journal ranks third with an h-index of 9, following *Current Issues in Tourism* (h-index = 12) and the *International Journal of Hospitality Management* (h-index = 11). The 10 most impactful sources are shown in Fig. 10.4.

Over 1,627 authors from around the world have produced 537 academic publications. Fig. 10.5 vividly displays the 25 most relevant authors, who collectively produced approximately 17% of all publications. According to the results, Han Heesup from Sejong University in South Korea and Law Rob from the University of Macau in China are the most prolific authors, with seven published papers each.

There are 1,627 authors affiliated with 848 different organizations around the world. Fig. 10.6 shows the top 25 affiliations of the most relevant authors. These organizations produced approximately 32% of all scientific research on this topic.

According to the figure, Hong Kong Polytechnic University ranks first among higher education institutions with 16 academic papers on this topic, followed by the University of Johannesburg with 11 papers and Sichuan University with 10 papers.

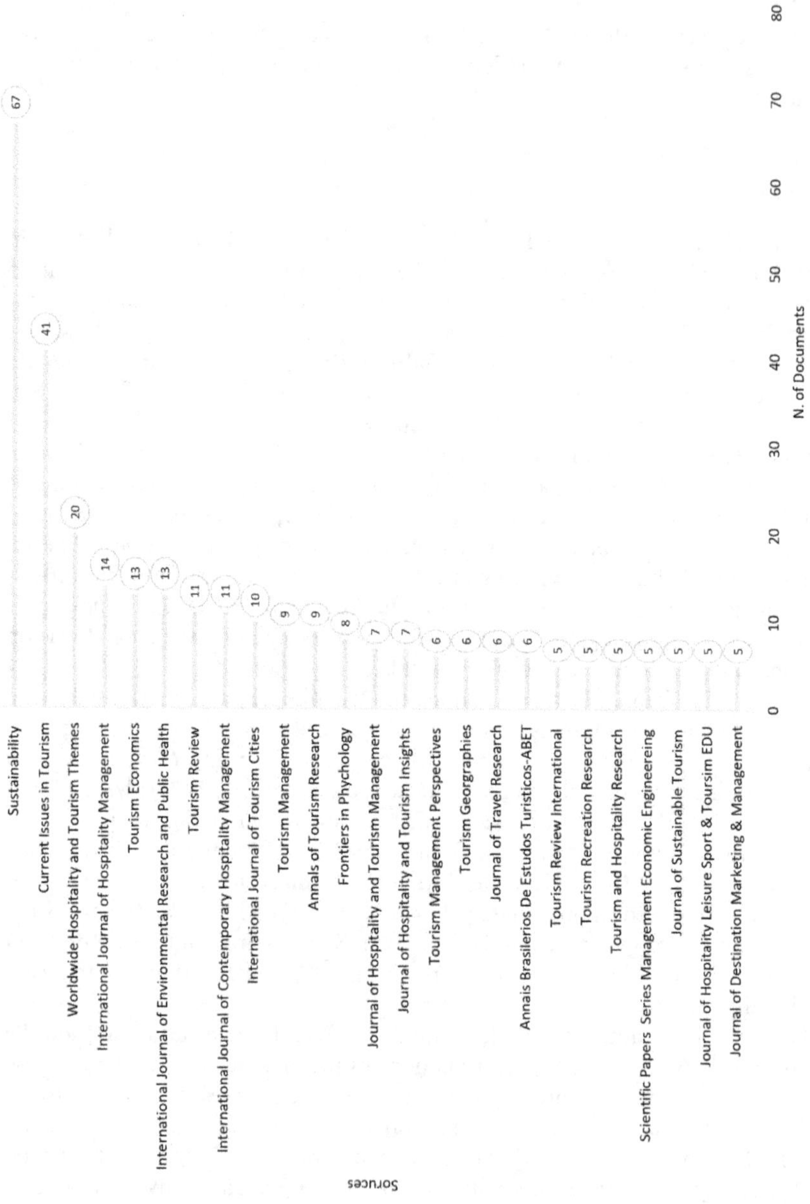

Fig. 10.3.   Most Relevant Sources.

Fig. 10.4. Source Local Impact.

Fig. 10.7 demonstrates the top 10 countries of corresponding authors who participated in scientific production on this topic, including China, Spain, India, the United Kingdom, the United States, Korea, and others.

The details of the top 10 countries are given in Table 10.2. According to the table, China is in the lead with 106 corresponding authors, 62 of whom are single (SCP) and 44 of whom are multiauthored (MCP Ratio = 0.42) papers. Spain has 37 corresponding authors, including 31 single-authored and 6 multiauthored publications, placing them in second place. India is ranked in the top three on this list, with 34 corresponding authors (29 single-authored and 5 multiauthored). We can see that this table contains countries with significant tourism potential, such as Spain, India, Tukey, and others.

Fig. 10.8 shows a list of the 25 most cited countries worldwide. China is currently leading in the list of most cited countries worldwide on this particular topic. Currently, China has 1,039 citations, followed by the United Kingdom with 466 citations, Turkey with 452 citations, Korea with 375 citations, Finland with 333 citations, and several other countries. The top 12 countries of corresponding authors are listed here, and they match the top 12 countries except for Indonesia.

Fig. 10.9 contains details about the most globally cited documents. In the current list, we can observe that the most cited documents are from 2020 and 2021. Hall, Scott, et al. (2020) published a paper entitled "Pandemics, Transformations, and tourism: Be Careful What You Wish For", in *Tourism Geographies*, which has received the most citations (333).

The next most cited paper, with 236 citations, belongs to Wen et al. (2020). The paper is titled "COVID-19: Potential Effects on Chinese Citizens' Lifestyle and Travel" and was published in *Tourism Review*. The paper titled "COVID-19 and China's Hotel Industry: Impacts, a Disaster Management Framework and Post-Pandemic Agenda" by Hao et al. (2020) is the third most cited with 172

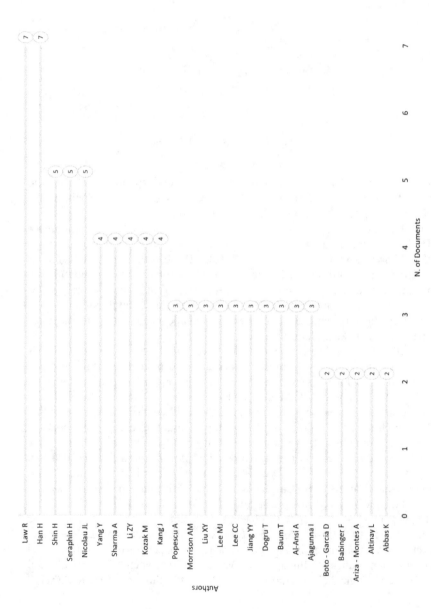

Fig. 10.5.   Most Relevant Authors.

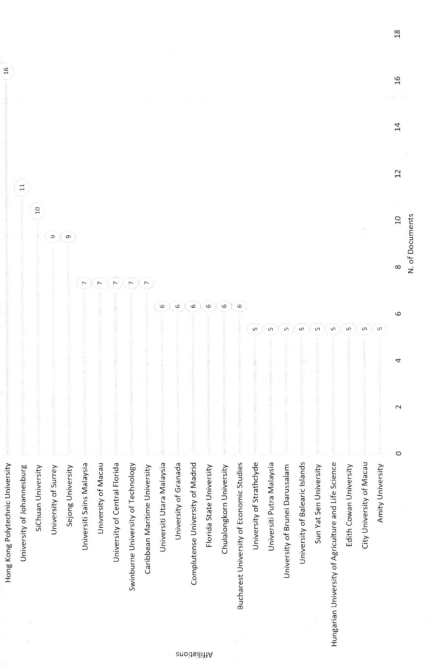

Fig. 10.6.   Most Relevant Affiliations.

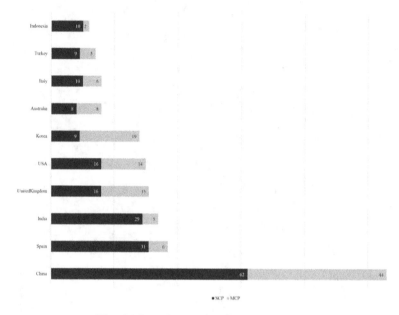

Fig. 10.7.   Corresponding Author's Country.

Table 10.2. Details of the Top 12 Countries.

Country	Cor. Authors	SCP	MCP	MCP Ratio
China	106	62	44	0.42
Spain	37	31	6	0.16
India	34	29	5	0.15
United Kingdom	31	16	15	0.48
United States	30	16	14	0.47
Korea	28	9	19	0.68
Australia	16	8	8	0.50
Italy	16	10	6	0.38
Turkey	14	9	5	0.36
Indonesia	12	10	2	0.17

citations. It was published in the *International Journal of Hospitality Management*. Although these three authors were not included in the top three most relevant authors list, their contributions have had a significant impact on this topic.

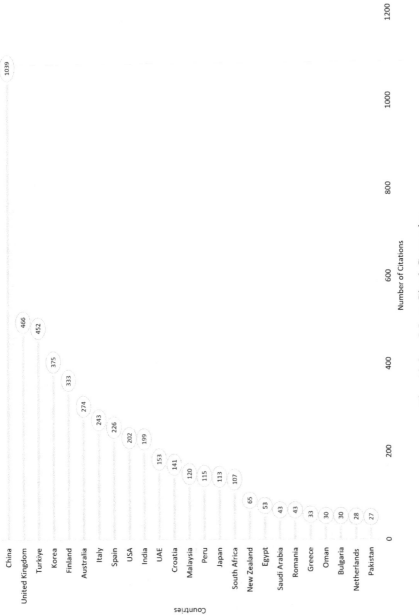

Fig. 10.8. Most Cited Countries.

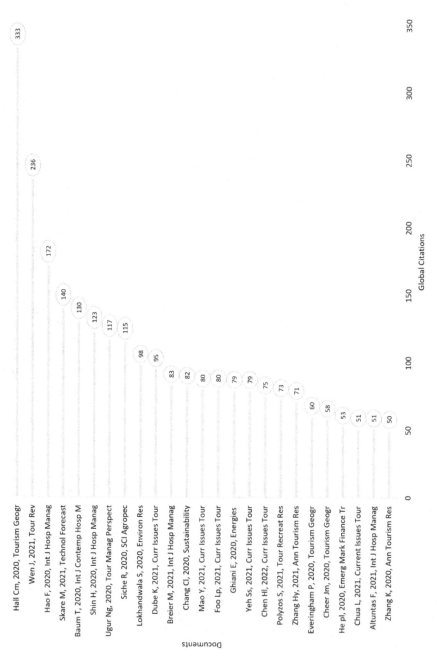

Fig. 10.9.   Most Global Cited Documents.

Conclusion

After the emergence of the COVID-19 pandemic, cases of COVID-19 spread rapidly around the world, putting countries in a serious stalemate. The congestion continued until the declaration of a pandemic, at which point countries began implementing strict measures. Afterward, international mobility came to a near standstill as most countries closed their borders and prioritized the protection of their citizens. Various measures and practices have been implemented to minimize the social, cultural, economic, and psychological negative impacts brought about by COVID-19. Some vulnerable sectors, such as the tourism industry, were among those that faced the most significant challenges and crises. Thus, COVID-19 has become one of the main challenges for the tourism industry worldwide, greatly reducing the speed of human mobility during the last years.

This situation has led to an increase in the academic research on this topic. Over the past three years, more than 500 academic papers, including articles, conference papers, and book chapters, have been published in sources indexed by WoS. Academic research on this topic is primarily presented in tourism-related academic journals. However, papers on this subject can also be found in academic periodicals outside of the tourism field, such as *Sustainability*, *International Journal of Environmental Research*, and *Frontiers in Psychology*. Furthermore, sustainability was identified as the most pertinent source among all academic journals. More than 1,600 authors from around the world are involved in academic research on this topic. Scholars from South Korea and China hold in the top positions on the list of most influential authors. The research fields of these top authors are related to the marketing, service marketing, consumer behavior, tourism, and hospitality. The countries with the most academic publications on this topic are those with significant tourism potential, such as Spain, India, and Tukey. China, Spain, India, the United Kingdom, the United States, and Korea are at the top of this list. Additionally, China, the United Kingdom, and Turkey are among the most cited countries in this field.

This study is important in terms of unveiling the overall status of academic research conducted on this topic in the past three years. However, like every academic study, this chapter also has some significant limitations. Firstly, this chapter is based on the academic publications indexed in WoS. However, future studies should focus on wider academic databases that have a significant contribution and influence on this topic. The second limitation of this study is related to its lack of detail in its content. This study aims to provide a broad overview of academic research. However, future studies should focus on specific details such as major subjects by year, identifying primary thematic clusters and conducting co-citation analysis.

Acknowledgments

Authors are profoundly grateful to Prof. Dr Serhat Burmaoglu (Kyrgyz-Turkish Manas University, Kyrgyzstan) for his valuable assistance and motivation.

References

Aslan, H. (2020). Covid-19 Pandemisineyönelikhazırlananerkendönemsosyalkorumat edbirlerininkarşılaştırmalıbiranalizi. *YönetimveÇalışmaDergisi.*, *4*(2), 266–291.

Baker, D. M. (2015). Tourism and the health effects of infectious diseases: Are there potential risks for tourists? *International Journal of Safety and Security in Tourism and Hospitality*, *12*(3), 1–17.

Budak, F., & Korkmaz, Ş. (2020). COVID-19 PandemiSürecineYönelikGenel Bir Değerlendirme: TürkiyeÖrneği. *SosyalAraştırmalarveYönetimDergisi*, *1*, 62–79.

Çeti, B., & Ünlüönen, K. (2019). Salgınhastalıklarsebebiyleoluşankrizlerinturizmsekt örüüzerindekietkisinindeğerlendirilmesi. *AHBVÜ TurizmFakültesiDergisi*, *22*(2), 109–128.

Chua, B. L., Al-Ansi, A., Lee, M. J.,& Han, H. (2020). Tourists' outbound travel behavior in the aftermath of the COVID-19: Role of corporate social responsibility, response effort, and health prevention. *Journal of Sustainable Tourism*, *1*(28), 879–906. https://doi.org/10.1080/09669582.2020.1849236

Donthu, N., & Gustafsson, A. (2020). Effects of COVID-19 on business and research. *Journal of Business Research*, *117*, 284–289. https://doi.org/10.1016/j.jbusres.2020. 06.008

Gürsoy, D., Sarıışık, M., Nunkoo, R., & Boğan, E. (2021). *Covid-19 and the hospitality and tourism industry* (p. 400). Edward Elgar Publishing. ISBN: 9781800376236, UK.

Gössling, S., Scott, D., & Hall, C. M. (2020). Pandemics, tourism and global change: A rapid assessment of COVID-19. *Journal of Sustainable Tourism*, *29*(1), 1–20. https://doi.org/10.1080/09669582.2020.1758708

Hall, C., Prayag, G., Fieger, P., & Dyason, D. (2020). Beyond panic buying: Consumption displacement and Covid-19. *Journal of Service Management*, *32*(1), 113–128. https://doi.org/10.1108/JOSM-05-2020-0151

Hall, C. M., Scott, D., & Gössling, S. (2020). Pandemics, transformations and tourism: Be careful what you wish for. *Tourism Geographies*, *22*(3), 577–598. https://doi.org/10.1080/14616688.2020.1759131

Hao, F., Xiao, Q., & Chon, K. (2020). COVID-19 and China's hotel industry: Impacts, a disaster management framework, and post-pandemic agenda. *International Journal of Hospitality Management*, *90*, 1–11. https://doi.org/10.1016/ j.ijhm.2020.102636

Hollingsworth, T. D., Ferguson, N. M., & Anderson, R. M. (2007). Frequent travelers and rate of spread of epidemics. *Emerging Infectious Diseases*, *13*(9), 1288–1294. https://doi.org/10.3201/eid1309.070081

ILO. (2020). ILO Monitor 2nd edition: COVID-19 and the world of work updated estimates and analysis context: Worsening crisis with devastating effects. https://www.ilo.org/wcmsp5/groups/public/—dgreports/—dcomm/documents/briefing note/wcms_740877.pdf. Accessed on May 03, 2020.

Karakaş, M. (2020). Covid-19 Salgınınınçokboyutlusosyolojisiveyeni normal meselesi. *İstanbul ÜniversitesiSosyolojiDergisi*. https://doi.org/10.26650/SJ.2020.40.1.0048

Li, Q., Guan, X., Wu, P., Wang, X., Zhou, L., Tong, Y., & Wong, J. Y. (2020). Early transmission dynamics in Wuhan, China, of novel coronavirus–infected pneumonia. *New England Journal of Medicine, 382*, 1199–1207. https://doi.org/10.1056/NEJMoa2001316

Lu, H., Stratton, C. W., & Tang, Y. W. (2020). Outbreak of pneumonia of unknown etiology in Wuhan, China: The mystery and the miracle. *Journal of Medical Virology, 92*, 401–402. https://doi.org/10.1002/jmv.25678

Okur, M. A. (2020). COVID-19 Salgını, Dünya Düzeni ve Türkiye. *Akademik Hasasiyetler, 7*(13), 311–335.

Oral, İ. O., & Sevinç, D. E. (2020). Covıd-19 eksenlisağlıkkrizininekonomiüzerind ekietkileriüzerinebirinceleme. *Journal of Management Theory and Practices Research, 1*(1), 58–70.

Pine, R., & ve McKercher, B. (2004). The impact of SARS on Hong Kong's tourism industry. *International Journal of Contemporary Hospitality Management, 16*(2), 139–143. https://doi.org/10.1108/09596110410520034

Pongsiri, M. J., Roman, J., Ezenwa, V. O., Goldberg, T. L., Koren, H. S., Newbold, S. C., & Salkeld, D. J. (2009). Biodiversity loss affects global disease ecology. *BioScience, 59*(11), 945–954. https://doi.org/10.1525/bio.2009.59.11.6

Ritchie, B. W., Crotts, J. C., Zehrer, A., & Volsky, G. T. (2014). Understanding the effects of a tourism crisis: The impact of the BP oil spill on regional lodging demand. *Journal of Travel Research, 53*(1), 12–25. https://doi.org/10.1177/0047287513482775

Rosselló, J., Becken, S., & Santana-Gallego, M. (2020). The effects of natural disasters on international tourism: A global analysis. *Tourism Management, 79*, 104080. https://doi.org/10.1016/j.tourman.2020.104080

Şahin, M. T. (2021). Literatür Taraması Üzerinden Covid-19 Salgınının Küçük ve Orta Büyüklükteki İşletmelere (KOBİ) Etkisini Anlamak: Kavramsal Bir Analiz. *Coğrafi Bilimler Dergisi/Turkish Journal of Geographical Sciences, 19*(2), 466–489. https://doi.org/10.33688/aucbd.956001

Seyfi, S., Hall, C., & Shabani, B. (2020). Covid-19 and international travel restrictions: The geopolitics of health and tourism. *Tourism Geographies Studies, 22*, 1–17. https://doi.org/10.1080/146166 88.2020.1833972

Sharma, G. D., & Mahendru, M. (2020). Lives or livelihood: Insights from locked-down India due to COVID19. *Social Sciences & Humanities Open, 2*(1), Article 100036. https://doi.org/10.1016/j.ssaho.2020.100036

Shin, H., & Kang, J. (2020). Reducing perceived health risk to attract hotel customers in the COVID-19 pandemic era: Focused on technology innovation for social distancing and cleanliness. *International Journal of Hospitality Management, 91*, 102664.

Shin, H., Sharma, A., Nicolau, J. L., & Kang, J. (2021). The impact of hotel CSR for strategic philanthropy on booking behavior and hotel performance during the COVID-19 pandemic. *Tourism Management, 85*. https://doi.org/10.1016/j.tourman.2021.104322

Sigala, M. (2020). Tourism and COVID-19: Impacts and implications for advancing and resetting industry and research. *Journal of Business Research, 117*, 312–321.

UNWTO (United Nations World Tourism Organization). (2022). Global and regional tourism performance, international tourist arrivals. https://www.unwto.org/tourismdata/global-and-regional-tourism-performance. Accessed on July 07, 2022.

Wang, D., Hu, B., Hu, C., Zhu, F., Liu, X., Zhang, J., & Xiong, Y. (2020). Clinical characteristics of 138 hospitalized patients with 2019 novel coronavirus–infected pneumonia in Wuhan, China. *JAMA, 323*(11), 1061–1069. https://doi.org/10.1001/jama.2020.1585

Wen, Z., Huimin, G., & Kavanaugh, R. R. (2005). The impacts of SARS on the consumer behaviour of Chinese domestic tourists. *Current Issues in Tourism, 8*(1), 22–38. https://doi.org/10.1080/13683500508668203

Wen, J., Kozak, M., Yang, S., & Liu, F. (2020). COVID-19: Potential effects on Chinese citizens' lifestyle and travel. *Tourism Review, 76*(1), 74–87. https://doi.org/10.1108/TR-03-2020-0110

WHO. (2022). *Coronavirus (COVID-19) dashboard.* https://covid19.who.int/. Accessed on July 01, 2022.

Wolfe, N. D., Dunavan, C. P., & Diamond, J. (2007). Origins of major human infectious diseases. *Nature, 447*(7142), 279–283. https://doi.org/10.1038/nature05775

Worthington, B. (2020). *The three tests Australia will need to pass before the coronavirus restrictions end.* ABC [Australian Broadcasting Corporation] News. https://www.abc.net.au/news/2020-04-13/coronavirus-greg-hunt-lockdown-social-distancing-isolation/12144576

Yang, Y., Hongru, Z., & Xiang, C. (2020). Koronavirus pandemic and tourism: Dynamic stochastic general equilibrium modeling of infectious disease outbreak. *Annals of Tourism Research,* 1–2. https://doi.org/10.1016/j.annals.2020.102913

Zheng, D., Luo, Q., & Ritchie, B. W. (2021). Afraid to travel after COVID-19? Self-Protection, coping and resilience against pandemic 'travel fear'. *Tourism Management, 83,* 104261.

Chapter 11

Green Labeling and Green Scapes in the Hospitality and Tourism Industry: A Perspective Study of Industrial Employees Attracting Brand Mark of Hospitality Organizations in UT Regions

Saanchi Grover, Sanjeev Kumar and Ankit Dhiraj

Lovely Professional University, India

Abstract

Green labeling and green scapes are generally associated with environmental practices known as eco-labeling. In the hospitality industry, the concept of green scapes and green labeling has been associated through the attraction of customers toward hospitality organization's brand mark. Green practices make a customer conscious and more tangible for a brand or product. Somewhere, green practices have the instinct to throw as an open-up strategy for futurism growth and to build the brand mark at the next market step of the industry. The determination of green practices of a hospitality organization is performed by the environment working employees (Villemereuil & Gaggiotti, 2015). The organization is advantageous only when the in-house environment is attractive. Green scapes are performed only on the criteria of key certification. The viewpoint of this chapter is to fulfill the criteria of green practices (Warren et al., 2008), attracting brand marks in the hospitality organizations of UT regions. This chapter will investigate the perceptions of industrial employees attracting the brand mark of any hospitality organization in UT states. This chapter will highlight the impact of B2B and B2C businesses connecting to the working environment toward attracting the brand mark of hospitality organizations in the UT states region. This chapter will be paying heed to discuss the enhancing effect of B2B businesses in the UT states market of the tourism and hospitality sector. The sample

Strategic Tourism Planning for Communities, 163–172

Copyright © 2024 Saanchi Grover, Sanjeev Kumar and Ankit Dhiraj

Published under exclusive licence by Emerald Publishing Limited

doi:10.1108/978-1-83549-015-020241013

collected for this chapter using closed ended questionnaire from hospitality organization or hotels in UT destination.

Keywords: Green labeling; green scapes; key certification; potential growth access; eco-labeling; B2B and B2C; green practices; in-house environment; hospitality organization; UT destinations

Introduction

Green labeling and green scapes are generally associated with environmental practices, which are, however, known as eco-labeling. In the hospitality industry (Moise et al., 2021), the concept of green scapes and green labeling has been associated since the attraction of customers toward the hospitality organization's brand mark. Green practices make a customer conscious and more tangible for a brand or product (Jeong et al., 2014). Somewhere, green practices have the instinct to throw as an open-up strategy for futurism growth and to build the brand mark at the next market step of the industry (Moise et al., 2021). The determination of green practices of a hospitality organization is performed by the environment working employees. Any organization is advantageous only when the in-environment is attractive. Green scapes are performed only on key certi-fication criteria (Littledyke, 2008).

The United Nations World Trade Organization (UNWTO) accounts for 5% of global carbon dioxide emissions, which is projected to increase by 130% in 2035. According to the research, the sustainability challenges in the hospitality and tourism industry (Jayawardena et al., 2013) have had a common effect in earlier times of the industry market (Tsarenko et al., 2013). This chapter is intended to enhance the attractiveness of brand mark using the sustainability of in-house criteria of employees. This chapter will review and discuss the most relevant literature on environmental management in hospitality and tourism businesses (Aragon-Correa et al., 2015). It will use strategic lenses to provide a specific framework for analysis and propose future research.

Literature Review

An Overview of the Historical Background Connecting Aspects of Re-Sustainability and Green Practices

Green labeling and green scapes are generally associated with environmental practices known as eco-labeling (Mesthrige Jayantha & Sze Man, 2013). In the hospitality industry, the concept of green scapes and labeling have been associated with the attraction of customers to hospitality organizations' brand marks. Green practices make a customer conscious and more tangible for a brand or product (Edwards & Laurance, 2012; Jeong et al., 2014). Somewhere, green practices have the instinct to throw as an open-up strategy for futurism growth and to build the brand mark at the next market step of the industry. The determination of green practices of a hospitality organization is performed by the environment working employees (Kim et al., 2016). That is why any organization is advantageous only when the in-environment is attractive. Green scapes are performed only on key certification criteria (Hansen et al., 2001). The UNWTO accounts for 5% of global carbon dioxide emissions, which is projected to increase by 130% in 2035. According to the research (Lenzen et al., 2018), the sustainability challenges in the hospitality and tourism industry have had a common effect in earlier times of the industry market (Kitamura et al., 2020). The paper is intended to enhance the attractiveness of brand mark using the sustainability of in-house criteria of employees (Kirk, 1995). The paper discussed the most relevant literature on environmental management in hospitality and tourism businesses, and the author used strategic (Schusler et al., 2009) lenses to provide a specific framework for analysis and propose future research (Le et al., 2006).

Connecting the Effect of B2B and B2C Over the In-House Environment of Hospitality Organizations

The environmental and sustainability factor has affected the industrial businesses setup of the tourism (Gunn, 2010) and hospitality sector, which is an inclusion of multiple strategies (Hu & Wall, 2005) such as entry and exit of employees, generation of new initiatives, and creation new techniques (Batle et al., 2018). The relationship between environmental criteria and business competition has developed a specific interest among the people (Eiadat et al., 2008). Some earlier research studies have undergone the factors to suggest that stringent environmental policies in the home country can lead to an improved comparative advantage for domestic firms abroad and deter foreign firms' access to the most stringent local markets. More recent analyses have focused on the internal and external features influencing a positive evolution of the firms' environmental approaches (Dincer & Rosen, 1999) in an international context (Ginevicius et al., 2017). A previous research study has generally found a positive relationship between environmental management and financial performance. Still, this relationship can change depending on multiple contingent differences (Silva et al., 2019).

Fig. 11.1 shows the cyclic process of three steps that are extremely dependable on each other in achieving brand marks at UT regions in a case where the perceptions of employees lead to the building of new and newer practices and making the effect of new customers, a hospitality organization brand mark in UT regions.

Research Methodology of the Study

The study's methodology has been articulated into key sections: selection of data approach and sampling design, data collection, and data analysis. However, the entire work in the study is all original in every manner.

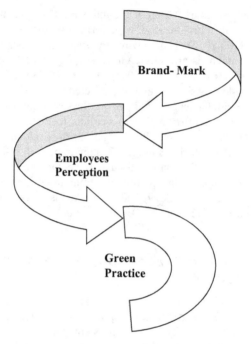

Fig. 11.1.   Cyclic Process Achieving Brand Marks.

Objectives of the Study

- To bring out the criteria of green practices achieving brand mark.
- To investigate the employee perception toward attracting brand mark.
- To study the futuristic impact of B2B and B2C businesses affecting the industrial mark.
- To connect the effect of the in-house environment with the external hospitality market of UT regions.
- To study the various strategies adopted to enhance the B2B and B2C and satisfy the industrial employees' perceptions connecting the link between the brand mark and in-house environment factor.

Hypothesis of the Study

Hypotheses are considered based on the objectives of the study.

H1. The effect of a rise in sustainability before the maintenance and implementation of green practices in hospitality organizations within UT regions for the aspect of the in-house environment.

H2. The effect of a rise in sustainability after the maintenance and implementation of green practices in hospitality organizations within UT regions for the aspect of the in-house environment.

Selecting Data Approach and Sample

A quantitative approach and probability random sampling had implied for the study to determine the impact of green practices on the hospitality organization's market mark. The approach and sampling technique worked for the study to keep a base view for adopting strategies to enhance the compatibility of the hospitality organization brand mark of the UT regions of Jammu and Kashmir region. Data approach and sampling pattern are shown in Fig. 11.2.

Data Collection

The data for the study were collected using a random sample design and going through the perception views of industrial employees using a questionnaire tool which required all closed-ended questions connecting the brand mark achievement through the help of employees' in-house environment of hospitality organizations in UT regions. Fig. 11.2 mentions that the quantitative approach, random sampling, and data analysis include a survey of the employee and achieving the brand mark.

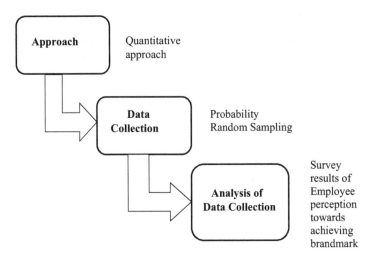

Fig. 11.2.   Shows the Techniques Used for Finding and Analyzing Results.

Analyzing Data

The data collected and analyzed are based on the perception views of industrial employees attracting brand mark of hospitality organizations in UT regions. A study using SPSS software through which a quantitative approach would be performed. The analysis of the collected data and use of the alternate hypothesis tool along with Z-test through which there is a possibility to prove that the brand mark of hospitality organizations has been achieved through in-house environment abilities, as mentioned in Table 11.1.

Z-test is likely to be used for the study because the sample size taken in the study is large as it requires the whole industrial employee staff of the hospitality organization of UT regions to achieve its brand mark by attracting customers. Using the alternate hypothesis tool with Z-test, it is known to be that the sample mean is not equal to the population mean. Z = (sample mean − population means)/(standard deviation) result shown in Table 11.2.

Findings of the Study

The study aims to prove that in-house environment abilities can achieve any hospitality organization's brand mark.

Table 11.1. Showing the Analysis Done of Achieving Brand Mark and Attracting Customers of Hospitality Organizations in UT Regions.

Employee	Customers
09	13
12	20
18	25
28	35
35	40
15	64
24	53
65	22
21	04
74	84
38	26
44	70
42	52
55	85
60	34
531	*627*

Table 11.2. Shows the Output of the Analysis Performed to Build Up the Brand Mark Using the Perceptions of Employees in Terms of Green Practices and Making the Effect of New Customers in a Brand Mark of UT Regions.

z-Test: Two Sample for Means

	Variable 1	Variable 2
Mean	36	41.8
Known variance	416.4,285,714	638.0285,714
Observations	15	15
Hypothesized mean difference	0	
Z	−0.69,176,591	
P(Z<=z) one-tail	0.244,542,174	
z critical one-tail	1.644,853,627	
P(Z<=z) two-tail	0.489,084,348	
z critical two-tail	1.959,963,985	

The study's findings have helped signify the effect of B2B and B2C in the hospitality market within UT regions during the challenging face of the in-house environment of organizations. However, the overall findings are intended to be highlighted based on results performance according to the responses received after surveying industrial employees' perceptive views, achieving brand mark, and attracting customers.

Results and Discussions

The results would like to depict and confine by collaborating the perceptive views and responses of the industrial employee staff of hospitality organization alongside achieving brand mark and attracting customers in the regions of UTs through using software named SPSS (need of the hour for every researcher) and EXCEL, connecting the environment of in-house.

The results of the study have been confined by evaluating the perception responses of industrial employees using a closed-ended questionnaire tool through which it can be depicted that there is a need to showcase the attraction of the brand mark of a hospitality organization in UT regions using the in-house environment factor. To reach out to the results (Warren et al., 2008), we have used statistical software named SPSS EXCEL based on hypothesis testing tools, that is, Z-test with an alternate hypothesis and one tail.

Discussions

The discussions are based on the survey results of the study to specify that there are significant chances in attracting the brand mark of a hospitality organization within UT regions which could be possibly done by connecting the in-house environment factor of employees, and that can be used in approaching and planning for future touristic growth of external hospitality market within UT regions as mentioned in Table 11.2.

Suggestions to Be Implemented

The suggestions for the study will be implied based on the analyzed survey results of industrial employee perceptions (Fig. 11.2) given attracting brand mark, through which we can have a look at the following suggestions:

- To satisfy and bring back their potential customers, green practices must be implemented regarding maintaining the in-house environment and its sustainability.
- To stabilize the running effect of B2B and B2C, it is necessary to adopt strategies according to the provided requirements of green practices.
- For the future aftereffect of enhancing businesses, it can be necessary to look after the publicity using different forms as per the recent trendsetter techniques.
- There can be a way for hospitality organizations and their industrial employee staff to redesign themselves in the hospitality economic UT region market, only by the effect of B2B and B2C.

Conclusion

Green labeling and green scapes are generally associated with environmental practices, which are, however, known as eco-labeling. In the hospitality industry, green scapes and labeling have been associated with customers' attraction toward hospitality organizations' brand mark. Green practices make a customer conscious and more tangible for a brand or product. Somewhere, green practices have the instinct to throw as an open-up strategy for futurism growth and to build the brand mark at the next market step of the industry. The determination of green practices of a hospitality organization is performed by the environment working employees. That is why any organization is advantageous only when the in-environment is attractive (Villemereuil & Gaggiotti, 2015). The study level is, although, paying heed to reach out in the achievement of its objectives with the help of using a closed-ended questionnaire tool to collect their responses on the aim of the study's perspectives and to use their responses in analyzing the results.

References

Aragon-Correa, J. A., Martin-Tapia, I., & de la Torre-Ruiz, J. (2015). Sustainability issues and hospitality and tourism firms' strategies: Analytical review and future directions. *International Journal of Contemporary Hospitality Management, 27*(3), 498–522. https://doi.org/10.1108/IJCHM-11-2014-0564

Batle, J., Orfila-Sintes, F., & Moon, C. J. (2018). Environmental management best practices: Towards social innovation. *International Journal of Hospitality Management, 69*, 14–20. https://doi.org/10.1016/j.ijhm.2017.10.013

Dincer, I., & Rosen, M. A. (1999). Energy, environment, and sustainable development. *Applied Energy, 64*(1–4), 427–440. https://doi.org/10.1016/S0306-2619(99)00111-7

Edwards, D. P., & Laurance, S. G. (2012). Green labeling, sustainability and the expansion of tropical agriculture: Critical issues for certification schemes. *Biological Conservation, 151*(1), 60–64. https://doi.org/10.1016/j.biocon.2012.01.017

Eiadat, Y., Kelly, A., Roche, F., & Eyadat, H. (2008). Green and competitive? An empirical test of the mediating role of environmental innovation strategy. *Journal of World Business, 43*(2), 131–145. https://doi.org/10.1016/j.jwb.2007.11.012

Ginevicius, R., Lapinskienė, G., & Peleckis, K. (2017). The evolution of the environmental Kuznets curve concept: The review of the research. *Panoeconomicus, 64*(1), 93–112. https://doi.org/10.2298/PAN150423012G

Gunn, C. (2010). Sustainability factors for e-learning initiatives. *ALT-J, Research in Learning Technology, 18*(2), 89–103. https://doi.org/10.1080/09687769.2010.492848

Hansen, B., Alrøe, H. F., & Kristensen, E. S. (2001). Approaches to assess the environmental impact of organic farming with particular regard to Denmark. *Agriculture, Ecosystems & Environment, 83*(1–2), 11–26. https://doi.org/10.1016/S0167-8809(00)00257-7

Hu, W., & Wall, G. (2005). Environmental management, environmental image, and the competitive tourist attraction. *Journal of Sustainable Tourism, 13*(6), 617–635. https://doi.org/10.1080/09669580508668584

Jayawardena, C. C., Pollard, A., Chort, V., Choi, C., & Kibicho, W. (2013). Trends and sustainability in the Canadian tourism and hospitality industry. *Worldwide Hospitality and Tourism Themes, 5*(2), 132–150. https://doi.org/10.1108/17554211311314164

Jeong, E., Jang, S. S., Day, J., & Ha, S. (2014). The impact of eco-friendly practices on green image and customer attitudes: An investigation in a café setting. *International Journal of Hospitality Management, 41*, 10–20. https://doi.org/10.1016/j.ijhm.2014.03.002

Kim, J.-Y., Hlee, S., & Joun, Y. (2016). Green practices of the hotel industry: Analysis through the windows of the smart tourism system. *International Journal of Information Management, 36*(6), 1340–1349. https://doi.org/10.1016/j.ijinfomgt.2016.05.001

Kirk, D. (1995). Environmental management in hotels. *International Journal of Contemporary Hospitality Management, 7*(6), 3–8. https://doi.org/10.1108/09596119510095325

Kitamura, Y., Ichisugi, Y., Karkour, S., & Itsubo, N. (2020). Carbon footprint evaluation based on tourist consumption toward sustainable tourism in Japan. *Sustainability, 12*(6), 2219. https://doi.org/10.3390/su12062219

Le, Y., Hollenhorst, S., Harris, C., McLaughlin, W., & Shook, S. (2006). Environmental management. *Annals of Tourism Research, 33*(2), 545–567. https://doi.org/10.1016/j.annals.2006.01.002

Lenzen, M., Sun, Y.-Y., Faturay, F., Ting, Y.-P., Geschke, A., & Malik, A. (2018). The carbon footprint of global tourism. *Nature Climate Change, 8*(6), 522–528. https://doi.org/10.1038/s41558-018-0141-x

Littledyke, M. (2008). Science education for environmental awareness: Approaches to integrating cognitive and affective domains. *Environmental Education Research, 14*(1), 1–17. https://doi.org/10.1080/13504620701843301

Mesthrige Jayantha, W., & Sze Man, W. (2013). Effect of green labeling on residential property price: A case study in Hong Kong. *Journal of Facilities Management, 11*(1), 31–51. https://doi.org/10.1108/14725961311301457

Moise, M. S., Gil-Saura, I., & Ruiz Molina, M. E. (2021). The importance of green practices for hotel guests: Does gender matter? *Economic Research-Ekonomska Istraživanja, 34*(1), 3508–3529. https://doi.org/10.1080/1331677X.2021.1875863

Schusler, T. M., Krasny, M. E., Peters, S. J., & Decker, D. J. (2009). Developing citizens and communities through youth environmental action. *Environmental Education Research, 15*(1), 111–127. https://doi.org/10.1080/13504620802710581

Silva, G. C., Regan, E. C., Pollard, E. H. B., & Addison, P. F. E. (2019). The evolution of corporate no net loss and net positive impact biodiversity commitments: Understanding appetite and addressing challenges. *Business Strategy and the Environment, 28*(7), 1481–1495. https://doi.org/10.1002/bse.2379

Tsarenko, Y., Ferraro, C., Sands, S., & McLeod, C. (2013). Environmentally conscious consumption: The role of retailers and peers as external influences. *Journal of Retailing and Consumer Services, 20*(3), 302–310. https://doi.org/10.1016/j.jretconser.2013.01.006

Villemereuil, P., & Gaggiotti, O. E. (2015). A new F_{ST}-based method to uncover local adaptation using environmental variables. *Methods in Ecology and Evolution, 6*(11), 1248–1258. https://doi.org/10.1111/2041-210X.12418

Warren, D. L., glor, R. E., & Turelli, M. (2008). Environmental niche equivalency versus conservatism: Quantitative approaches to niche evolution. *Evolution, 62*(11), 2868–2883. https://doi.org/10.1111/j.1558-5646.2008.00482.x

Chapter 12

Ayurveda Wellness Tourism: An Overview of the Sri Lankan Context

R. L. T. D. S. Rajapakshe[a] and R. S. S. W. Arachchi[b]

[a]Ayurveda Hospital, Sri Lanka
[b]Sabaragamuwa University of Sri Lanka, Sri Lanka

Abstract

Tourism is one of the key economic activities in the world. Sri Lanka is a country that deeply relies on income from tourism. Hence, identifying new horizons to develop the tourism sector is vital. Since wellness tourism is a trending concept in world tourism, this chapter aimed at Ayurveda-based wellness tourism and ways to uplift the existing outfit through lessons from other Asian counterparts. The researcher conducted 19 in-depth interviews with industry professionals to collect qualitative data inputs to understand the real scenario in Ayurveda wellness service providers. Results showed that Sri Lankan Ayurveda wellness tourism (AWT) is impacted by the actions of three main stakeholders, tourism-related authorities, Ayurveda-related authorities, and service providers. Tourism and Ayurveda-related authorities identified the importance of AWT to some extent, but actions are insufficient or rather bottleneck the sustainable development in the industry. Further, the bureaucracy of authorities prevents the expansion of AWT through medium- or small-scale service providers. The results suggest that Sri Lankan AWT requires long-, mid-, and short-term-based corrective actions.

Keywords: Ayurveda wellness tourism (AWT); Sri Lankan Ayurveda tourism; new trends in wellness tourism; current issues; strategies

Introduction

Tourism is one of the key contributors to economics for most countries as well as for the world. In 2019, tourism contributed to 10.3% of global gross domestic

Strategic Tourism Planning for Communities, 173–195
Copyright © 2024 R. L. T. D. S. Rajapakshe and R. S. S. W. Arachchi
Published under exclusive licence by Emerald Publishing Limited
doi:10.1108/978-1-83549-015-020241014

product (GDP) and 4.3% of the total investment of the world as well as offering 330 million jobs and became 1 in 10 jobs around the world (Economic Impact, World Travel and Tourism Council (WTTC), n.d.). As per the same report, 10.3% of GDP and 11% of job opportunity generation are done by the tourism sector in Sri Lanka. Further, the tourism sector is the third contributor to foreign exchange earnings in Sri Lanka which accounted for 711,961 million rupees in 2018 (Sri Lanka Tourism Development Authority, 2018). Tourism is a fast-growing industry in the world, due to its importance and economic signifi-cance. Now tourism is a little bit different, and there are new trends. Among them, health tourism is used largely in many countries.

As per the study conducted by the Global Wellness Institute (GWI), wellness tourism is now widely recognized as a fast-growing, high-opportunity niche segment. GWI estimates that wellness tourism expenditures reached $639.4 billion in 2017, as compared to $563.2 billion in 2015. The sector's 6.5% annual growth rate from 2015 to 2017 is more than double the 3.2% annual growth rate for general tourism. Wellness trips account for 6.6% of all tourism trips but represent 16.8% of total tourism expenditures (GWI: Global Wellness Economy Monitor, 2018). This is because wellness travelers tend to spend much more per trip than the average traveler. Therefore, whoever can tackle this trending market in the future could be able to gain a competitive advantage in the tourism sector.

Health tourism is defined as a primary motivation for contributing to physical, mental, and/or spiritual health through medical and wellness-based activities which increase the capacity of individuals to satisfy their own needs and function better as individuals in their environment and society (Exploring Health Tourism Executive Summary, 2018). Health tourism has two distinct subcategories, well-ness tourism and medical tourism. Wellness tourism is a type of tourism activity that aims to improve and balance all the main domains of human life including physical, mental, emotional, occupational, intellectual, and spiritual. Medical tourism is a type of tourism activity that involves the use of evidence-based medical healing resources and services (both invasive and noninvasive). This may include diagnosis, treatment, cure, prevention, and rehabilitation (Exploring Health Tourism Executive Summary, 2018).

At present, health tourism is a trending concept in a world where indigenous and unique features of the medical system of any country are integrated with tourism which provides a win-win situation for both the recipient and service provider. When it comes to Southeast Asia and Thailand, they promote their traditional Thai massage to boost their tourism industry. International tourists are flocking to Thailand for its unique Thai hospitality, exotic beaches, enter-tainment opportunities, and medical treatments. Vietnam and Myanmar promote their traditional foot massage therapies to promote their tourism. On the other hand, China is promoting its traditional Chinese medicine in health tourism promotion.

India is one of the top countries that use Ayurveda medicine to promote health and wellness tourism (Karai, 2018). In 2017, India ranked seventh in the top 20 wellness tourism markets and tenth among the top 20 spa markets in the world, while ranking third in both the top 10 wellness tourism markets and top 10 spa markets in the Asia Pacific. According to the reports, Indians made 56 million wellness-related trips, both domestic and international, in 2017 (a growth of 45% over 2015), which included expenditures worth $16.3 billion. Also, India ranked 2nd in terms of leading growth markets for wellness tourism, depicting an average annual growth rate of 20.3% from 2015 to 2017, adding a little over 17 million wellness trips in the same period (Kumar, 2019). As per the initiatives of the government of India, they are expecting to grow health tourism at a compounded annual growth rate of nearly 12% for the next 5 years and to reach the US $9 billion mark by 2020 (Karai, 2018).

Considering the Sri Lankan context, several advantages warrant further expansion of health and wellness tourism (Sri Lanka Export Development Board: National Export Strategy of Sri Lanka – Wellness Tourism Strategy, 2018). Sri Lankan culture is inherently attached to and shaped by Ayurveda and traditional medicine as a core. As same as Sri Lanka, geographic location is another positive factor to attract visitors who love wellness based on Ayurveda. Further, the climate is also supporting to promote health tourism linked with other value-added features such as sandy beaches, forestry, and heritage sites. The stability in the political and security situation after the Elam war was one of the advantages in general. However, the Easter Sunday attack and COVID-19 pandemic situations negatively affected tourism in Sri Lanka.

Considering the existing context in wellness tourism, it is worthwhile to study the Sri Lankan scenario in Ayurveda wellness tourism (AWT) which could provide a better pathway to maximize the AWT market share in Sri Lankan tourism.

Literature Review

Trending Concepts in Ayurveda Health Tourism

As per the United Nations World Tourism Organization (UNWTO), wellness tourism is "tourism associated with travel to health spas or resort destinations where the primary purpose is to improve the traveller's physical well-being through a regiment of physical exercise and therapy, dietary control, and medical services relevant to health maintenance" (Peršić & Janković, 2013). Connell (2006) described that global healthcare service has been booming recently. In the international healthcare tourism industry, nearly 30 countries including Thailand, Malaysia, Singapore, Korea, Hungary, Poland, Jordan, India, Turkey, and the United States are considered the major players in the international health tourism market (Eissler & Casken, 2013).

In India, government support for medical tourism is in a remarkable stage. They provide visa facilitation, hospital accreditation, and public–private sector partnership (PPP), including marketing. The government improved airport infrastructure to smooth the arrival and departure of medical tourists (Medical and wellness tourism – lessons from Asia, 2014). In the contemporary world, the healthcare tourism component is not new. It has existed for many centuries in many countries of the world, including Switzerland, Germany, Austria, Jamaica,

Hungary, the United States, and the United Kingdom. It is a good concept to approach health tourism with a deliberate marketing strategy. Healthcare tourism can be the basis of a positioning strategy for some hotels or resorts in a world that is becoming more health conscious.

Health and Wellness Tourism in Sri Lanka

Satisfaction toward Ayurveda medical tourism was high when the tourists' perception of tangibility, responsiveness, and empathy was high (Arachchi & Kaluarachchi, 2019). It possibly should be enhanced by providing more attention to the dimensions of service quality which indicated a significant and positive influence on the medical tourists' satisfaction. It is identified that the promotion of Ayurveda and indigenous medicine boosts immunity and promotes distress and counseling programs with the Eastern way of thinking embedded with the Buddhist philosophy, Hinduism, and Ayurveda (Samarathunga, 2020).

According to the *International Medical Travel Journal*, Sri Lanka Tourism has also been in discussion with the European Union (EU) office in Colombo; they offered a grant help to recover from the crisis. This grant would be used to support and promote wellness tourism, including Ayurveda and Sri Lanka's own indigenous traditional medicine, *helawedakama*. Sri Lanka, Tourism has agreed with the EU to use the money on product development, branding, marketing, and certification of wellness resorts, focusing on Ayurveda and *helawedakama*. As per the said report, Sri Lanka tourism is working with the Ministry of Health to finalize regulations relating to Ayurveda and *helawedakama* and capacity building, after which, product development and promotional campaign will be launched (Pollard et al., 2020).

As per the national export strategy (2018–2022), the government of Sri Lanka has implemented strategies to promote wellness and medical tourism introducing economic incentives and simplified project approval procedures for companies investing in wellness-related developments. The expected goals of this strategy are to coordinate the development of traditional and modern health and medical tourism, establish a quality assurance system for wellness and traditional health systems, and provide an information system for the Sri Lankan health tourism sector and its target markets. To achieve these goals, Export Development Board (EDB) has planned to establish the Sri Lanka Wellness Tourism Association comprised of Western medicine companies, indigenous Ayurveda practitioners, and many others engaged in wellness tourism-related activities.

Methodology

This study followed a qualitative research design based on the postpositivist philosophy. The researcher conducted this study as a case study where the Sri Lankan wellness tourism sector was subjected to study. This study was mainly depending on primary interview data. Purposive sampling was the technique adopted for this research.

The expertise of the field of Ayurveda who are at the higher management level such as Ayurveda Commissioners, directors of Ayurveda research institutes, teaching hospitals, training institute key appointment holders of government Ayurveda medical officers' associations, members of Hospital and Education committees, expertise in the tourism sector such as Directors of Tourism Development Authority, members of EDB, Economic expertise in the hotel sector related to AWT such as key appointment holders in recognized hotel groups were the population of this study.

In this study, the sample was selected according to experience. All interviewees have experience of more than 5 years. They had experienced the COVID-19 pandemic (and the Easter Sunday attack) during this situation. Finally, 19 professionals were interviewed until the data collection became saturated. There were six Ayurveda medical officers, five Ayurveda administrators, five managers from reputed hotel chains related to AWT, and three professionals from Sri Lanka Tourism Development Authority (SLTDA) and EDB who were interviewed until the data were saturated. The qualitative data analysis method was used as the analysis method; the researcher followed the steps data analysis method described by Creswell and Creswell (2018).

Data Analysis and Discussion

As discussed in the methodology, the researcher coded all 19 interviews before analysis. During the analysis, the researcher formulated four categories related to research objectives with relevant subcategories thereon: Ayurveda in Sri Lankan tourism, contribution from tourism-related authorities, contribution from Ayurveda-related authorities, and contribution of AWT service providers (hotels/resorts).

Ayurveda in Sri Lankan Tourism

Ayurveda is identified as a part of Sri Lankan tourism, and it has been contributing in different calibers to the field. One of the objectives of this research is to understand the present status/scenario of Ayurveda in Sri Lankan tourism. For a better understanding and analysis, this category was further subdivided into four subcategories. They are: positive contributions to Sri Lankan tourism, adverse bearings of Ayurveda tourism in Sri Lanka, peripheral opportunities that are available to develop Ayurveda in Sri Lanka, and optimistic prospects about AWT development.

All the interviewees showed that Ayurveda is one of the strengths that Sri Lankan tourism can rely on. The same kinds of expressions about Ayurveda were given by managers, doctors, owners, and Ayurveda and tourism administrators. This could be taken as a good positive point about Ayurveda. Below are some of the opinions expressed by professionals in different segments:

> Our authentic Ayurveda has high potential with proven results which we need to create awareness. There is a bigger demand in the market for the same. (Shanaka, Personal Communication, July 26, 2021)

It was revealed that the present trend of providing Ayurveda services in a hotel become a norm due to several reasons such as the world trend for wellness tourism, wellness tourism becoming a part of leisure tourism, extended stays by wellness tourists and the tendency for revisit is higher by wellness tourist. Due to these reasons, there is a tendency to promote star-class hotels as "Ayurveda Resorts and Spa" instead of just as "Hotels".

> I can say that Ayurveda has become very popular in European countries, especially Germany, Switzerland, and Canada countries. (Dushan, Personal Communication, September 05, 2021)

Another fact was the standards of Sri Lankan Ayurveda. Even though there were contradictory opinions about the standards of Ayurveda in the wellness sector, managers and doctors of reputed Ayurveda resorts stated that the standards of the high-end service providers are good and attract more customers, particularly to the Ayurveda wellness sector.

> Sri Lankan Ayurveda standards are better than that of India, hygienically and quality-wise. (Nishan, Personal Communication, September 12, 2021)

Ayurveda in Sri Lankan tourism is identified as a niche segment by several respondents. On a positive aspect, specialized service and a specific customer base can be developed by being in a niche segment. On the other hand, becoming a niche segment could cause restrictions on development in the mainstream tourism umbrella.

> Ayurveda is used as a niche market in Sri Lankan tourism. But as for me, this is blooming and it has had a good market for four years. (Surandi, Personal Communication, August 19, 2021)

Discussing on adverse bearings of Ayurveda tourism in Sri Lanka, several factors were unveiled. As per the respondents' view, the history of Ayurveda usage in tourism was not acceptable. Collective analysis of the past revealed that Ayurveda was adapted wrongly to tourism so the impression of Ayurveda is bad within the tourism sector. This caused to underutilizing of or neglect of this important avenue for tourism development. In addition, it was revealed that Ayurveda was used as a tool to promote or fill the promotional gaps in the past through which the real value of Ayurveda was diluted.

Earlier, Ayurveda was not properly used as an interesting area in tourism. But with time, it has become one of the factors of identity in Sri Lankan tourism. But the way it is used is not very acceptable to my knowledge. (Buddhi, Personal Communication, July 27, 2021)

Another negative fact found through analysis was the identification of the potential of Ayurveda by relevant authorities. Due to this reason, target customer bases and areas to be focused on are not properly identified. Ayurveda was used in tourism without having a solid national strategy. This restricts the development of the field. One of the key areas in this aspect is promotion. Most of the respondents opine that there is no collective promotional drive for Ayurveda in the international market, instead individual organizations do their promotional campaigns and Ayurveda is promoted either as a main or secondary service provided by them as per individual strategy.

There is no major promotional campaign internationally about Sri Lanka as a destination with Ayurveda treatment.... Most of the guests get to know about Sri Lankan Ayurveda only after arriving here. (Dickson, Personal Communication, August 11, 2021)

We don't focus on it. I mean those who are even doing Wellness tourism don't have the exact knowledge about Wellness tourism and what areas they are looking for. (Mangala, Personal Communication, August 09, 2021)

Another area that was highlighted through analysis was the place given to Ayurveda in Sri Lankan tourism. One respondent opined that Ayurveda is not a key factor in tourism as well and Sri Lanka is not a symbol of Ayurveda in the international market. This view indicates that Sri Lankan tourism doesn't consider Ayurveda as an important factor to consider in drafting strategies.

In Sri Lanka tourism, Ayurveda is not a key factor...Even though some hotels contribute to Ayurveda tourism, Sri Lanka is not a symbol of Ayurveda. (Dickson, Personal Communication, August 11, 2021)

In addition to the above adverse comments, the general effects of the Easter Sunday attack and the COVID-19 pandemic, regulatory issues in Ayurveda were identified as barriers to the AWT sector in Sri Lanka.

Considering the opportunities in Sri Lankan AWT, important factors were identified. Considering Sri Lanka, identities such as our localities, climate infrastructure related to Ayurveda, serene beaches, jungle hideouts, hospitality, Ayurveda cuisine, Indigenous medicine, and Theravada Buddhism become advantages to developing AWT. Further, the good hygienic concerns of Sri Lankans were highlighted as a competitive advantage for the sector.

> We have good Ayurveda medical methods, and practices. Our
> localities, climate and other infrastructure related to Ayurveda
> are good. In addition, we have lots of serene beaches, jungle
> hideouts. (Buddhi, Personal Communication, July 27, 2021)

Some respondents identified the flexibility for a guest to schedule their treatment process as one of the advantages that we have compared with the competitors. Further, world recognition of quality service providers is also an advantage for us in developing AWT.

Despite the negative aspects and loopholes in developing AWT in Sri Lanka, interviewees were optimistic about the future of Sri Lankan AWT. Respondents provided their views in different dimensions, mostly regarding the geographical setting. They opined that Sri Lanka could utilize these advantages to boost Ayurveda wellness since all these geographical settings are favorable for Ayurveda.

> We can use Sri Lanka as a destination for delight. Ayurveda
> systems, fauna and flora, meditations, and even rowing also can
> be taken into the Ayurveda spectrum. We have sound and colour.
> (Parakrama, Personal Communication, August 31, 2021)

In addition, respondents believe that the quality of Sri Lankan people would be a good strength. In that, our inherent hygienic concerns and cleanliness as a country were highlighted as strengths. They have seen the improvement in these areas in Sri Lanka and identified the added advantage of it in the development of the field.

> There was a trend to select India but nowadays this trend has
> leaned towards Sri Lanka as well. Sri Lankan Ayurveda standards
> are better than that of India, hygienically and quality-wise. That
> means our field is in good marketable standard and there is a good
> trend in Sri Lankan Ayurveda. (Nishan, Personal Communication,
> September 12, 2021)

Another highlighted point was the necessary support. Respondents expect support and attention to the Ayurveda wellness field. So, it would be developed to a higher status. In that, they highlighted the "attention" which indicates the present situation of the field.

> I think, if necessary if support and attention are given, we could
> see more income from this. (Kalpana, Personal Communication,
> July 28, 2021)

Overall expectations of all respondents were that, with the necessary support, Ayurveda could be used and developed to become a game changer in Sri Lankan tourism.

Contribution From Tourism-Related Authorities

When discussing tourism, it is mandatory to discuss tourism-related authorities since they are the rightful and responsible authorities for national-level involvement. There are several institutions that were identified in this category. Ministry of Tourism Development, SLTDA, EDB, and Sri Lanka Tourism Promotion Bureau (SLTPB) are the competent authorities that undertake activities on national-level policymaking, regulating, and promoting. To achieve the first objective of the research, the researcher formulated a category to gauge the contribution given by aforesaid institutions to develop AWT in Sri Lanka. This category was further divided into two subcategories for easy analysis; they are the positive contribution from the tourism-related authorities toward AWT and the detrimental acts of the tourism-related authorities toward AWT.

But these positive comments mainly originated from the respondent who represented one of the aforesaid institutions. Other respondents expressed mixed ideas about such institutions, and those are more leaned toward negative aspects. One of the positive views expressed about tourism-related authorities was that these institutions have identified the value and importance of Ayurveda in developing the overall tourism sector in Sri Lanka.

> Yes. . .I say Ayurveda has a Richer, Big export Market for that. So we work on Ayurveda . . ., you know in Ayurveda It produces eye touch products. (Dushan, Personal Communication, September 05, 2021)

> They know that tourism is promoted by Ayurveda. (Guruge, Personal Communication, August 31, 2021)

Another positive comment made was that these institutions are trying to promote Ayurveda in their promotional campaigns. But some comments are related only to primitive and isolated acts which can't be taken as deliberate or purposeful efforts. Some comments were focused on the theoretical aspects where actual attention is questionable.

> Yes, we get lots of support from SLTDA. Promotional articles are added to Sri Lankan Airlines magazines. (Dayangani, Personal Communication, August 24, 2021)

The respondents of SLTDA elaborated on three of their strategies to promote Sri Lankan Ayurveda in the international arena. They facilitated individual institutions/hotels to exhibit their services in international travel exhibitions. Another strategy is to invite foreign journalists around the country to explore Ayurveda resorts and experience the service. Then they expect those journalists to publish their experience in international forums/magazines and other media so that indirect publicity is expected. Another way of promoting Ayurveda is to conduct discussions with travel agents and facilitate them in arranging guests in Sri Lanka.

> They, try to do something,. . . We also joined their programs. They merge with us to do seminars and conferences. With these actions, they try to promote Ayurveda in other countries. (Akila, Personal Communication, July 30, 2021)

Expressions of the same kind were observed from most of the respondents, and it indicates that the contribution from authorities is merely sufficient to say that it is a good contribution. When discussing unfavorable impressions, lots of drawbacks were highlighted by the respondents, especially managers and owners of Ayurveda-related service providers. The main factor highlighted here was the promotional issues. Though promotional efforts were praised, the focus on promoting Ayurveda was neglected by authorities.

> They by experience do and answer about where can visit, what can see, and what can buy but if anybody asks about Ayurveda treatments, cultural values, and the benefits of Ayurveda, they can't answer. (Achala, Personal Communication, September 05, 2021)

On the other hand, the unavailability of the governmental or national-level promotional strategy was highlighted. Most of the managers, doctors, and owners opined that only individual-level marketing is done about Ayurveda, and it is not sufficient. They urged for a national-level promotional effort, mostly handled by tourism-related authorities.

> Most of the time, the private sector promotes them on their own. There is no large promotional campaign from the government side. (Thakshila, Personal Communication, September 01, 2021)

> For example, I can promote my place as a doctor and it is what exactly happens there where individuals promote their businesses. But the government is doing nothing. Sri Lanka is promoted to this level because of the effort made by private and individual organizations. (Achala, Personal Communication, September 05, 2021)

Further, both tourism-related authorities and Ayurveda-related authorities were collectively criticized by the respondents due to the unavailability of coordination and communication between the two parties. This issue is deeply elaborated on by the respondents who know both sectors such as doctors who work in tourism-related authorities and Ayurveda administrators. Mostly, these allegations focused on regulation and registering areas where the present legal framework does not allow small-scale operators to get their centers registered and demanding unachievable thresholds in providing approvals for Ayurveda wellness facilities. In addition, the two parties were criticized for not sharing knowledge about each other whereby the AWT sector is stuck at the same level.

There is a big gap between Ayurveda professionals who don't know much about tourism and tourism people who don't know much about Ayurveda. (Kalpana, Personal Communication, July 28, 2021)

Lack of knowledge about potentials, requirements, necessities, and ground reality of Ayurveda wellness by tourism authorities was also highlighted. This dilutes the effect of existing promotional drives on Sri Lankan tourism.

I think they have no whatsoever like interfering with Ayurveda tourism or Wellness tourism. (Mangala, Personal Communication, August 09, 2021)

During the analysis of tourism-related authorities on their contribution to AWT, it was found that such authorities have made sufficient effort for the development of the Ayurveda field. In that, their attempt was recognized by respondents provided that extra effort is needed to make such effort worthy in developing AWT in Sri Lanka.

Contribution From Ayurveda Authorities

When considering the AWT, it is required to understand the involvement and contribution of Ayurveda-related authorities since all Ayurveda-related matters are the responsibilities of such institutions. Ministry of Indigenous Medicine, Ayurveda Department, Provincial Ayurveda departments, National Institute of Traditional Medicine (NITM), and Bandaranaike Memorial Ayurveda Research Institute (BMARI) are the key institutions in Sri Lanka that work toward the operation and upliftment of Ayurveda. To achieve the objective, the researcher formulated a category to assess the contribution of such authorities to the field. The following subcategories were identified in assessing such contributions on either end: the positive contribution from the Ayurveda-related authorities toward AWT and the detrimental acts of the Ayurveda-related authorities toward AWT.

With the analysis concerning positive contribution, few were found relating to positive aspects. Further, those were mainly from the Ayurveda administrators' category of respondents. As per them, they are doing the regulation process continuously. In addition, they stated that these processes are done in a standard method and without unnecessary delays.

We issue the license after thorough investigations okay? (Guruge, Personal Communication, August 31, 2021)

It is highlighted that the Southern provincial Ayurveda department is contributing actively to the field. They have set up a treatment center for foreigners and willing to expand it to other areas as well. In addition, the Southern province has established a separate institution to handle tourism-related activities.

> To have good attraction, we established a separate institution in the Southern Provincial Council. We, together with the Southern Provincial Tourism Bureau established a treatment centre ......
> We generated about 10–12 lakhs profit before the pandemic. (Guruge, Personal Communication, August 31, 2021)

To maintain the quality of the service, the technical section of the department has taken actions to remove spas and treatment centers that are using the Ayurveda name for such facilities and to cease operations of illegal and unethical locations. This helped to clean the tarnished image of Ayurveda in the field as well as within the general public.

> We removed every place which highlights the name and operation as Indigenous and Ayurveda. .... It is evident in most places that they don't have any Ayurveda drugs instead, use some cream or lotion. .... Most places are found guilty of such unacceptable things. (Shanthi, Personal Communication, August 12, 2021)

At present NITM is progressing to introducing a therapist training course to fill the therapist vacuum. This was one of the good signs of contribution from the Ayurveda side to the wellness industry of Sri Lanka.

> There is a training course for therapists conducted by NITM these days. This has to be dealt with hospital and education committee. They already prepared the syllabus for NVQ level 3–4 qualifications. (Shanthi, Personal Communication, August 12, 2021)

During the data analysis process, the researcher found lots of adverse comments regarding the contribution from Ayurveda-related authorities. Those comments were received from most of the respondents, and they expressed displeasure about such authorities. The general assessment showed that the contribution from such authorities is less.

> As a person in the field, I would see that the contribution from the department is very low. (Surandi, Personal Communication, August 19, 2021)

Initial responses from almost all respondents, other than Ayurveda administrators, were like the above quotes. This indicated the impression of such authorities within the field. In addition, there were serious critics of authorities that they do not have an idea about the AWT sector, its requirements, and the benefits of supporting wellness tourism in Sri Lanka. This has to be considered critical since the Ayurveda-related authorities are one of the main pillars in developing AWT.

Neither the department nor the personnel working there have an idea about Ayurveda tourism and its benefits to Sri Lanka. (Dickson, Personal Communication, August 11, 2021)

Respondents further urged Ayurveda authorities to participate actively in the betterment of the field. That illustrated again the contribution from such authorities is insufficient to fulfill at least basic requirements.

Mostly what they do in the first impression is just say no, no, no. This is bad. (Mangala, Personal Communication, August 09, 2021)

There were other supportive comments related to the above-mentioned idea. Therefore, It could be considered true since the whole field stands on these few pillars.

Actually. . ., therapists who trained and worked under me are also open treatment centres with few experiences. That is very wrong and the department can act against these things. (Kalpana, Personal Communication, July 28, 2021)

Another allegation toward competent authorities was that they only look for registration fees. This was criticized by respondents stating that authorities were keen to look for annual fees and other money collection means without really looking at the contribution part. This caused to dilute the reputation of authorities and increased displeasure within the field. It is to be noted that nobody objected to a subscription, but they expect honorary service for the subscriptions which is not given by the authorities.

Registration renewals are done by the Ayurveda department. Annual inspections are also carried out. Other than that, nothing happened. (Thakshila, Personal Communication, September 01, 2021)

Another highlighted area was the regulation process. Even though Ayurveda administrators stated that there is a solid regulation process, all others expressed views opposed to that. Operators and doctors in the field opined that there are lots of shortcomings in the regulation process. By analyzing the codes related to this aspect, it was found that this is one of the key areas which Ayurveda authorities must look into and the area where they lack attendance.

Officers only check registered places and they check for timely payment in registered locations. But they don't visit and check unregistered locations as well. Even if they visit such a location, owners bribe them and nothing happens afterwards. (Achala, Personal Communication, September 05, 2021)

As an extension of this regulation process, it was highlighted that these authorities were unable to fulfill the statutory requirements to run the wellness field smoothly. In that, the Education and Hospital board of the Ayurveda department was not summoned for a long period. The importance of this board is to approve training institution and their syllabus. Since it has been inactive for a long time, important decisions related to the wellness field are held up. The committee for regulation of Ayurveda hospitals, dispensaries, and drug stores is responsible for the formulation of regulations for all Ayurveda services in Sri Lanka, but this committee is inactive and does not formulate any regulations for the betterment of either the Ayurveda wellness sector or general Ayurveda medical sector.

> Training institutes can't be established in Sri Lanka since the Ayurveda department does not have the facility in this regard. Only 4 institutions can train therapists and such authority is also given by the Education and Hospital Committee in the department .... Even this committee is not summoned for a longer time. (Dickson, Personal Communication, August 11, 2021)

In addition, there are lots of regulations that are to be standardized and to be gazette but have not yet materialized. This has been highlighted even by Ayurveda administrators. Those regulations are essential for the development of the wellness sector. Further, it was highlighted that these areas are neglected knowingly by the authorities, and no attempt to correct such.

> For example, massage is to be done man-to-man and woman-to-woman. It is not gazetted but there is medical ethics for that. (Shanthi, Personal Communication, August 12, 2021)

This regulation issue includes provisions to get registration for treatment centers. It proved that existing registration categories of Ayurveda centers is extremely rigid and it restricts the entrance for small or medium-scale locations since there are no provisions to operate treatment center with minimum requirements.

> At the moment there is no category to register institutions. Either it should be a hotel or a dispensary. In between, there is no room to register any institution. (Dickson, Personal Communication, August 11, 2021)

Another area that was highlighted was that Ayurveda authorities are acting irresponsibly regarding the issues in the wellness sector; it is found that without providing viable solutions, authorities have put additional restrictions which caused more complications in developing the field.

Department registered 'Panchakarma' centres. But with time, those panchakarma centres became Spas. What the Department must have done is investigate such misuses and close such places. Instead, the department stopped registering panchakarma centres. (Dickson, Personal Communication, August 11, 2021)

Insurance claims for treatment were another fact found through analysis. As to one respondent, it is said that international insurance companies do not cover Ayurveda treatments in Sri Lanka through their travel insurance. This caused a reduction in the guest income since long-stay treatment schedules would incur high costs and without recovery means in Sri Lanka; those guests opted to proceed to other countries like India which provide valid claiming procedures. His justification for nonacceptance by international companies was that Sri Lanka does not have gazetted/standardized treatment plans for illness/wellness treatments. Without this legal coverage, insurance companies would not accept the bills produced for illness/wellness treatments. Through the analysis of this fact, it is found that Ayurveda authorities' inefficiency caused to delay in the standardization and legalization of treatment processes to be used in the wellness sector in Sri Lanka.

Anyway, there is a legal issue in this aspect. There is a good reason for this... it is the silence of the authority. The Ayurveda department is responsible for the standardization and specification of treatments. That means they are to set out treatment profiles ... These protocols are not yet set out in Sri Lanka. But India........... When inquired with the department, they said that they were going to do it. ...all those are to be approved by the government and to be gazetted. Then only they become legal and binding to insurance companies. (Parakrama, Personal Communication, August 31, 2021)

Most of the respondents criticized Ayurveda institutions like the technical section, BMARI and NITM heavily for not doing their job properly. For example, the technical section has lots of responsibility to provide registration and facilitation which are not done, BMARI is a dedicated research institute not only for the wellness sector but also for the whole of Ayurveda in Sri Lanka which is not conducting quality research for the betterment of the field, and NITM which is responsible for the training and development of a workforce for entire Ayurveda field which was unable to provide at least qualification for Ayurveda wellness workers.

Out of all Ayurveda institutions, critics of the Ayurveda department and technical section have to be taken seriously since most of the respondents expressed heavy displeasure on that. These critics include they do not even know the basics of the Ayurveda wellness sector and even no person is competent in the general responsibilities of the section. If the situation is such, AWT is unachievable since they are responsible for most authentication and standardization activities.

> There is no place/ person to get information about Ayurveda tourism if we visit the Ayurveda department, at least a Clark... Even in the technical branch, they do only registration of hotels or institutes but there are no plans for promotion or support to establish Ayurveda institutions. (Dickson, Personal Communication, August 11, 2021)

Another critique was that these institutions only collect facts for the sake of doing so and do not even produce accurate factual content provided for better forecasting and plans. This shows the irresponsible behaviors of these institutions.

> One of the great backdrops in the Ayurveda field is the lack of statistics. The development section sends lots of erotic reports and if we look at the Central Bank report, we can see how small the budget is for Ayurveda. (Parakrama, Personal Communication, August 31, 2021)

Another important area that was highlighted is the contribution of provincial Ayurveda departments; it is found that provincial departments' contribution is less to the well-being of the field. Within this, it was highlighted that provincial departments lack the necessary authority to act on some issues due to the legal framework of such departments. In addition, the individuality of provincial commissioners was also found to be a matter in addressing the issues of the AWT field.

> Contribution from us (Provincial Ayurveda department) is less. ...
> We can't do much from the Provincial council level. (Guruge, Personal Communication, August 31, 2021)

Contribution of AWT Service Providers

The fourth category of the research is related to the first objective, and it is about the contribution of AWT service providers. This includes hotels providing Ayurveda treatments to a guest, Ayurveda resorts, *Panchakarma* centers, and any other Ayurveda treatment center focusing on foreign guests. Respondents were asked to provide details on this category in a general context without focusing on one particular area such as owning a hotel or a small-scale business. This category was divided into three subcategories: the positive contribution from AWT service providers, detrimental acts of AWT service providers, and issues in providing better service to service providers.

When analyzing those codes, it is found that there is a difference between services provided by large-scale hotels and small-scale hotels. Generally, large-scale operators pay more attention to maintaining the standards in all aspects of guest treatment which includes quality of the treatments, hospitality, food and beverages, infrastructure, and ensuring the Sri Lankan identity in wellness tourism.

> I know most big hotels pay much attention to service quality... Those are up to the standard and usually maintain good quality standards. (Buddhi, Personal Communication, July 27, 2021)

These hotels/resorts provide service which is customized to fit the guest's expectations and customers are happy with the service received from such reputed institutions. Further, senior management's commitment was praised by the respondents since they satisfied most of the management's decisions regarding the advancement of the wellness tourism field.

> We provide customer-based treatments. Treatment is decided according to customer type. We even, customized food as well. ... We require upgrading the general health of the customer whilst fulfilling his wishes. (Akila, Personal Communication, July 30, 2021)

Another area that comes with a positive aspect is promotion. Even though there are no signs of having a national strategy to promote Sri Lankan Ayurveda internationally, these individual hotels do promote them in the international forum which contributes commendably to the wellness sector. Ayurveda administrators highlighted the advantages of having government-owned wellness facilities. The trust among guests is expected to be high in government-run facilities and unemployed doctors could be used in these facilities. On the contrary, another Ayurveda administrator opined that there are restrictions to entering the Ayurveda wellness sector by government entities. As an example, it is highlighted that there are protocol restrictions and payment irregularities to entering a business venture in the field.

> Now we can't do it. But the private sector could. There are rules and regulations to admit to our government hospital where we can't accommodate tourists since there are other protocols to be followed and security should be ensured. ... Local and foreign rates should be different, So, we can't per se charge different rates from a foreigner and we can't even charge the same rate like 300 Rs. Both are wrong. (Dayangani, Personal Communication, August 24, 2021)

On the detrimental aspects, there were 11 codes related to the area. The main thing highlighted was the standards of the small-scale facilities are lesser than large-scale entities. This standard degradation was identified due to the lack of space available in such places. Owners of such restricted locations tend to include everything haphazardly and ill-equipped to provide quality service, thereby degrading the architectural and mental freedom of guests.

> There is a problem with small-scale hotels and wellness service providers. In such a place resources are less, so they tend to dilute the service. (Buddhi, Personal Communication, July 27, 2021)

> But in some other places, they don't even have the feeling of relaxation. Ill-equipped and substandard. (Achala, Personal Communication, September 05, 2021)

Again, these small-scale operators were criticized for not following proper and standardized treatment processes as well as not using proper tools and equipment for treatments. This would again dilute the quality of Sri Lankan Ayurveda.

> No proper treatment process and required equipment were also not available. By looking at some equipment, we can see that they are only exhibits and aren't used for treatments. (Guruge, Personal Communication, August 31, 2021)

Another aspect that is highlighted as detrimental aspect is staffing. It was highlighted that there is a qualified staffing problem all over the field. This is not restricted to small-scale service providers, but large-scale operators also have this problem. This caused the trust among guests that negatively affected to wellness field.

> If we look at HR matters, there are no qualified personnel. For example, only kedumbindum or sarpavisha doctors are there and they don't know about treatments. They are not qualified. (Guruge, Personal Communication, August 31, 2021)

Limited large-scale service providers are available. In Sri Lanka, it was highlighted. Related to this, it is not directly related. It was pointed out this vacuum caused the development since the competition was not there. Further, the lack of new entrants to the medium and small-scale sectors was also highlighted.

> However, there are very few new entrants to this field. Considering Southern province, it is very less, even; I can name all the places. This is not a good trend. (Dickson, Personal Communication, August 11, 2021)

During interviews, respondents were asked about issues, particularly service providers. In this, it was found that there are centers that are owned by foreigners. This was highlighted by the owners' category of interviewees, and they expressed displeasure toward such facilities since they would drain out foreign earnings that must be directed to Sri Lankans.

> We earn money as Sri Lankans and it is for the country. But there is a foreign lady who runs a spa and she earns a profit and sends it to her country. (Achala, Personal Communication, September 05, 2021)

Another issue that is highlighted is the unavailability of a therapist training facility in the Southern province even has the highest Ayurveda wellness facilities in Sri Lanka. It highlighted that this caused the extra effort to go to Colombo for training and practically it is not happening. Finally, it highlighted the issue of insurance claiming inability that was discussed previously under the contribution from Ayurveda-related authorities' category.

> All the training institutes are located in Colombo whereas most Ayurveda centres are located in the Gall suburb. So, it would be difficult to come to Colombo to get trained. (Dickson, Personal Communication, August 11, 2021)

Discussion

This research was conducted to study the context of AWT in Sri Lanka. In that, the researcher focused on strategic aspects of the sector where AWT was looked at. While doing a preliminary study about the subject matter, the researcher understood that there are issues in the strategic outfit of the industry which drag the development of the industry. Hence, this study was structured to achieve three objectives of Sri Lankan AWT. In summation, the research was able to achieve all three objectives through the findings. An expanded discussion is presented hereunder.

In understanding the present status of Sri Lankan AWT, the researcher found that Ayurveda was one of the strengths Sri Lanka tourism possessed. Due to world trends in tourism, standards of the Sri Lankan Ayurveda wellness sector, geographical setting, and culture, the field seems to be developing gradually. During data analysis, it was found that changing world tourism trends toward wellness tourism, Sri Lankan tourism operators also identified the fact that Ayurveda wellness is one of the force multipliers in tourism. Therefore, most service providers are keen on converting to providing Ayurveda wellness or adopting wellness principles for their strategic developments. The transition of designation from "hotel" to "hotel and spa" and further to "Ayurveda resort" indicates this trend in the Sri Lankan hotel industry. Though the present trends are positive, findings affirmed that mismanagement and misuse of Ayurveda in past scenarios incur negative impacts on the sector. The bad image created by such activities is posing high resistance for the AWT in the present-day context, mostly toward the perception of society. This is one of the reasons dragging the expansion of the sector in rural but high-potential localities. Community resistance against setting up new ventures and staffing issues are the outcomes of such a bad image created in past. Nonidentification of the real potentialities of

Ayurveda by authorities is another adverse factor in the present context, which diverted due attention. Despite negativities, all respondents were very optimistic about the future of AWT and Sri Lankan tourism in general. This is a good sign of prosperity in the field since optimism could be converted to good trust to boost the field by all stakeholders and with necessary support from authorities.

In the analysis of individual stakeholders of AWT, tourism-related authorities, Ayurveda-related authorities, and service providers were contrasted. The findings of tourism-related authorities unveiled some interesting factors. Respondents from tourism-related authorities have stressed lots of positive contributions to the sector, whereas others such as operators and doctors have expressed mixed expressions about the contribution. This creates a question of whether the efforts made by authorities are suited or worthwhile to the operators'/doctors' point of view. So, understanding between two parties would be unsatisfactory. This could lead to misunderstanding and misconception ultimately degrading the effectiveness of the effort made by authorities. Findings have shown that authorities have understood that AWT is an important sector, but necessities have not been properly identified. This distracted the focal point of authorities where centers of gravity are not addressed. The researcher, based on such findings, opined that this is the reason for operators'/doctors' dissatisfaction with authorities.

Respondents from Ayurveda-related authorities confirmed their active contribution to the sector. However, operators and doctors were under a different purview. The findings of the study were exciting with related to Ayurveda authorities. Initially, these authorities have done little to the sector, but it is gloomy to state that acts of Ayurveda authorities were destroying the sector rather than developing it. Findings revealed that authorities were fully absent in mind about the sector, and it is astonishing to state the unconsciousness in supporting this important generator. Findings revealed that though tourism authorities were not fully focused on the sector, their actions helped to sustain the industry. But Ayurveda authorities are concerned their contribution is negligible and absentminded about AWT. Without a proper understanding of the AWT, its core functions, and the responsibility of Ayurveda authorities, support from Ayurveda authorities cannot be expected and findings proved such misunderstanding on the part of Ayurveda authorities. Due to these reasons, vast resources and capabilities that are wasted by Ayurveda authorities are not utilized for the betterment of the AWT. In addition, being the authorities, necessary policy support concerning the sector is not met, further degrading the international legality of AWT as a means of healthcare service.

Considering the service providers, interesting factors were unveiled. One of the facts was the inter-relationship between the scale of the business and service quality. Evidence from the research proved that service quality is proportional to the scale of the business. Large-scale service providers maintain the exceptional quality of overall service, whereas quality is degraded when coming down to being small-scale. The researcher identified several factors in this regard. The capital requirement was one of the reasons why small-scale operators were facing difficulties in meeting such expenses. On the other hand, issues in two authorities (Ayurveda and tourism authorities) made small-scale operations difficult due to the reasons discussed in the above paragraphs. Generally, these small-scale operators find it difficult to meet the specifications demanded by those two authorities, hence trying to fulfill all requirements with limited funds/resources, thereby degrading the service quality. Another revealed fact was that there is a tendency to immerging small to medium centers owned by foreigners where such centers threaten the local operators in the industry.

An in-depth discussion on points related to the whole study was presented in previous paragraphs. A summary of the discussion points is given herewith. Due to several reasons such as world tourism trends, standards of Sri Lankan Ayurveda and AWT have become one of the strengths that Sri Lankan Tourism. The present context shows a gradual increment in the sector; findings proved that there were issues in managing and using Ayurveda in the tourism sector. The effects of such issues are still there in the sector. Tourism-related authorities, Ayurveda-related authorities, and service providers filled the majority of seats at the stakeholder round table. Considering the contribution from each portion, tourism-related authorities were found to be supportive to a considerable extent of the sector, but there are grey areas that drag the development of AWT. When discussing Ayurveda-related authorities, it was found that such authorities are not in the correct picture at all. Even their actions would imply negative impacts. An interesting thing found about service providers was the relationship between the size of the business and service quality. It was found that these are proportional to each other due to reasons within and out of their control of them.

Conclusion and Implication of the Research

Conclusion

Tourism is one of the ways that humans use for easing their stresses in day-to-day life. The general outfit of this tourism is subjected to various factors where operators would tackle the ever-changing scenarios and reshape their strategies to get the advantages of these changes. Wellness tourism is one of the trending concepts in world tourism. As such, every country which welcomes tourists is changing its existing strategies to tackle this changing scenario. Sri Lanka has no exceptions to this phenomenon. As one of the tourism service providers to overseas tourists and dependent on income generated by tourism, Sri Lanka has identified the importance of securing a considerable portion of the world wellness tourism trend and opted to capitalize on wellness tourism through Ayurveda. However, there is an ambiguity about whether Sri Lanka is properly doing the needful to use optimum potentialities to catch the desired portion of wellness tourism. To find answers, the researcher extensively studied about Sri Lankan scenario and other country profiles, guided by three objectives.

The findings of the study proved that Sri Lankan AWT has great potential to grow, but those potentialities were not managed properly. In addition, several administrative bottlenecks drag the development. Further, it was revealed that a lack of whole-country effort would further dilute the expansion of AWT in Sri Lanka. Interestingly, Sri Lanka still has a chance to grow in the sector by applying several corrective measures to the existing outfit of the AWT of Sri Lanka. Finally, this qualitative research would contribute to the development of AWT by providing possible recommendations for actions in a practical scenario and the expansion of the existing knowledge base about AWT in Sri Lanka.

Implications of the Research

Since the study was about AWT, two identical sectors can be identified, tourism and Ayurveda. Theoretically, this study focused on Ayurveda in the tourism eye, and findings proved that the Sri Lankan Ayurveda sector is not orientated to tourism in general. When tourism is seen through the Ayurveda eye, the tourism sector has a comparatively higher understanding of Ayurveda, its pivotal points, and its importance. However, findings suggest that both sectors are not in the correct perspective or rather not synchronized. Hence, Ayurveda authorities need to focus on the wellness sector because it is identified as one of the trending tourism motives in the world. Findings have clearly shown that our counterparts in the industry are moving ahead with the proper application of Ayurveda and other indigenous medical systems in the tourism sector. Hence, Sri Lanka needs to focus on national policy implementation for AWT. Those policies could bridge the communication gaps between authorities, provide necessary alternations in Ayurveda education and application systems, guide human resources planning for staffing, and enlighten society at large about the importance of AWT.

Another theoretical implication derived from this study was the expansion of the existing knowledge base regarding AWT in Sri Lanka. This study covered a full spectrum of the specific subject which supported filling the lacuna of AWT. This study would provide good insights into the sector which contributes to the development of AWT in Sri Lanka as well as guide future researchers in developing the knowledge base.

References

Arachchi, D. E., & Kaluarachchi, I. P. (2019). Ayurveda medical tourism in Sri Lanka: Service quality & tourists' satisfaction. *Journal of Tourism Economics and Applied Research, 3*, 1. http://jtear.uoctourism.com/publication/2019volume1/ayurveda_medical_tourism_in_sri_lanka.pdf

Connell, J. (2006). Medical tourism: Sea, sun, sand and surgery. *Tourism Management, 27*(6), 1093–1100. https://doi.org/10.1016/j.tourman.2005.11.005

Creswell, J., & Creswell, D. (2018). *Research design* (5th ed.). SAGE Publications.

Eissler, L. A., & Casken, J. (2013). Seeking health care through international medical tourism. *Journal of Nursing Scholarship, 45*(2), 177–184. https://doi.org/10.1111/jnu.12014

Global Wellness Institute. (2018). *Global wellness economy monitor.* https://globalwellnessinstitute.org/industry-research/2018-global-wellness-economy-monitor/

International Trade Centre. (2014). *Medical and wellness tourism: Lessons from Asia.* https://www.intracen.org/uploadedFiles/intracenorg/Content/Publications/Medical%20and%20wellness%20Tourism%20-%20lessons%20from%20Asia_L.pdf

Karai, V. K. (2018). Ayurveda: Bringing India to the top of wellness tourism. *Entrepreneur India.* https://www.entrepreneur.com/article/324424

Kumar, A. (2019). Wellness tourism: Taking a step forward. https://www.traveltrendstoday.in/news/india-tourism/item/7482-wellness-tourism-taking-a-step-forward

Peršić, M., & Janković, S. (2013). The assessment of opportunities and assumptions of the Croatian health tourism development. *Journal of Business Management & Economics, 1*(1), 88–104. https://www.ba.lv/wp-content/uploads/2015/08/no6jbm_issue-6.pdf#page=88

Pollard, K., Jenkins, J., & Youngman, I. (2020). Sri Lanka looks to promote health tourism. *Laing Buisson News.* https://www.laingbuissonnews.com/imtj/news-imtj/sri-lanka-looks-to-promote-health-tourism/

Sri Lanka Export Development Board. (2018). *National export strategy of Sri Lanka – Wellness tourism strategy.* https://www.srilankabusiness.com/national-export-strategy/nes-wellness-tourism.html

Samarathunga, W. (2020). Post-COVID-19 challenges and the way forward for Sri Lanka Tourism. *SSRN Electronic Journal,* 1–12. https://doi.org/10.2139/ssrn.3581509

UNWTO. (2018). *Exploring health tourism executive summary.* https://www.e-unwto.org/doi/book/10.18111/9789284420308

World Travel & Tourism Council (WTTC)/Economic impact. (n.d.). https://wttc.org/Research/Economic-Impact. Accessed on October 4, 2020.

Chapter 13

Redefining and Revitalized Community-Based Tourism: An Evaluation of Green Tourism Practises in Turkey

Elif BAK ATEŞ[a] and Gül ERKOL BAYRAM[b]

[a]Ministry of Industry and Technology, Turkey
[b]Sinop University, Turkey

Abstract

This chapter aims to highlight practices that ensure a livable climate and support the creation of a greener and more sustainable environment for community-based tourism in the case of Turkey. Green tourism needs to be improved and enhanced integrally from the perspective of tourism stakeholders, including tour operators, travel agencies, hotels, guests, and the host community. Turkey is the first country in the world to apply the green tourism certification system. It is a system very similar to the safe certificate system applied in tourism facilities. In Turkey, 4–5 star hotels are obliged to switch to this system. Community-based tourism is an alternative tourism approach that meets the needs and wishes of the host people, provides a more sustainable economy compared to other economic activities, and does not harm local culture and traditions. Global climate change and tourism are in a relationship with each other, and this relationship is even more evident for nature-based tourism types. Climate, natural environment, and personal security are seen as three main factors in the selection of a tourism center, and it is predicted by the Intergovernmental Panel on Climate Change that global climate change will have significant effects on these factors at the regional level. The United Nations World Tourism Organization accepts that the tourism industry should develop its potential to adapt to global warming, considering that the tourism industry is an economic sector that is open to the direct and indirect effects of climate change and is dependent on climate.

Keywords: Global climate change; green tourism; certification; GSTC; Turkey

Strategic Tourism Planning for Communities, 197–209
Copyright © 2024 Elif BAK ATEŞ and Gül ERKOL BAYRAM
Published under exclusive licence by Emerald Publishing Limited
doi:10.1108/978-1-83549-015-020241016

Introduction

In a general definition, climate is the weather conditions that occur over a very long time in large geographical areas. Climate includes extreme weather events. In addition, the climate also affects the vegetation of the region (Meteroloji). Global warming is the increase in global temperature over some time. This temperature increase has reached such dimensions that it will affect many ecological balances. The biggest impact of this global temperature increase is on the climate system. Changing climate structure with global warming is the change in the structure of greenhouse gases naturally present in the atmosphere, and accordingly the overheating of the earth and the occurrence of some ecological imbalances. Many factors cause climate change, and most of these factors are human-induced greenhouse gas emissions. Events such as economic development, increasing population, excessive energy consumption, and use of fossil fuels cause carbon emissions and deforestation. The rapid rise of global warming today has caused many disasters. It threatens the life of lively life, creates changes in the seasons, and causes the glaciers to melt (Karakaya & ve Özçağ, 2004).

Climate is important in directing the demand of tourists in the tourism sector. The climate determines the destination choice of tourists, the season they will travel, and the duration of their stay. Tourism types such as ski tourism, nature tourism, sea tourism, and ecotourism are closely related to the issue of climate change, as they require certain climatic conditions (Amelung et al., 2007). However, previous research on climate and tourism has ignored the vulnerability of tourism to climatic events. Previous national and international reports have focused more on government policies. But nature dominates everything. A flood or earthquake disaster that we experience affects not only that region but the whole world. In addition, natural disasters in any part of the world trigger each other.

The importance of climate change in the tourism sector has also been realized with the tangible effects of global climate change on natural areas, living spaces, human life, and economic sectors. Increasing temperature values, changes in sea level, changes in age, amount, and frequency, and destruction and destruction of natural areas have changed the demand for tourism (Solomon et al., 2007). Climate change raises many security concerns. Disasters such as storms, snow, and hurricanes pose a great threat to potential tourists. In addition, the increasing temperatures in the destinations visited for sea tourism in summer and the dominance of the desert season become a season that tourists avoid over time (Grillakis et al., 2016; Scott, 2003). With the changing climatic conditions, the course and direction of tourism are also changing. At this point, countries that adopt a stable and more resistible development model emerge as the society that is least affected by the negative effects of climate change.

Global Climate Change

Climate refers to the average state of weather conditions observed in a particular region or place of the world over many years. In other words, the climate is the statistical definition of weather conditions occurring over at least 3 years. Climate change, on the other hand, is the natural climatic variation detected in comparable periods and seasons. In addition, climate change can be defined as the variation in climate and seasons after human activities that directly or indirectly disrupt the structure of the global atmosphere (United Nations, 1992). With a broad definition, climate change is the noticeable changes that occur in weather events such as precipitation rate and temperature level in a certain region and that make their effects felt for a long time (Uysal, 2022). According to the United Nations environmental convention, which was prepared under the leadership of the United Nations and took its place in history as the first convention on global warming, climate change is defined as "changes directly or indirectly attributed to human activity, in addition to natural/normal climatic variability observed over comparable periods, which ultimately differentiate the composition of the global atmosphere" (UNFCCC, 1992).

The industrial revolution has deeply affected many living things in the world. After the industrial revolution, the increasing use of coal and oil, fossil fuels, and forest areas and natural resources have been destroyed to a large extent with the increasing carbon dioxide gas emissions after World War II. The occupation of forest areas by urbanization has also increased the natural greenhouse effect by affecting the heat holding capacity of the atmosphere (Kadıoğlu, 2008). Climate change, which is one of the important consequences of global warming; they are important changes that occur for a long time in climatic events such as temperature, precipitation, evaporation, and wind (Türkeş, 2008). Studies on climate change; the state that the world will gradually warm up, glaciers will melt, strong weather events will occur frequently and severely, sea level will rise, precipitation regimes will change, climate zones will change, drought, desertification, and increase in waterless areas will cause many negative changes (Karadeniz et al., 2018). According to İncecik (2007), the life of all living things is in danger with climate change. When the literature is reviewed, natural and human-related factors are among the causes of climate change. Some studies have included cultural elements in these effects. The general judgment is that the destruction of natural resources caused by consumption causes climate change (Başdemir, 2008). We can express the natural factors that cause climate change as follows (Schurer et al., 2015):

• changes in Earth's orbit;
• scarce drifts;
• changes in solar radiation;
• ocean temperature changes;
• volcanic eruptions.

Climate change is going to be a very difficult and costly process in terms of the future of the world and the transfer of resources to future generations. Solutions and actions to be taken regarding climate change are possible with the cooperation of many different institutions and stakeholders. Unfortunately, very few institutions can do their part. Levin et al. (2012) emphasized some features of climate change regarding the solution to the issue. We can express these features as follows:

• Climate change has a complex structure, and its solution is quite difficult.
• The time to take action on this issue is getting shorter, and resources are running out fast.
• Problems are produced by both the causes of the problems and those affected, and solutions are sought.
• Classical analyses and interpretations of climate change are quite inadequate.

Activities related to combating global warming and climate change are carried out by many international organizations such as the United Nations. This struggle started in the 1970s. The International Conference on the Human Environment, held in Stockholm in 1972, has a key role in the fight against climate change. This conference drew attention to the fact that environmental problems related to climate change are international rather than regional or national. He also emphasized that the solution is possible with international cooperation. Established in 1972, the European United Nations environment program aims to discuss many environmental issues, including climate change, in an international context. The purpose of the IPCC, established by the United Nations and UNEP, is to prepare special reports and technical assessments on climate change–related issues. In the reports published by the IPCC in different periods, it has been clearly emphasized that the greenhouse gases created by individuals cause climate change (Arıkan & Özsoy, 2008). At the conference held in Paris, France in 2015, the Paris Agreement, which constitutes the framework for climate change implementation, was accepted (Uysal, 2022).

Effects of Global Climate Change on Tourism Destinations

Tourism has been accepted as the basic development tool of many world countries with the increase in the income level and leisure activities of the working population, after the World War II. According to the World Tourism and Travel Council, tourism is the world's largest industry with the highest employment. With this definition, it is possible to say that tourism is the main tool of economic development and the way out of economic crises. There are three main sources of attraction for destinations that have a dominant role in the development of the tourism sector. These areas have tourist attractions, ease of access, and accommodation. Touristic attractions have a fundamental role in tourists' preference for a destination. For example, the biggest reason for choosing a destination can be a famous museum or restaurant in the world. Another factor: Access is related to adequate and convenient transportation facilities. This suitability may be related to geographical conditions and climate structure. Having a suitable climate for tourists to have a holiday in the region they visit is a distinguishing factor in their satisfaction with their holidays. Climate is one of the main motivational factors in choosing a destination. Suitable climatic conditions have an essential role in the sea-sun-sand trio, which has an important potential for world tourism (Özgüç, 2007).

Tourists prefer more suitable areas in terms of climate. Areas that are not suitable for climate are less preferred by tourism stakeholders. For example, people from Norway prefer warmer areas as they have cold weather conditions. Arabian tourists prefer destinations with cold weather conditions (Corobov, 2007). According to Güçlü (2010), climate change is closely related to tourism. Tourism generally covers tourism activities carried out in open areas. Recreational activities are mostly carried out in open areas, and adverse climatic conditions may adversely affect satisfaction levels. In this context, climate comfort has an important place in site selection.

The tourism sector has a seasonal concept. In tourism, which is divided into the summer season and winter season, there is a tourism season mainly based on sea-sun-sand tourism in summer. Tourists visiting these destinations usually come from regions that live in cold climates. In addition, tourists living in hot climates are seen in destinations where winter tourism activities are carried out (Kozak, 2014). It is important to know the current climatic conditions well for an effective marketing and promotion activity in the tourism sector. When the literature is reviewed, it is possible to express the serious effects of climate change on tourism. Bayazıt (2018) stated that climate change has significant effects on tourism, which is an important development factor for Turkey, and that if climate change damages the tourism sector, it will cause many economic and social losses. According to Sevim and Zeydan (2007), health problems occur due to climate change, flooding of coastal hotels and beaches, landslides in coastal areas and the destruction and disappearance of coastal areas, drought, desertification, and the gradual decrease in access to clean water resources and extreme heat (Aydemir & ve Şenerol, 2014). Tourism management should improve its scope depending on changing climatic conditions and living conditions. Sector representatives should make innovations and review the necessary planning in order not to be harmed by seasonal differences. For example, tour operators adapt quickly to seasonal changes and change their tour programs according to weather conditions. Tourism managements provide services in different scopes and qualities all over the world. Deserts, poles, mountains, and hills are among attractive destinations around the world. Tourism management should be sensitive and adaptable to different climates and include them in their decision-making processes (Lemieux & Scott, 2010).

There is a two-way relationship between the tourism sector and climate change. As in all activities carried out by people, greenhouse gases formed after tourism activities create a warming and cooling effect in the atmosphere. However, the greenhouse gases formed generally have a more warming effect. As the atmosphere warms, it changes and changes climates. Changing climates cause the world to warm and sea level to rise, and some sudden and big weather changes occur. Some sudden changes in meteorology affect the tourism sector indirectly and directly. For example, tourism cannot be carried out effectively in very hot destinations, and many tourism activities cannot be realized in destinations where very intense winter conditions are experienced. Although temperatures in the summer season, which are above seasonal conditions, attract the attention of tourists and strengthen the demand for destinations, the long-term negative effects will negatively affect the future of tourism. Tourism season, demand, and the number of tourists change and differentiate with climate change (Giles & Perry, 1988).

Tourism is a comprehensive sector that includes many different sectors such as agriculture, animal husbandry, and business. Most of the touristic services offered to tourists are provided by subsectors that supply goods and products to tourism. In this context, besides the direct effects of climate change on tourism demand, there are also negative effects on subsectors. The raw materials of the tourism sector are natural areas, cultural heritage, and architectural structures. Climate change, which directly affects these factors, will decrease the value of free goods (Olalı & Timur, 1988). Climate change creates stress and negative emotions in local people living in destinations. With the rise in sea level, psychological negative effects may occur on individuals and epidemics may occur. The threats faced by tourism express its fragile and sensitive nature (Sevim & Zeydan, 2008; Viner & Agnew, 1999).

As stated before, climate change, which is mainly related to tourism, has a close relationship with different types of tourism. For example, climate change is important in the success of alternative tourism types such as mountain tourism, ecotourism, agricultural tourism, and sea tourism. At the same time, tourism is in direct relationship with sectors sensitive to climate change such as agriculture, energy, and transportation. The world tourism organization (UNWTO, 2008) expressed the effects of climate change on tourism destinations as follows:

- High temperature affects destinations, changing seasonality, heat stress for tourists, cooling costs, plant and insect populations, changes, and infectious diseases.
- Reducing snow cover and melting glaciers affects destinations, lack of snow in winter sports, increased skiing cost, and shorter winter sports season.
- Frequency of extreme storms and increase in density affect destinations, risk for tourism facilities, increased cost of insurance, and business outage costs.
- Decreased precipitation and increased in some areas evaporation affects destinations; water scarcity, competition for water among sectors, desertification, forest fires that threaten infrastructure increase.
- Increased in some areas heavy rainfall frequency affects destinations, flood damage to historical and cultural assets, and damage to tourism infrastructure.
- Sea-level rise affects destinations, coastal erosion, loss of coastal area, and coastal protection costs.
- Sea surface rising temperatures affect destinations, increased coral bleaching and marine esthetic deterioration with sources.
- Terrestrial and marine in biodiversity changes affect destinations, natural attraction in tropical–subtropical countries, loss of species, and high disease risk.

- More often and larger forest fires increased risk of flooding, damage to tourism infrastructure.
- Soil changes affect destinations, archeological sites with their effects on target locations, and loss of assets and other natural resources (UNWTO, 2008; Climate Change and Tourism Responding to Global Challenges).

Climate change affects environmental resources that are essential for tourism such as snow, temperature, precipitation, forest fires, biodiversity, water levels, and the functioning of tourism. The positive and negative effects of climate change vary according to the destination and the services it offers. Destinations should minimize the existing risks and try to take the necessary plans and policies in this direction. These priorities are to create economically, socially, and environmentally sustainable opportunities. Making use of sustainable opportunities is possible with a strong adaptation and coordination process to climate change (UNWTO, 2008).

Certification Systems in Sustainable Tourism

It is seen that the terms monitoring, control, licensing, and voluntary certification are used among the sustainable tourism tools offered by the United Nations Environment Program and the World Tourism Organization in order to carry out sustainable tourism principles in a healthy way (UNEP/WTO, 2005). In the development plans specific to Turkey, sustainability goals in tourism and the repetition of these goals in the Turkish Tourism Strategy, the determination of standards for them and the establishment of measurement and monitoring systems are included (Ministry of Culture and Tourism, 2007). At this point, one of the main ways used to actively support, fulfill, and follow sustainability studies in the tourism industry is "certification".

The systems and processes in which these functions of certification are carried out are multilateral. Key players of certification: The supporting body that is the entrepreneur and financier of the program, the awarding body that is the program executive, the verification body that creates the criteria and inspects the businesses accordingly, the applicant business that wants to have a certificate and the tourism market that is expected to recognize and approve this business and the certificate program (Font, 2002).

Although most of the tourism certification programs are based on voluntary membership, the application varies in terms of scope and quality. One of the groupings made in this field in the literature is the grouping made according to the certification program executive. Considering the ISO, environmental labeling programs classification, the programs are divided into two according to the executive. If the executive is also the enforcer, this defines first-party environmental labeling programs. Here, a business implements its own environmental sustainability program. If the executive is an organization other than the implementer, that is, the enterprise, these third-party environmental labeling programs are defined (Kından, 2006).

The Importance of Certification in the Tourism Industry

The place and importance of the certification system in the tourism industry: It is possible to evaluate it in terms of sustainable tourism, international dependency principle, marketing and tourists. The importance of sustainable tourism should be evaluated through mass tourism. As a matter of fact, there is a high number of accommodation supply and demand in mass tourism. On average, half of the total number of tourists coming to developing countries such as Turkey consists of tourists who take part in mass tourism activities, especially in the summer season. Despite this feature, unless the necessary control and monitoring mechanisms are established, economic, sociocultural and environmental sustainability related to mass tourism can be mentioned. Negative effects of mass tourism through sustainable tourism certification: It can be monitored by third-party independent observers at the scale of the enterprise, eliminated or minimized with the control mechanism to be provided. Thus, this touristic activity, which is important in terms of employment and tourist potential, becomes sustainable and supportable by all parties affected by it, especially the environment and local society. In terms of governments, measures are taken in areas of struggle such as health, safety, environment, and social stability in a certified industry without government tools being involved. A hotel that carries out concrete activities related to local development, which is guaranteed through certification, is more accepted in the society than a hotel business that hosts a tourist who does not go out of the hotel with an all-inclusive system and is only interested in the money he earns from it. Thus, the industry rises to an advantageous position for local stakeholders (Poser, 2009).

Certification, which offers marketing and effective/efficient management assistance in terms of business and destination, also provides different advantages for tourists. It is very easy for tourists to access environmentally friendly travel options within certification programs, especially through online systems. Environmentally sensitive tourists gain confidence that the tour operator, destination, or accommodation they choose is truly environmentally friendly. Terms such as permanent guest, customer loyalty, network marketing refer to important marketing elements, especially in terms of medium-term profitability of accommodation businesses. As a result of the marketing activities before the season, the guest attracted to the establishment, if he is satisfied with the service he receives, he is likely to choose the same business on his next trip without the need for too many marketing people. In this way, it is possible to provide customer loyalty and continuous guests by creating customer satisfaction. Studies on accommodation businesses where certification systems are applied show that the eco-label of a business affects post-travel satisfaction rather than its effect on pre-travel decisions (Seyhan & Yılmaz, 2010).

In a study conducted in Spain, customer satisfaction was compared in hotels that have ISO 14001 certification and those that do not. While doing this, the guest evaluation scores on the web pages of the hotels and on the website of "booking.com", a world popular online reservation system and travel advice/evaluation platform, were used as data (Signes et al., 2014).

According to the 2014 Annual Report of the World Tourism Organization, guest reviews and hotel classes have decisive roles in the pre-travel search process. Hotel classes act as a pre-search filter, while guest reviews play a key role in final decisions. In this context, it is planned to integrate guest evaluations into the hotel classification system with the "QualitMark Norway" program, an application that is planned to be implemented in Norway (UNWTO, 2015). If this situation is considered together with the positive effect of certification on continuous guest and network marketing, it can be said that certification will constitute an important component among the determining factors of quality in the future.

Among the first examples of the certification system in Turkish tourism, in a campaign that started to be implemented by the Ministry of Culture and Tourism in 1993, the "Environmentally Friendly Organization Certificate and Plaque" was given to the enterprises as a result of the evaluation made in order to create environmental awareness in enterprises and to contribute to environmental protection. Within the scope of the program, which is also known as PINE-CHIP-YUNUS, the plaques given for yacht operators have the symbols of "Dolphin", the plaques given for marinas have the symbols "Anchor", and the plaques given to accommodation and catering establishments have the symbols of "Pine". With the "Green Star" certificate coming into effect in 2008, the PINE-CHIP-YUNUS program came to an end (Official Gazette, September 22, 2008). In the same period, the Blue Flag application, which is an international certificate, came into force in Turkey in 1993. The Blue Flag, an international environmental award given to beaches, marinas, and yachts that meet the necessary criteria, is run by the Turkish Environment and Education Foundation (TÜRÇEV) (Blue Flag, 2016; Özçoban, 2012). In addition to these, the White Star Project, which was put into practice by the Turkish Hoteliers Federation (TÜROFED) in 2008, and the "Greening Hotels" project, which was initiated in 2009 under the leadership of the Turkish Hoteliers Association (TUROB), are other certificate programs implemented in Turkey.

Green Tourism Certificate System

According to the Minister of Culture and Tourism Mehmet Nuri Ersoy, within the scope of the changes in the law numbered 2634, all hotels will be certified by the Ministry until the end of July, and a single standard system will be adopted. He also stated that the Safe Tourism Certification will be converted into a Green Tourism Certification by the end of the year (CNN Türk News, 2022).

He emphasized that they implemented the "Safe Tourism Certificate" program during the COVID-19 epidemic and achieved a high degree of success due to very good inspection. Emphasizing that the certification program is an example to the world, the Minister stated that the Paris Agreement was signed in 2021, and now the issues that the world should consider jointly are sustainability and green (space). Therefore, it is planned to move to the second stage of the certification system. Until the end of 2022, the relevant rules and implementation methods will be determined and the name of the certificate will be changed from "Safe Tourism Certificate" to "Safe and Green Tourism Certificate" by 2023.

Pointing out that there are sustainable and environmentally friendly facilities under the Ministry of Culture and Tourism, Minister Ersoy stated that the number of these facilities has reached 451. Ersoy stated that the facilities in Turkey will be subject to certification on a facility, region and country basis gradually and said, "The 2023, 2025 and 2030 targets include these. If the needs are determined, an extra financing for them, if necessary for transformation, they will meet with the Treasury and the Ministry, and they will be informed about it. ...We will prepare packages, but at the moment, a certain part of our facilities are ready for this. We will prepare a certain part of them gradually" (Anadolu Agency, 2022).

In order to establish the strategy regarding the certificate, a 3-year protocol was signed as the Ministry with the Global Sustainable Tourism Council (CSTC), which is the highest specialized authority in the world. Certificate details were shared with industry representatives. By the end of the year, the certification will be ready and implemented. Reminding that Turkey signed the Paris Convention last year, Ersoy stated that the sectors also have commitments to fulfill as a country and a region as per this contract.

In order to be the preferred country and the preferred destination in the tourism of the future, it is essential to complete the certified criteria related to sustainability. If the relevant criteria are not met and the costs are not incurred, the countries exporting passengers to Turkey will have a tax return. This phased system needs to be established. According to CSTC's discourse, Turkey is the first country in the world to coordinate this work on a state basis. Turkey will be the first country to reach these criteria (Ministry of Culture and Tourism, 2022).

Conclusion

The tourism sector is a sector that can be a tool for the protection of environmental and cultural heritage when implemented in a responsible and sustainable framework. However, the way tourism is implemented needs to be managed. A balance must be struck between its economic, social, cultural, and environmental impacts. Conservation of biological diversity, protection of natural and cultural heritage, protection of living human treasures, and respect for society are the main objectives of sustainable tourism policy. Visitors are now focused on green tourism. For example, if the hotel has waste water management, the relevant destinations are more preferred. Climate change adaptation programs are prepared by the Ministry of Culture and Tourism. Turkey is the third country with the most blue flag beaches in the world.

The first country in the world to implement the green tourism certification system is Turkey. It is a system similar to the secure certificate system applied in tourism facilities. In Turkey, 4–5 star hotels are obliged to switch to this system. Businesses, if they implement their own environmental policies, they make membership in and compliance with certificate programs much easier.

Certification, on the other hand, can provide companies with brand, standardization, and reliability elements in terms of marketing in an intensely competitive environment. In addition, through membership in these programs, businesses can achieve significant savings in energy expense items and establish the necessary performance monitoring mechanisms through periodic reporting. Faster results can be obtained if the studies in line with the goal of economic, social, and cultural sustainability of tourism, which is among the items in the Turkish Tourism Strategy and 10th Development Plan, are supported by current and future certification programs in the industry. While doing this, the integration of existing national certificate programs into international accreditation mechanisms will contribute to the recognition and reliability of these programs. Certification programs carried out by nongovernmental organizations (NGOs) will be at least technically supported by official institutions, which will be effective in the professionalization of these organizations. In this direction, the Ministry of Culture and Tourism can provide supervisory personnel support. Establishing more effective economic incentive mechanisms, especially in programs run by the state, will increase the demand for these programs (Satar & Güneş, 2017).

References

Amelung, B., Nicholls, S., & ve Viner, D. (2007). Implications of global climate change for tourism flows and seasonality. *Journal of Travel Research*, *45*(3), 285–296.

Anadolu Ajansı. (2022). https://www.aa.com.tr/tr/kultur-sanat/kultur-ve-turizm-bakani-ersoy-sertifikamizin-adini-guvenli-ve-yesil-turizm-sertifikasi-olarak-degistirecegiz/2473602. Accessed on April 20, 2022.

Arıkan, Y., & Özsoy, G. (2008). *A'dan Z'ye İklim Değişikliği Başucu Rehberi*. REC Türkiye.

Aydemir, B., & ve Şenerol, H. (2014). İklim Değişikliği ve Türkiye Turizmine Etkileri: Delfi Anket Yönetimiyle Yapılan Bir Uygulama Çalışması. *Balıkesir Sosyal Bilimler Enstitüsü Dergisi*, 381–416.

Başdemir, H. Y. (2008). Küresel ısınma ve çevre ahlakı. F. Kayadibi (Yay. haz.), *in Uluslararası çevre ve din sempozvum*. Yalın yayıncılık.

Bayazıt, S. (2018). İklim Değişikliği ve Turizm İlişkisinin Türkiye İç Turizmi Açısından İncelenmesi. *Anatolia: Turizm Araştırmaları Dergisi*, 221–231.

Blue Flag. (2016). First Blue Flag Beaches in Asia — Blue Flag. Accessed on March 11, 2024.

CNN Türk Haber. (2022). *Oteller tek belgeli ve yeşil sertifikalı olacak*. https://www. cnnturk.com/ekonomi/oteller-tek-belgeli-ve-yesil-sertifikali-olacak#:~:text=K% C3%BClt%C3%BCr%20ve%20Turizm%20Bakan%C4%B1%20Mehmet,Sertifikas %C4%B1'na%20d%C3%B6n%C3%BC%C5%9Ft%C3%BCr%C3%BClm%C3% BC%C5%9F%20olaca%C4%9F%C4%B1n%C4%B1%20a%C3%A7%C4%B1klad %C4%B1. Accessed on April 20, 2022.

Corobov, R. (2007). Climate change and Moldova's tourism: Some indirect consequences. In B. Amelung, K. Blazejczyk, & A. Matzarakis (Eds.), *İçinde climate change and tourism – Assessment and coping strategies* (pp. 173–189), Maastricht – Warsaw –Freiburg.

Font, X. (2002). Environmental certification in tourism and hospitality: Progress, process and prospects. *Tourism Management, 23*(3), 197–205. https://doi.org/10. 1016/S0261-5177(01)00084-X

Giles, A. R., & Perry, A. H. (1988). The use of temporal analogue to investigate the possible impact of projected global warming on the UK tourist industry. *Tourism Management, 19*(1), 75–80.

Grillakis, M. G., Koutroulis, A. G., Seiradakis, K. D., & Tsanis, I. K. (2016). Implications of 20 C global warming in European summer tourism. *Climate Services, 1*, 30–38.

Güçlü, Y. (2010). Doğu Karadeniz Bölümü Kıyı Kuşağında İklim Konforu Şartlarının Kıyı Turizmi Yönünden İncelenmesi. *Coğrafi Bilimler Dergisi, 8*(2), 111–136. https://doi.org/10.1501/Cogbil_0000000108

İncecik, S. (2007). İnsan Kaynaklı İklim Değişimi ve Türkiye. *1. Türkiye İklim Değişikliği Kongresi, 11–13 Nisan.* İTÜ.

Kadıoğlu, M. (2008). Küresel İklim Değişimi ve Etik. *TMMOB İklim Değişimi Sempozyumu, 13–14 Mart, 2008 Ankara* (s. 393–424).

Karadeniz, C. B., Sarı, S., & ve Çağlayan, A. B. (2018). İklim Değişikliğinin Doğu Karadeniz Turizmine Olası Etkileri. *1. Uluslararası Eğitim ve Sosyal Bilimlerde Yeni Ufuklar Kongresi Bildiriler Kitabı, İstanbul.*

Karakaya, E., & ve Özçağ, M. (2004). Sürdürülebilir Kalkınma ve İklim Değişikliği: Uygulanabilecek İktisadi Araçların Analizi. *Kırgızistan-Türkiye Manas Üniversitesi I. Maliye Konferansı, Geçiş Ekonomilerinde Mali Politikalar.*

Kından, A. (2006). *Bir Eko-Etiket Olarak Mavi Bayrak'ın Türkiye Kıyı Turizminde Bir Pazarlama Unsuru Olabilirliğinin Araştırılması.* Yayımlanmamış Yüksek Lisans Tezi, Ankara Üniversitesi Sosyal Bilimler Enstitüsü.

Kozak, N. (2014). *Turizm Pazarlaması.* Detay Yayıncılık.

Kültür ve Turizm Bakanlığı, Ankara. (2007). *Türkiye Turizm Stratejisi 2023: Eylem Planı 2007–2013.* T.C. Kültür ve Turizm Bakanlığı Yayınları.

Kültür ve Turizm Bakanlığı, Ankara. (2022). https://basin.ktb.gov.tr/TR-317124/ kultur-ve-turizm-bakani-ersoy-antalya39da.html. Accessed on April 20, 2022.

Lemieux, C., & Scott, D. (2010). Weather and climate information for tourism. *Procedia Environmental Sciences*, 146–147.

Levin, K., Cashore, B., Bernstein, S., & Auld, G. (2012). Overcoming the tragedy of super wicked problems: Constraining our future selves to ameliorate global climate change. *Policy Sciences, 45*(2), 123–152.

Olalı, H., & Timur, A. (1988). *Turizm Ekonomisi.* Ofis Ticaret Matbaacılık.

Özçoban, E. (2012). *Yeşil Yıldız: Turizm endüstrisinde bir sosyal sorumluluk örneği.* Orion Kitabevi.

Özgüç, N. (2007). *Turizm coğrafyası* (5. baskı). Çantay Kitabevi.

Poser, E. A. (2009). *Setting standards for sustainable tourism: An analysis of US tourism certification programs.* Yayımlanmamış Yüksek Lisans Tezi, Duke University.

Satar, İ., & Güneş, G. (2017). Turizm Sertifikasyonu: Ankara Radisson Blu Otel'de Örnek Uygulama. *Ankara Üniversitesi Sosyal Bilimler Dergisi, 8*(2). https://doi.org/ 10.1501/sbeder_0000000139. Accessed on April 20, 2022.

Schurer, A. P., Hegerl, G. C., & Obrochta, S. P. (2015). Determining the likelihood of pauses and surges in global warming. *Geophysical Research Letters, 42*(14), 5974–5982. https://doi.org/10.1002/2015GL064458. Accessed on April 20, 2022.

Scott, D. (2003). Climate change and tourism in the mountain regions of North America. In *1st international conference on climate change and tourism* (pp. 9–11).

Sevim, B., & Zeydan, Ö. (2007). İklim Değişikliğinin Türkiye Turizmine Etkileri. *Çeşme Ulusal Turizm Sempozyumu, 21–23 Kasım, Çeşme, İzmir.*

Seyhan, G., & Yılmaz, B. (2010). Sürdürülebilir Turizm Kapsamında Konaklama İşletmelerinde Yeşil Pazarlama: Calista Luxury Resort hotel. *Dokuz Eylül Üniversitesi İşletme Fakültesi Dergisi, 11*(1), 51–74. https://dergipark.org.tr/tr/pub/ifede/issue/25421/268211

Signes, A. P., Ona, M. V. S., Verma, R., Jimenez, J. M., & Vargas, M. V. (2014). The impact of environmental Certificationo hotel guest ratings. *Cornell Hospitality Quarterly, 55*(1), 40–51.

Solomon, S., Qin, D., Manning, M., Averyt, K., Marquis, M., & Tignor, M. M. (Eds.). (2007). *Climate change 2007-the physical science basis: Working group I contribution to the fourth assessment report of the IPCC* (Vol. 4). Cambridge University Press.

Türkeş, M. (2008). Küresel iklim değişikliği nedir? Temel kavramlar, nedenleri, gözlenen ve öngörülen değişiklikler. *İklim Değişikliği ve Çevre, 1,* 45–64.

UNEP/WTO. (2005). *Making tourism more sustainable: A Guide for policy makers.* https://wedocs.unep.org/20.500.11822/8741. Accessed on April 20, 2022.

UNFCCC. (1992). *United nations framework convention on climate change.* https://unfccc.int/. Accessed on April 20, 2022.

United Nations (UN). (1992). *United nations framework convention on climate change (UNFCCC Report No. GE.05-62220 (E) 200705).* United Nations Framework Convention on Climate Change. https://unfccc.int/resource/docs/convkp/conveng.pdf. Accessed 2004.2022.

UNWTO. (2015). *UNWTO annual report 2014.* https://www.unwto.org/archive/global/annualreport2014. Accessed on April 20, 2022.

Uysal, Y. (2022). İklim değişikliği ve küresel ısınma ile mücadelede yerel yönetimlerin rolü: Tespitler ve öneriler. *Kesit Akademi Dergisi, 8*(30), 324–354.

Viner, D., & Agnew, M. (1999). *Climate change and its impact on tourism.* http://awsassets.panda.org/downloads/tourism_and_cc_full.pdf. Accessed on April 15, 2022.

World Tourism Organization. (2008). *Climate change and tourism responding to global Challenges.* UNWTO.

Chapter 14

Transforming Women's Role for the Opportunity in Tourism

Priya Sodani (Choudhary) and Shruti Arora

University of Kota, India

Abstract

Tourism is considered to be one of the fastest growing industries with huge potential for economic development and economic reform, especially in developing countries. It directly contributes in the economy not only by earning foreign exchange but also makes a direct contribution through multiplier effect. Diversified tourism methods that promote employment opportunities and business practices provide new innovations and methods to meet the diverse needs of tourists in domestic and international markets. The contribution of women in the global business world has increased in recent years, especially in the hospitality and tourism industry. Their contributions are not only restricted as employees but also equally in business and entrepreneurship. These women have become major actors in the tourism entrepreneurial arena despite facing inequality in a perceived male-dominated environment. In the tourism industry, the proportion of women working in the industry is high, but their roles are mainly engaged in unskilled, low-paid jobs. This chapter will emphasize the opportunities for women in the tourism industry. A brief discussion on the various challenges women face, mainly in terms of a lack of appropriate training and education within the tourism industry sector that might adequately support their business ventures, as well as in relation to lacking sufficient access to finance for their business(es), is provided in this chapter. Significant and rapid measures are needed to support the tourism industry; henceforth, this chapter will also focus on the significant policies and strategies adopted by government and private players to change the role of women in this industry.

Keywords: Tourism industry; women; entrepreneurship; government and private player; low-paid jobs

Strategic Tourism Planning for Communities, 211–220
Copyright © 2024 Priya Sodani (Choudhary) and Shruti Arora
Published under exclusive licence by Emerald Publishing Limited
doi:10.1108/978-1-83549-015-020241017

Introduction

Tourism is one of the world's biggest and fastest developing industries. In many nations, tourism, entrepreneurship, and education are booming sectors of the 21st century. These sectors don't seem to be only better for individual boom but also for development of the whole nation. In many nations, it acts as an engine for improvement via foreign exchange earnings and therefore the creation of direct and indirect employment. Tourism contributes 5% of the world's GDP and 7% of jobs worldwide (Ramchurjee, 2011). It accounts for 6% of the world's exports and 30% of the world's exports in services. In developing countries, tourism generates 45% of the entire exports in services (United Nations World Tourism Organization [UNWTO]).

Tourism has since long been considered a leisure activity. The principal reason of tourism has been to seek solace from the busy and hefty schedule of city lifestyle and spend some leisure time for self-improvement. Further, the governments and policymakers started to perceive the economic benefits from the development of tourism, when the number of tourists started to grow. The monetary benefit is especially due to the foreign exchange earnings brought in by the overseas tourists and the consumption expenditure made through the domestic vacationers. Thus, as the tourism enterprise flourished, the economic system began to gain the monetary blessings and the externalities, including infrastructure improvement, improvement of allied industries, employment opportunities, related to it. September 27 is celebrated as World Tourism Day across the world. Since the 1980s, the UNWTO has observed the day to boost awareness on the role of tourism within the global community and the way it affects social, political, and cultural values worldwide. Over the past decades, international tourists have gone from 25 million international arrivals in 1950 to over 1.3 billion in 2017. UNWTO forecasts that the sector is expected to continue growing 3.3% annually until 2030, a year in which 1.8 billion tourists will cross borders (UNWTO, 2023). Similarly, revenue earned by tourist destinations from across the world has grown from 2 billion US dollars within the 1950s to 1,260 trillion in 2015. The sector also contributes around 10% of the world's GDP and 1 in 10 jobs globally.

The Draft Tourism Policy 1997 sees the emergence of tourism as a very important instrument for sustainable human development including poverty alleviation, employment generation, environment regeneration, and advancement of women.

Tourism has proven its ability for creating jobs and encouraging income-generating activities to benefit local groups in destination areas. But less attention has been paid to the unequal methods in which the benefits of tourism are dispensed between men and women, particularly in the growing world. The tourism sector certainly provides numerous access factors for women's employment and possibilities for developing self-employment in small- and medium-sized income-generating activities, thus developing paths toward the elimination of poverty of women and nearby communities in developing countries.

Objective of the Study

The study revolves around broad objectives: The first aim is to provide the readers a basic knowledge of the position of women in the tourism industry. Then, the work tries to outline the issues and challenges faced by the women workforce in the tourism industry and the role played by government and other private players to promote women group of workers. This chapter will also provide few suggestive mechanisms with the aid of which the tourism industry can make a contribution greater in the direction of reaching gender equity.

Methodology Adopted

This work is designed as a conceptual paper that takes its cues from the desk overview of both online and offline materials. Numerous articles in reputed journals have been first searched through Google and other online resources. Tourism, Women Empowerment, and Gender had been used as the keywords to extract the resources. Further, many websites of various government and nongovernment agencies have been accessed to trace out any policy measures related to this topic. Offline sources like books, notes, and publications had been collected and ultimately were assimilated to draw the logical structure of the chapter. The thematic content analysis was implemented to derive particular information from vast records.

Literature Review

The Fifth Sustainable Development Goal is to "achieve gender equality and empower all women and girls," and UNWTO, a specialized UN body in the field of tourism, is dedicated to strengthening the positive impact of tourist development on women's lives. For women, the travel and tourism industries offer distinctive job prospects. A woman is typically felt in the tourism industry, acting as an air hostess on flights only. When the tourism industry was just getting started in the early 1970s, it was believed that there were very few positions in this sector that were suited for women. But today, she is everywhere from Ministers for Tourism in Several States, Bureaucrats in Ministries of Tourism in the Governments, Chairpersons and Managing Directors, managing big hotels, marketing aviation business, managing travel and visa Services, planning executing holiday packages, etc. It is amazing to note that several Indian women are heading key positions in various tourism sectors in other countries also (Krishna Kumari, 2014). But Alrwajfah et al. (2020) determined a set of challenges varied between social stigma for women participation in the tourism sector, difficulty balancing between working requirements and family needs, and the lack of education for females in the requirements of the tourism sector. With an empirical investigation pertaining to roughly 90 developing nations, Amin and Islam (2014) affirm that women typically manage businesses in the service sector, particularly in the retail rather than the wholesale sector. Additionally, businesses run by women typically have a small staff and are located in towns with a tiny population. Women have an advantage when dealing with tourism-related activities since they are seen as being understanding and soft-spoken, which could help to empower women and raise their economic status (Abou-Shouk et al., 2021). Dabrowski et al. (2019) assert that empowered women can contribute to sustainable tourism development through their capacity to make decisions on real estate, company planning, and other business-related matters. Tourism involves duties that are primarily performed by women as part of their everyday routines, including guiding, giving lodging, and providing food. Women are therefore deemed to do these tasks better (Lama, 2000). Additionally, most parts of the world only engage in tourism on a part-time basis. Because of the nature of the work, ladies who finish their housework can engage in leisurely tourism-related activities. Women are said to engage with nature more frequently than males since they are always gathering food and fodder and caring for the house's grounds (Scheyvens, 2000). Attempts to increase the number of women working in the tourism sector frequently result in groundbreaking innovations. Women are reshaping tourism for the better in a variety of ways, including by giving women more possibilities for employment, coaching the next generation of female leaders, and recognizing women's historical contributions to create more respect. Women are therefore more sympathetic to nature than men. But moving on to issues facing women in the tourism industry, sexual exploitation of women there seems to be a key issue (Jeffrey et al., 2020). Women are more likely to experience harassment when working part time, seasonally, casually, or for low pay in the tourism industry. Furthermore, poverty forced women to accept these occupations in the tourism industry, which puts them in danger, particularly if they are the breadwinners and in desperate need of money, food, or any other necessities (Jeffrey et al., 2020). Because of their established social customs, women participate in tourism to a greater extent in other Asian nations than in India. Women are likely to perceive tourism differently according to their positions in their respective sociocultural and socioeconomic surroundings, Apostrolopoulos et al. (2001, pp. 235–237) found. This is especially true in developing nations. They contend that women are exploited by the patriarchal tendencies of global capitalism and that both tourists and tour operators live in a world that is gendered, with varied effects on tourism depending on the environment in which each gender is present. No industry has a profession that a woman cannot flourish in, but we must acknowledge that there is still a gender gap in the tourism sector. For women, rural areas, and other historically marginalized populations, tourism has been a tool for integration, empowerment, and income generation. Another important pillar for the preservation of our natural and cultural heritage is tourism. Tourism can support the advancement of equality on a local, national, and international level with careful planning and the incorporation of strong gender perspectives.

Women's Role in Tourism

Women around the world have achieved higher levels of education than ever before and today constitute greater than 40% of the worldwide workforce. Yet, their percentage of management positions remains unacceptably low, with just a tiny proportion succeeding in breaking through the "glass ceiling". There are various interconnected factors which help to keep gender segregation of the labor market. Among them are gender stereotyping, traditional gender roles, and gender identity – women are visible as being suitable for certain occupations and they see themselves as suitable. In addition, traditional gender roles assign to women the main duties for raising children, caring for the elderly, and doing household jobs. Thus, women are often forced to select casual labor, part-time, and seasonal employment. Tourism offers both opportunities and challenges for gender equality and women's empowerment. The contribution of women in the business world has elevated in recent years, even though women are underrepresented in management and leadership. In the tourism industry, the share of women who work in the industry is excessive; however, their function is dominated by unskilled, low-paid jobs. The tourism sector definitely provides numerous access factors for women's employment and possibilities for developing self-employment in small- and medium-sized income-generating activities. Tourism presents an extensive range of income generation opportunities for women in both formal and informal employment. Tourism jobs are very flexible and can be carried out at numerous different locations such as the workplace, community, and household. Moreover, tourism creates a wide range of possibilities for women through the complex value chains it creates in the destination economy.

Gender stereotyping and discrimination mean that women specially tend to perform jobs such as cooking, cleaning, and hospitality. A good amount of tourism employment is seasonal and fluctuates according to the changing nature of the industry. If a strong gender attitude is integrated into planning and implementation procedures, tourism can be harnessed as a vehicle for promoting gender equality and women's empowerment at the family, community, national, and worldwide level. At the same time, more gender equality will contribute to the overall quality of the tourist experience, with a considerable impact on profitability and quality across all aspects of the industry.

But there are some situations under which this potential may be used more effectively. This requires collaboration of all stakeholders – governments and intergovernmental bodies, local government, industry, trade unions, local groups and their different member groups, nongovernmental organization (NGOs), etc. The increase of using tourism's ability while safeguarding the natural surroundings and cultural heritage and increasing social and financial justice should be the intention of further tourism development.

Apart from direct employment through tourism, women are also indirectly engaged in tourism-associated activities. In an indirect manner, tourism-associated activities like in hotels, restaurants, cafeterias, small and medium enterprises (SMEs), various household businesses, tea stalls, travels, handlooms and handicraft, etc., they are employed and have occupied a substantive position worldwide. Even in seasonal homes (homestays), the participation is noticeable. Tourism is a service-oriented, labor-intensive, and multi-dimensional area that is related with many other sectors of the economy like transportation, hotels, restaurants, travels and tour businesses, seasonal home (homestay), etc., and offers a larger opportunity for employment. Therefore, there is wide scope for women's empowerment in each, formal and informal sectors of tourism industry. The tourism industry is pivotal in its capacity to promote gender equality and the empowerment of women worldwide. The pandemic's impact on hospitality, travel, leisure, and all associated sectors has presented the industry a completely unique possibility to assess the significance of diversity and representation in both its workforce and patron demographics. Now more than ever, journey ventures throughout genres and geographies are well-placed to rethink internal frameworks and service offerings as a way to serve to bridge the gender gap. According to a study launched in 2021 by the UNWTO which spans four global regions – Africa, Asia, and the Pacific, Latin America and the Caribbean, and Europe – and four key tourism industries – digital platforms and technology, hotels and accommodation, tour operators, and community-based tourism: women presently constitute 54% of people employed in tourism (Global Report on Women in Tourism Second Edition, October 12, 2023), 27% of tourism ministers, and 20% of government ministers.

Issues and Challenges

Women are, by default, at a drawback when accepting the chance of entrepreneurship, simply due to the fact that they could lack the important resources in terms of financial resources, networks, and the management expertise to begin their very own business. Beyond this, in a developing country context, women have a tendency encounter challenge referring to employment, including pressures within the workplace, struggles to stabilize all the elements of the existence of a homemaker who works, and in relation to the general status of unemployment as experienced within the country wherein they reside.

Women workforce faces many obstacles. The first impediment is being a female. The second one is the type of business (in tourism) linked to restaurants or businesses that offer the possibility of meeting many people. The third is when women want to broaden their businesses in places dominated by large international tourism firms.

Tourism as a sector offers women massive alternatives for entrepreneurship that do not require heavy start-up financing. However, women continue to face challenges with limited or no access to security, finance and markets to start or grow tourism businesses. Women's tourism entrepreneurship is also held back by a lack of access to technology, information, business skills, education, and training. In order to develop sustainably, the tourism industry needs to make certain equal participation of women in the tourism development process. However, many challenges hinder the way for women as they march forward. Some of those challenging situations are highlighted below:

• Women literacy stands as one of the largest challenges in ensuring women empowerment. Many women don't get to finish their education necessary for obtaining jobs as they have to take care of the family or due to the fact that they get married.

- Gender stereotypes are nevertheless common in developing countries wherein women are considered not fit for many jobs.
- Pay gaps are a common phenomenon in which women are paid less for the equal post of job or for the identical work performed than men. This stands as a tremendous impediment in the direction of development.
- Lack of support by male counterparts is one of the major factors which hinder the growth of women in the tourism industry.
- Orthodox and conventional mentality, e.g., women in the house should not have interaction with tourists and strangers, are very common. Eliminating such misconceptions could be a great challenge for policymakers.
- Religion-based issues for women, that is thinking about a woman impure while she is having her periods and not permitting to work during those days, need due consideration.

Government and Private Players Push for Women Empowerment in Tourism

The policies best geared toward increasing women's employment in travel and tourism are those that support employment in the sector by encouraging women to join the labor force and through addressing inequalities at the workplace.

To facilitate women ought participation within the labor force and to deal with inequalities in employment, countries and organizations to undertake family-friendly policies and conditions, increase the representation of women in decision-making positions, eliminate discriminatory salary gaps and pay attention to women from disadvantaged minority groups. Within the workplace specifically, this action can require setting company-wide goals and the measuring and monitoring of progress. Strengthening company regulations in this regard is a must.

The most effective policies are those that:

- Improve women's access to high satisfactory jobs and promote equal access to opportunities.
- Promote women's education and training.
- Ensure women earn similar to men for comparable work.
- Promote women's leadership.
- Provide attractive childcare, tax, social benefits, maternity protection, and incentives to return to work.
- Increase flexible work arrangements.
- Combat unconscious bias.
- Inform/educate employers about the benefits of employing women.
- Promote women's entrepreneurship and facilitate the identical access to start-up grants.

To ensure women are empowered, the government of India plays important roles to enable their welfare in various sectors. Whether it's providing free cooking gas and education schemes or enabling women to leverage technology, some of the schemes have been launched in recent years to empower women to be independent in their lives. Some of the schemes are:

Mahila-E-Haat

Under the purview of the Ministry of Women and Child Development, the government launched Mahila-E-Haat in 2016. It is a bilingual online marketing platform that leverages technology to assist aspiring women entrepreneurs, self-help groups (SHGs), and NGOs to showcase their products and services.

Mahila Shakti Kendra

The government launched the Mahila Shakti Kendra in 2017 to empower rural women with opportunities for skill development, employment, digital literacy, health, and nutrition. The Mahila Shakti Kendras will run through community engagement through student volunteers' most backward districts. Each Mahila Shakti Kendra will provide an interface for rural women to approach the government to avail of their entitlements through training and capacity building. It works at the national, state, district, and block levels.

Support to Training and Employment Program (STEP) for Women

The STEP scheme was founded to provide skills to women in order that they will take up gainful employment. It also provides the correct competencies and training for women to become entrepreneurs. Open to every woman above the age of 16, it is run through a grant given to an institution/organization including NGOs directly. According to the Ministry website, the help under STEP Scheme is going to be available in any sector for imparting skills associated with employability and entrepreneurship, including but not limited to the agriculture, horticulture, food processing, handlooms, tailoring, stitching, embroidery, zari, handicrafts, computers, and IT-enabled services together with soft skills and skills for the workplace, such as spoken English, gems and jewellery, travel and tourism, and hospitality.

The Government of India's Ministry of Tourism runs a variety of programs for Indian entrepreneurs and citizens working within the tourism industry, including: capacity building for service providers (institutes), hotel accommodation, marketing development assistance (MDA), motels accommodation, public relation and marketing, Rahul Sankrityayan Paryatan Puraskar Yojna, refresher courses for regional level guides, stand-alone restaurants, tented accommodation, timeshare resorts, travel trade. Private players encourage women to take part in the active travel and tourism industry by way of ensuring that equal opportunities are provided to both men and women. In fact, a lot of leading positions in the company are held by women. Women are also encouraged to guide massive group trips.

Conclusion

Women entrepreneurs, women employees, and women travelers alike constitute an extensive and growing segment of the market. Pro-women business models will show to be more resilient, innovative, sustainable, and profitable in the long run. It is, therefore, no surprise that in latest years, reviews surveying tourism have proven that firms are adopting unified strategies to make sure inclusivity and the upliftment of women across operations. We conclude that recognizing the issue of gender discrimination in the labor market is a common issue and should not mean that it is not addressed in tourism discussions. Bringing the necessary adjustments about requires efforts in all sectors. However, the tourism industry seems to be specifically proper for putting in efforts toward the development of women. Because of its size, its fast growth, and its extremely diverse and dynamic nature, the tourism industry has huge flexibility. This could enable the industry to develop key tasks for the advancement of women so that other industries can benefit from initiatives and techniques in the tourism sector as models for their own development.

Women have proven to be the dealers for building capacities of sources in the tourism sector in comparison to men. Hence, it is crucial that the degree of issues faced by women in the tourism sector call for quantification along with the qualitative approach. Since there are no data sources on the actual number of women contributing to the tourism sector in various roles, a proper categorization is lacking. Much needs to be done from the government, agencies, and other associated organizations to uplift women not only in the name of empowerment but in the name of protecting them with social safety mechanisms such as insurance, protection from external harm, and their well-being.

Suggestions

We can encourage women through offering some tourism-related activities and business mainly for females like, hotels, model tea houses, trainings in travels, and providing seasonal home business (homestays) for them/or in the name of women of the home, and licensing of cafeterias for women. Apart from these, the tourism-related workshops, seminars, conferences, and exhibitions should be organized, mainly for women, within nation and later for internation.

To ensure equal participation of women in the tourism industry, many structural changes need to take place. Some of the suggestive mechanisms have been stated below:

- Undertake reforms to provide women equal rights to economic resources like loans, credits, bank services, etc.
- Organize awareness camps to enhance gender equality and women empowerment.
- Providing a better workplace for women and ensuring their safety and security.
- Taking measures to eliminate any form of discrimination against women.

- Taking actions to recognize and value the unpaid work performed by a female workforce and provide remuneration or rewards.
- Motivation and support of the friends and family must be provided for women workforce in the tourism industry.
- Adopting and strengthening of policies as well as enforceable legislations for the promotion of gender equality and the empowerment in the tourism Industry.
- It is not only the duty of the government, but also it is the duty of individual, institutions, organization (both profitable and nonprofitable), SHGs, SMEs, micro financial institutes, banks, and all other stakeholders of tourism to facilitate and encourage women to participate in tourism-related activities. Finally, it may be emphasized that the women themselves have to come forward and make it as a major and alternative means of livelihood.

References

Abou-Shouk, M. A., Mannaa, M. T., & Elbaz, A. M. (2021). Women's empowerment and tourism development: A cross-country study. *Tourism Management Perspectives, 37*, 100782.

Alrwajfah, M. M., Almeida-García, F., & Cortés-Macías, R. (2020). Females' perspectives on tourism's impact and their employment in the sector: The case of Petra, Jordan. *Tourism Management, 78*(1). https://doi.org/10.1016/j.tourman.2019.104069

Amin, M., & Islam, A. (2014). Are there more female managers in the retail sector? Evidence from survey data in developing countries. *Journal of Applied Economics, 17*(2), 213–228.

Apostrolopoulos, Y., Sonmez, S., & Dallen, J. (2001). *Women as producers and consumers of tourism in developing regions.* Greenwood Publishing Group, Inc..

Dabrowski, D., Brzozowska-Woś, M., b-Andrzejak, E. G.Î, & Firgolska, A. (2019). Market orientation and hotel performance: The mediating effect of creative marketing programs. *Journal of Hospitality and Tourism Management, 41*, 175–183.

Jeffrey, H., Eger, C., & Vizcaino, P. (2020). *Tourism and gender-based violence: Challenging inequalities.* CABI Publishing.

Krishna Kumari, J. (2014, September). Woman empowerment through entrepreneurship in service sector with special reference to SHGs in tourism. *Research Paper, 3*(9). ISSN No 2277 – 8160.

Lama, W. B. (2000). Community-based tourism for conservation and women's development. *Tourism and Development in Mountain Regions*, 221–238.

Ramchurjee, N. (2011, December). *"Tourism- A vehicle for women empowerment: Prospects & challenges" department of studies in environmental science.* University of Mysore.

Scheyvens, R. (2000). Promoting women's empowerment through involvement in ecotourism: Experiences from the third world. *Journal of Sustainable Tourism, 8*(3), 232–249.

UNWTO. (2023, October 12). *Global report on women in tourism* (2nd ed.). https://www.e-unwto.org/doi/book/10.18111/9789284420384

UNWTO. (2023, October 13). *'Overtourism'? Understanding and managing urban tourism growth beyond perceptions.* https://www.e-unwto.org/doi/book/10.18111/9789284420070

Chapter 15

Motivation in Community-Based Tourism: Linking Locals to Internationals in Promoting Community Development and Conservation of Natural Resources

Md. Wasiul Islam, Shakil Ahmed and Raisa Tasnim Mahin

Khulna University, Bangladesh

Abstract

Community-based tourism (CBT) is known as a strong strategy and tool to promote community development and conservation of natural resources through its various virtues in both developing and developed economies. Local people's active and functional participation is considered as the focal point in CBT practice and development. However, their functional participation doesn't always come instinctively; rather, it requires proper extrinsic and intrinsic motivation in the form of both tangible and intangible, which ultimately help them to influence their behavior and pursuit of goals that may ensure their participation in CBT and to receive various benefits. These benefits are linked to the sustainability of CBT development including community development. Therefore, strategic CBT planning and its implementation are essential to ensure sustainable CBT which can also safeguard the link between the local community people and their guests as well as other stakeholders including internationals to facilitate local community development. This chapter focuses on various theories and concepts of motivation from various fields of research, and efforts have been taken to apply those in the field of CBT development to explore its optimum potential for the sake of human welfare. Moreover, attempts have been taken to use various CBT initiatives in Bangladesh to relate these theories and concepts to evaluate these initiatives as well as to provide some suggestive measures to improve the performance of CBT and to facilitate more community development as a whole.

Keywords: Community-based tourism; motivation; behavior; local community; development; sustainability; participation; multi-stakeholder

Strategic Tourism Planning for Communities, 221–245
Copyright © 2024 Md. Wasiul Islam, Shakil Ahmed and Raisa Tasnim Mahin
Published under exclusive licence by Emerald Publishing Limited
doi:10.1108/978-1-83549-015-020241018

Introduction

Community-based tourism (CBT) is one of the types of sustainable tourism which promotes the active participation of residents in operating and managing small tourism projects as a means of poverty reduction and offering an alternative source of income generation for local community members. It is a pro-poor strategy in a local community setting that aims to facilitate respect for local cultures, norms, traditions as well as natural heritage (SNV & University of Hawaii, 2007). In other words, CBT refers to any tourism business or activity that is local community-based which may either be privately owned or managed or operated with the active involvement of local community people. It warrants to develop community linkages and promote responsible tourism practices to consider sociocultural, economic, and environmental sustainability (Giri et al., 2008; Islam, 2010; Islam et al., 2013; Spenceley et al., 2016).

According to the World Bank Enterprise Survey (2013), insufficient access to commercial finance is globally known as one of the most crucial challenges (31% of all challenges) for small and medium enterprises (SMEs). Private sector investment is one of the major drivers of development in the tourism sector which is also recognized as a focal innovator in shaping business partnerships with local communities for tourism development around the world. Joint ventures between local communities and private investors in the tourism sector are recognized as a great contributor in addressing such challenges provided that such ventures are designed and managed properly. Such ventures bring new income, jobs, and know-how directly to residents living in remote areas, as well as create shared responsibility for protecting and conserving cultural and natural resources (WBG & WWF, 2014).

In this regard, various motivations are applicable for establishing and pro-moting such joint ventures and partnerships. However, a single partnership model is not appropriate in all cases to develop a commercially attractive tourism business which warrants various models of partnerships with varying interests and motivations of different stakeholders starting from local communities to inter-national donors where government and nongovernmental organizations (NGOs) can play important roles. Such commercially attractive business is the major incentive for the private sector (WBG & WWF, 2014). There are many areas of CBT where such motivations play crucial roles in contributing to community development as well as conserving the natural resources of a destination.

Considering the importance of motivation in CBT, this chapter focuses on the application of various theories and concepts of motivation in CBT development to explore its optimum potential for human welfare, particularly in community development and conservation of natural resources. Moreover, various CBT initiatives in Bangladesh have been discussed to relate with these motivation theories and concepts so that community development and the conservation of natural resources of the destination might be facilitated.

Motivation for CBT

The word "motivation" is derived from the word "motive," which means needs/desires/wants/drives within the individuals. More specifically, motivation is a psychological phenomenon or process which initiates, causes, guides, and maintains/continues/terminates goal-oriented human behaviors at a given time by fulfilling such needs/desires/wants/drives of an individual. Human behavior is goal-oriented where motivation stimulates people to actions to achieve such human behavior. In other words, it is the driving force behind human or other animals' actions to perform some behavior whether to continue or terminate it. As an example, people's behavior may desire for fulfilling some basic physio-logical needs, having resources, job-satisfaction successes, recognition, teamwork, and so on. Therefore, responsible management personnel try to create willingness among their employees by arousing their interests so that they can perform their best according to their capabilities, and hence, the organization can perform outstandingly (Cherry, 2022; MSG, 2022).

There are three major stages of the motivation process (Brown, 2007; Hinds et al., 2010; Seo et al., 2004):

(1) *Activation/direction:* This denotes the decision to initiate an action/behavior. It is a felt need or drive which entangles the biological, emotional, social, and cognitive forces that activate to perform a certain action/behavior in a certain time frame.
(2) *Persistence/continuation:* It means the continued efforts toward achieving the goal. It also involves the factors (also called stimuli in which needs have to be stirred) that direct and maintain these goal-directed actions (though such motives are rarely directly observable). As a result, we often have to infer the reasons why people do the things that they do based on observable behaviors.
(3) *Intensity/efforts:* It is the concentration and vigor to achieve the goal. It is the measure of satisfaction when a specific need/goal is achieved or accomplished.

There are three components of motivation. These are: (i) biological compo-nent, (ii) learned component, and (iii) cognitive component. Any behavior is processed by an interaction of these three components where brain circuits are activated, learned responses are triggered, and control is taken by making plans. In short, these three components of the motivation process are performed by our head, heart, and hand, respectively. The biological component arouses the functions of several chemicals (like hormones), whereas the learned component inspires a rewarding activity which facilitates people to cope with their undesired conditions. On the other hand, the cognitive component focuses various benefits of that particular activity by reducing those undesired conditions. Here, the beliefs, attitudes, values, stereotypes, and behavior of a person influence them to carry out that particular activity (Baldassarre, 2011; Hidi, 2006; Huitt, 2001).

Learning is governed largely by attention, and attention is partially governed by motivational processes. In the attention process, the focus is given to the sensory receptors to sensitize the source of information, analyze (attending), and organize the information. Therefore, learning is dependent on receptors orientation and selective attention which causes deliberate and incidental or passive learning. Associative learning is the interaction or association between stimuli and responses (S-R learning). Habits are developed as a result of repetition of some responses or sequences of responses (Greer, 2016; Thompson et al., 1997; Wasserman & Miller, 1997). Such learning is also influenced by social incentive theory (Killeen, 1981), cognitive dissonance theory (Harmon-Jones & Harmon-Jones, 2012), implicit theories (Dweck, 2012), attribution theory (Kelley & Michela, 1980), locus of control theory (Lefcourt, 2014), Herzberg's two-factor theory (Alshmemri et al., 2017), Maslow's hierarchy of needs (McLeod, 2007), self-determination theory (Deci & Ryan, 2012), and so on.

There are different types of motivation. Motivation may be intrinsic or extrinsic. Intrinsic motivations are resulted from within the individual for their satisfaction, not for getting rewarded by someone. Conversely, extrinsic motivations are resulted from outside of the individual and usually encompass various types of rewards or incentives. However, intrinsic motivation can be influenced by the external environment/rewards. Motivation is not fixed; rather, it is controlled by intrinsic and extrinsic motivational factors. According to self-determination theory, persistent education systems can build intrinsic motivation which is also influenced by surrounding environmental factors and driven by autonomy, competence, and relatedness (Baldassarre, 2011; Deci, 1971; Tranquillo & Stecker, 2016).

Moreover, motivation may be both positive and negative. Positive motivation encourages people to perform their jobs in the best possible manner to improve their job performance and to be rewarded (financial/tangible and nonfinancial/intangible). On the other hand, negative motivation focuses on regulating the negative effects of the job and targets to generate a sense of fear for the employees where people have to suffer for their poor performance. For example, if an employee can't achieve their targeted outputs, they should be punished (Matsumoto & Hikosaka, 2009; Singh, 2022; Usmanovna & Oybekovna, 2018). Some motivations are short term (like eating for satisfying hunger) and some are long term (like getting a promotion for performance).

Psychologists suggest different theories to illuminate what motivates human behavior. There are several key theories of motivation. One of them is the "instinct theory." This theory of motivation implies that human behaviors are motivated by instinct characteristics which are permanent and inborn, i.e., genetically hard-wired behaviors. Several psychologists have proposed various basic human drives that motivate human behaviors. These instincts might include some biological instincts such as seeking, fear, anger, cleanliness, love, panic-grief, care, pleasure, denial, lust/greed, and revenge, which are crucial for an organism's survival (Myers & Smith, 2012; Pianka, 2012).

The drives and needs theory suggests that human being has some basic biological drives to perform a specific behavior which is influenced by the need to fulfill these drives. For example, human behaviors like eating, drinking, and taking rest are motivated by our biological system based on the biological needs for food, water, and take rest. Consequently, human being is motivated to do these certain actions/behaviors like eat, drink, and taking rest (Siegling & Petrides, 2016).

The arousal theory of motivation suggests that individuals are motivated to engage in certain behaviors that assist them to support their optimal level of arousal (Hockenbury & Hockenbury, 2010). An individual with a low level of arousal needs might pursue an activity with a relaxing attitude such as playing football, while individuals with high arousal needs might be motivated to engage in any exciting and thrill-seeking behaviors like hiking in the forests (Cherry, 2022).

It has already been mentioned that motivation is concerned with those processes which can generate goal-directed behaviors. Therefore, the basic elements of the motivation process are (i) motives, (ii) behavior, and (iii) goal (see Fig. 15.1). Motives promote people to perform actions. In other words, motives are the primary stimulants or ways of behavior. These ways can stimulate behavior in many ways. However, they are cognitive variables which are generally subjective and denote the mental feelings of human beings which generally construct a state of disequilibrium, physiological, or psychological imbalance within the individuals, whereas behavior is known as a series of activities which are usually motivated by a desire to achieve a goal. Motives are pointed toward goals which are the ends to deliver the satisfaction of human needs or wants. Achieving a goal facilitates reinstating physiological or psychological balance or equilibrium and helps to reduce human tension (Paper Tyari, 2022).

The Link Between Community Development and CBT

Tourism is one of the world's fastest-growing sectors and a significant source of income for many nations where CBT has been a growing interest as a viable alternative to traditional tourism. It has the potential to benefit our economy, society, and environment and is perceived as a tool for community development by linking poverty alleviation and resource conservation; it helps to pave the way for rural economic development (Islam, 2021; Ruiz-Mallén et al., 2015).

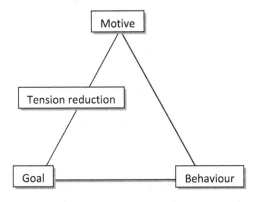

Fig. 15.1.   Motivation Process.

Community development aims to provide individuals and groups with the skills they need to make a positive change in their communities as well as to empower community members and build better and more connected communities. CBT creates jobs and income-earning opportunities for local people, as well as generates funds for infrastructural and socioeconomic development. It offers direct job opportunities such as tour guiding, resource management, cultural performances, and housekeeping, as well as indirect job opportunities in agriculture, transportation, and trade (Mensah & Afenyo, 2022). It intends to boost the well-being of communities by increasing community participation and promoting community control over tourism development (Stem et al., 2003).

Tourism particularly CBT has the capability to contribute to all of the Sustainable Development Goals (SDGs) whether directly or indirectly (Kostoska & Kocarev, 2019), and these goals can be grouped into three pillars of sustainability (Fig. 15.2): economic, environmental, and social (Delli Paoli & Addeo, 2019).

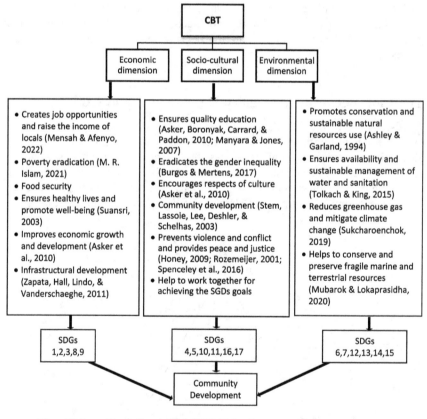

Fig. 15.2.   Contributions of CBT in Community Development Considering Sustainability Dimensions and SDGs.

CBT promotes peaceful coexistence between residents of host communities and strangers, increases recreational and sporting activities, which attracts many tourists to the host communities, and encourages enlightenment, education, and interpersonal relationships, all of which help people develop socially (Mbagwu et al., 2016). CBT is treated as a viable development approach for maximizing socioeconomic benefits while minimizing its negative environmental consequences (Moscardo, 2008; Tolkach & King, 2015).

CBT can enhance local incomes and jobs while also developing skills, institutions, and empowering locals (Ashley & Garland, 1994). It provides an alternate source of income. It has the potential to create jobs and generate entrepreneurial opportunities for people from a variety of backgrounds, skills, and experiences, including rural communities and especially women (Islam et al., 2011). In the age of globalization, the social contribution of tourism to community development cannot be overlooked by countries, states, communities, and individuals with positive development goals, since no nation on earth can afford to overlook tourism's economic, social, and cultural value (Ezeani, 2015).

Importance of Local People's Participation in CBT

CBT entices a specific type of tourism that is created, developed, planned, owned, and managed by the community for the sake of that community. It is guided by cooperative decision-making, responsibility, access, ownership, and benefits (Jamal & Getz, 1995). CBT is a long-term strategy that focuses on communities, and objectives are to provide economic, sociocultural, and environmental benefits to the community. Its goal is to diversify the local population's economic activity through a bottom-up process of local participation in decision-making, capacity building, and neoliberal economic diversification (Johnson, 2010). Communities' involvement in tourism development is crucial in empowering communities and minimizing the harmful effects of tourism (Jamal & Dredge, 2014).

CBT development will only be achieved if the community participates actively at all phases and when all stakeholders work together (Onderwater, 2011). Participation in the community aids in the equitable distribution of material resources as well as knowledge sharing and self-development (Connell, 1997). In CBT, the local communities living near the main destination are increasingly emphasized. By assuring their active participation in CBT planning and development, local people establish ownership, which supports conservation sustainability and economic benefits (Islam, 2010).

When the local community is aware of the planning and participation goals, tourism development can be successful (Miskowiak, 2004) and strengthen local communities, increase local skills, foster community ownership, and can lead to local development (Leballo, 2000). Local participation is a driver of long-term tourism development that improves opportunities for destination communities and would foster a good attitude among the community toward the growth of tourism and preservation of natural resources (Tosun & Timothy, 2003).

Local communities can make better decisions in the planning and development processes because they are the most informed about their requirements and the nature of their resources (Tosun, 2006). So, they should be involved in the design, development, implementation, and evaluation of CBT. They also participate in the decision-making process, express their views, and share their expertise and ideas with others (Karacaoğlu & Birdir, 2017). Locals play a key role in CBT's planning and growth. Local tourism participation is growing in popularity around the world and contributes to rural development and poverty reduction. More local people's involvement in the decision-making process and management will ensure community development (Chebus, 2018).

Community participation is important to promote sustainable tourism (Okazaki, 2008) and is essential to the tourism industry's success (Choi & Sirakaya, 2005). CBT management is done by community members who can positively impact decision-making, development, and monitoring processes (Lwoga, 2019). As a result, participation is important in promoting long-term growth that includes transparency and efficiency (Stiglitz, 2002).

Local people, one of the most important stakeholders of CBT, can be motivated in various ways (like providing various types of tangible and intangible motivations) to participate in a CBT business through the initiatives taken by either government or private tourism stakeholders which ultimately promote community development as well as natural resource conservation of that CBT destination (see Fig. 15.3).

Interactions Among Different Stakeholders in Promoting CBT

CBT's success hinges on effective interactions, participation, collaborations, and partnerships with important stakeholders (Giampiccoli & Mtapuri, 2017). They ensure identifying and implementing the appropriate corrective action to minimize tourism's negative environmental, economic, and sociocultural effects and also emphasize achieving and maintaining tourist satisfaction and promoting sustainable tourism practices to them. Relevant stakeholders can work together on each issue to ensure long-term sustainability in terms of environmental, economic, and sociocultural aspects (Amin, 2018).

Fig. 15.3.   Local Community Participation in CBT to Enhance Community Development and Natural Resource Conservation.

The active participation and interaction of all relevant stakeholders as well as dedication are required for the CBT development and management (Byrd, 2007). The involvement, empowerment, and ability of relevant stakeholders to participate in the tourism decision-making process are needed for tourism development (Tosun, 2000). The implementation of a CBT program relies heavily on the presence of active participation from host communities and other important players in the sector (Adongo et al., 2017). Within an institutional framework, providing opportunities for learning and knowledge sharing among stakeholders is essential (Wray, 2011). All relevant stakeholders should be involved, but missing a single major stakeholder group could result in the entire process failing (Clarkson, 1995).

Therefore, a strategic plan for motivating all these stakeholders (including tourists/guests), particularly the local community, is essential. Such motivation (either intrinsic or extrinsic) can control human behavior to be environment friendly and culturally sensible which will promote the practice of responsible/sustainable CBT to improve the performance of CBT products and services (see Fig. 15.4). Here, good practices by tour operators, eco-cottages, eco-guides, or any other service providers can motivate stakeholders to be responsible stakeholders by boosting their knowledge and experiences to facilitate sustainable CBT practice. Such initiatives will motivate local people and nonlocal stakeholders to practice CBT.

The community benefits from the stakeholders' assistance in improving the region's infrastructure and superstructure, as well as its marketing and promotion. Stakeholders offer various forms of assistance to community members to help them enhance their capacity and occupational skills (Karacaoğlu & Birdir, 2017). So, stakeholder participation and motivation have been required for successful CBT development (Björk, 2000).

CBT Initiatives in Bangladesh

CBT is the ideal option to acquire a magnificent experience of ethnic life, culture, and the peacefulness of panoramic nature, as well as the preservation of historic art, music, and literature. However, CBT is a relatively recent concept in Bangladesh. Just a few organizations have been working on CBT in Bangladesh for the last few years. Among these organizational initiatives, the Forest Department's Nishorgo Program (several projects under the program) played a

Fig. 15.4.   Responsible/Sustainable CBT Practice Through
Stakeholder Motivation.

significant role in the field of CBT development in the forested destinations of Bangladesh.

Initially, CBT was implemented (limited scale) in five protected areas of Bangladesh, viz. Lawachara National Park, Satchari National Park, Rema-Kalenga Wildlife Sanctuary, Chunoti Wildlife Sanctuary, and Teknaf Game Reserve (now it is Teknaf Wildlife Sanctuary) under the above program. By this time, several efforts have been taken to develop CBT in and around these protected areas along with some other protected and nature-based areas in Bangladesh. Some of these efforts are: ecotourism micro plan, eco-cottages development, eco-guides development, elephant ride, motivation of local community on CBT, training for local entrepreneurs (e.g., various handicrafts, souvenirs), and so on.

The Sundarbans (the single largest mangrove forest in the world) and Cox's Bazar (the largest unbroken sea beach in the world) are ideal nature-based destinations to practice CBT since the entire neighborhood exudes a desire to return to one's roots. The socioeconomic position and environmental factors of a location are highly dependent on the community's overall development. The researchers need to develop a method for selecting CBT destinations and assess the link between CBT and sustainability (Patwary et al., 2019).

Recently, there have been some CBT developments in the Sundarbans region. Some new eco-cottages and eco-resorts have been developed at the fringe of the Sundarbans which are becoming popular after the relaxing COVID-19 pandemic. Both local people's ownership and private tour operators' investments have been noticed there which are attracting both domestic and foreign tourists. At present, the United States Agency for International Development (USAID) Ecotourism Project under the initiatives of Bangladesh Ecotourism and Conservation Alliance (BECA) is ongoing particularly at Dacope and Mongla upazila of Khulna and Bagerhat districts, respectively. Under this initiative, various interventions are currently implanting at the field level to develop, manage, and promote community-based ecotourism so that it can facilitate the welfare of the local people through various small businesses as well as to improve their environmental education and awareness. Various activities are being implemented there targeting to improve the biodiversity conservation efforts of the Sundarbans.

Though the entrance of the tourists is banned for 3 months (June–August), but tourists can easily visit those Sundarbans adjacent villages to enjoy the beauty and attractions of the mangrove forest as well as the local community and their culture. Bangladesh Forest Department, Bangladesh Tourism Board, Tour Operators' Association of Sundarbans, and few NGOs organize training on tourism operations and tour guides for the Sundarbans. However, a strategic plan for such tourism training as well as certification of such training courses is warranted to ensure quality services for the Sundarbans destination.

CBT Motivations: A Case Study on the Sundarbans

The Sundarbans (area covers 601,700 hectares) are located in the southwestern part of Bangladesh at the Bay of Bengal's shoreline. The Sundarbans have significant roles in saving the coastal people from natural disasters like a mother. This world-famous mangrove forest is very rich in biodiversity including the home of Bengal tigers (*Panthera tigris tigris*). CBT is a type of niche tourism that is getting popularity day by day around the Sundarbans where tourists visit and experience the cultural and natural heritages. The Sundarbans has global ecological significance due to its abundant biodiversity, attractive landscapes and seascapes, the diversified livelihood of local people, welcoming host population, and pleasant weather.

Around 3.5 million people are directly or indirectly reliant on the Sundarbans for their livelihoods (BFD, 2019). Due to a lack of income opportunities, education, and environmental awareness, most of them are completely or partially reliant on the Sundarbans' natural resources, posing a hazard to the forest. CBT is a potential alternative source of income for the local people living around the Sundarbans (CEGIS, 2021). Local poor people can participate in a variety of economic activities which can allow them to earn money while also raising environmental awareness to promote natural resource conservation. Here, earning money for their livelihoods is the main motive for engaging in CBT interventions which leads them to avoid illegal resource extractions from the Sundarbans which ultimately facilitates them to achieve their goal of improving their socioeconomic condition which eventually has a direct positive impact on the natural resource conservation of the Sundarbans.

Nowadays, the local people around the Sundarbans villages have a positive attitude toward CBT development as it is facilitating their legal economic activities to improve their living standard. They believe that the Sundarbans is the main attraction of CBT in this region. They have various tourism products and services, such as embroidery quilts (*nokshi katha*), handkerchiefs, bed sheets, pillow covers, glass coasters, pickles, intangible cultural heritage, the amazing beauty of their villages, honey, shrimp farming, agricultural farming, etc. Moreover, they can make a wide range of items from soil and bamboo. They can also design towels with symbols of the animals of the Sundarbans which is a national treasure.

They have recently started growing watermelon in their farming lands which may be a CBT attraction for this region. The tourism services that the local community provides are eco-cottage services, tour guiding, cooking, boat (both paddle and engine boats) services, other transportation services, and traditional cultural performances according to the demands of the tourists. *Bonobibi* and *Gazikalu* worship are the two most important local intangible cultural heritages. Tourists are interested in enjoying these local CBT products and services which motivated the local people to be engaged more in CBT interventions.

The active participation of all concerned stakeholders in the Sundarbans is one of the major criteria for the development and management of CBT. Several NGOs and government agencies are currently working in the villages to help with CBT development, particularly for community development and promoting the conservation of the natural resources of the Sundarbans. These activities are motivating the local people to reduce human–tiger conflicts, deer hunting, and other illegal forest operations to some extent. These activities have improved public awareness of the Sundarbans and its biodiversity conservation.

Very recently, USAID has come forward with a pilot project "USAID Ecotourism Project" (2021–2024), particularly designed for CBT development around the Sundarbans. This project aims to empower the local community by improving their socioeconomic status as well as to promote the conservation of the natural resources of the Sundarbans. This is the first-ever project in the Sundarbans which is dedicated to developing CBT which is currently motivating the local people to engage themselves in this business to receive diversified benefits out of the business and to change their fate. Another project "USAID Protibesh Project" currently implemented in and around the Sundarbans is also facilitating some of the activities of CBT, particularly the capacity building of CBT-related local people and entrepreneurs (BECA, 2023).

Nevertheless, the overall rate of CBT development in the Sundarbans is slow. The main reason is the demotivation of most of the tourism businessmen and tour operators due to the fear of losing their traditional liveaboard/launch-based tourism businesses. This is why they are not interested in promoting and investing in CBT businesses around the Sundarbans with some exceptions. There are 112 tour operators involved in operating tourism businesses in the Sundarbans. Among them, very few of them (not more than eight) understand the CBT business which causes such demotivation.

Moreover, the local people face several challenges in managing and marketing their CBT products and services, particularly international tourists. Some of these challenges are language (mainly English) barrier, lack of information about digital marketing of these products and services, insufficient capacity building initiatives, poor internet network, absence of a good platform through the website and social media, lack of financing, guiding to this business, support for the Forest Department, among others. Moreover, still there are community needs for safe drinking water, electricity, road communication, medical facilities, post-disaster management, loan facilities, jetties, extensive capacity-building facilities, and so on, among others. These challenges are warranted to be solved for the betterment of CBT development in the Sundarbans region as well as to motivate the local people and external investors in this business.

Adopting suitable CBT marketing techniques can be a critical component of increasing revenues that can contribute to the growth of the local economy of the Sundarbans. It will also motivate consumer loyalty while reaching out to new guests at the various destinations of the Sundarbans.

Factors Affecting the Involvement of Private Players to Motivate Local People

The private sector of the tourism industry including travel agents, tour operators, hoteliers, and destination managers among others must be involved in CBT projects. The earlier this engagement occurs and the stronger the connection becomes, the more likely it is to be successful (George et al., 2007). The following main factors are responsible for making the involvement of private players functional and effective.

Publicizing their development efforts: Private sector especially NGOs implement various development activities toward motivating the locals and promoting CBT by providing various training programs, education incentives utilizing any skills and human potential within the community, etc. When the local people take their support and adapt, they can visualize their development activities (Suansri, 2003).

Positive relationships with local people: Developing positive relationships with local people can be the foundation for a successful tourist enterprise in a specific destination. Mutually beneficial connections can aid in increasing local acceptance of tourism activities and reducing conflict risks. Along with other forms of cooperation, assisting CBT ventures could be regarded as a manner of generating profits at the community level. Second, promoting a CBT product is a niche market investment. Even if it isn't the most profitable alternative, it can complement a tourism company's existing portfolio and serve as a tool for acquiring new consumer groups. Finally, participating in CBT provides potential for image building and public relations. It boosts the company's profile as a socially responsible business, which could help to gain market share in the long run.

Marketing for profitability: While private sector institutions have a wide range of interests, they are primarily concerned with the profitability of their businesses. They must develop a high level of experience in the marketing of tourism services in a competitive setting. As a result, they may be able to provide substantial marketing help to CBT ventures. Tourism businesses must constantly acquire market data to customize their programs to the interests and expectations of their target audiences. As a result, a private-sector partner might be a source of market data for a CBT endeavor. Such data, especially on the demands of foreign tourists from various cultural and economic backgrounds, look to be critical for the development of commercially viable CBT businesses.

Act as an intermediate medium: Private operators can act as an intermediate medium for providing the goods which are made by the locals as the locals face difficulties to sell their products and services for their poor market access and can promote market development. The private sector combines different tourism services to create new products, and their main function is to sell different tourism products and services. CBT also helps them to gain access to new markets and work with the community to decrease the risk of their investment (Forstner, 2004).

Effective use of the community as a tourism destination: Private sector uses community services such as guides, transportation, and food service. They use their knowledge of tourists and experiences in business and marketing. They abide by the rules and regulations set by the community.

Gaining government funding: Private sector contributes to society by investing in the community and providing expertise. Villager participation brings stability and can build a good image. They also show that the private sector can participate in supporting the community and natural resources conservation. These things are probably able to obtain government funding easily (Suansri, 2003).

Investment benefit: The public partner retains ownership and overall management of the public asset or system under the private operation and maintenance option. Another method is for a public partner (federal, state, or local government agency or authority) to enter into a contract with a commercial partner to operate, maintain, and manage a facility or system that provides a service. The public partner retains ownership of the public facility or system under this contract option, but the private party may spend its capital on the facility or system. Any private investment is thoroughly assessed in terms of its contribution to operational efficiencies and cost savings over the contract's duration. The longer the contract duration, the greater the chance of increased private investment because there is more time to recoup any investment and generate a reasonable return (George et al., 2007).

Factors Affecting the Involvement of Government Players to Motivate Local People

Formulating policy framework and supporting rules and regulations: The government's role is essential in the establishment of regulatory and policy frameworks and in ensuring their enforcement (George et al., 2007). Policies need to be formulated expressly to encourage local participation in tourism in natural and remote places. It does not allow for the appropriation of benefits through self-management schemes. Policies are intended to address specific public issues. Therefore, only those who are affected may validate them. Rather than a descriptive assessment of policy document content, it was thought that the practical challenges and enabling variables encountered by communities when implementing CBT would be a better basis for the development of evaluation criteria (Yanes et al., 2019).

Although the majority of CBT operations take place on a local level, they must fit into national-level structures. Government officials and policies can readily help or hinder the development of CBT. When it comes to building a CBT business, the government can be a valuable partner, especially if a community is located near a protected area (Malek-Zadeh, 1996). What communities do in the tourism industry is determined by their possibilities and power, as well as the incentives and pricing they confront, as well as their access to skills, training, finance, and markets. Government laws and regulations have an impact on all of these (George et al., 2007).

The United Nations Development Programme (UNDP) (2011) defines administrative governance as "the system for the implementation of policies, which requires the existence of well-functioning organizations at central and local levels." It should be included in the following operations:

Institutional coherence: This is reflected in the clear division of responsibilities and jurisdictions, which guarantees that the population is not misled by the authorities involved, as is frequently the case in developing nations. An agency whose institutional duty is the sustainable management of the place and a tourism promotion group whose interest is more economic may issue contradictory guidelines. When government departments have a disjointed power structure, local coordination suffers, resulting in fragmented planning, failed tourism program execution, and poor tourism regulation within tourist hotspots.

Authority and institutional presence: It is a crucial concern for communities in protected areas affected by public order difficulties because their involvement is contingent on the protection of their right to participate, referred to as an authority and institutional presence. It also presents itself in the institutional presence that follows and supports community actions in some locations, especially peripheral regions. Peripherality is a problem for many distant towns, not just in terms of accessing markets but also in terms of gaining the attention and financial and administrative assistance of local governments (Yanes et al., 2019).

Promoting sustainable use of natural and cultural resource utilization: People are increasingly conscious of the significance of their community assets, such as their culture, tradition, food, and way of life because of community-based development. It motivates them to turn them into revenue-generating projects while providing tourists with a more varied and worthwhile experience. Every person should be schooled in small business management, environmental awareness, product development, and marketing as a potential business partner. This kind of "people-centered" tourism fosters a sense of "ownership," which bodes well for the industry's long-term viability. CBT's methodology and objectives for conservation and development are based on the idea that increasing involvement intensities can offer communities an extensive economic and other benefits as well as decision-making authority. These financial benefits serve as incentives for participants as well as a means of motivation in conserving the natural and cultural resources that are used to generate their income (George et al., 2007; Suansri, 2003).

Income generation and creating jobs: Government uses CBT as a cost-effective way for income generation and creates job opportunities in rural communities because CBT provides many earning sources to local people by providing services to the tourists. Providing accommodation, food, transportation facility, and selling handicrafts are some examples of services of the locals. In this way, CBT can earn foreign exchange which will raise the gross domestic product (GDP) of the country.

Community development: CBT develops a community by building the capacity of the community (Suansri, 2003). In general, community capacity refers to the community's combined knowledge and ability, which are then used to define challenges and options from inside the community. According to the UNDP, the concept of capacity building for communities entails the creation, utilization, and retention of capacity to achieve goals such as poverty reduction, enhancement of self-reliance, and improvement of lives. The UNDP denotes that increasing capacity necessitates the accumulation of human skills, institutional capacities, and chances to put those talents and networks to good use in societal transformation (Imbaya et al., 2019).

It strengthens people's and organization's ability to solve problems and achieve their objectives. It ensures social equity, helps to achieve local peoples' economic and environmental goals, social equity, and motivates them toward sustainable development aspirations. It also helps to build and increase community leadership. It has been viewed as a bottom-up approach, focusing on local solutions to help the poor (Franco & Tracey, 2019).

Monitoring and evaluation: Once the program is fully operational, monitoring and evaluation begin. It aids in the identification of issues, repercussions, and advantages, as well as the operation's long-term viability. It looks at how well the project is accomplishing its goals. It should also lead to strategies and initiatives to compensate for flaws, fix problems, change systems, and improve the program. Government is mainly responsible for monitoring and evaluating the CBT process. This may include stakeholders' proper participation, local people's involvement, and their arising problems regarding CBT (George et al., 2007).

Getting taxes and revenues: The introduction of tourism within a community's government can earn money by allocating taxes for providing services and goods to tourists (Reed, 1997).

Moreover, the government can play important roles in motivating the local community people through promoting volunteerism, good governance in all levels and sectors, improving stakeholders' competencies by creating easy access to skills and support, improving tourists' facilities, setting standards for tourism services, financial and technical support, equitable benefit sharing mechanism, improving environmental education and awareness, biodiversity conservation, improving ownerships, adopting management approach of CBT destination, stakeholders' commitments, involving local government and other supporting agencies which will eventually promote CBT development at a destination.

Factors Affecting the Involvement of International Investors in CBT

The involvement of international investors in CBT plays a crucial role. Sometimes, the development of CBT requires big investments as, generally, the tourism industry is very capital-intensive due to the high cost of infrastructure and creating various facilities including the safety and security of the guest and host population. Therefore, many times such CBT developments require foreign direct investment (FDI). These investments are ensured through the proper channel of government where national policy for foreign investments, concerned rules, and regulations can strongly influence. Such foreign investment is an important means to build good relationships between these investors and local people of CBT destinations. Moreover, it can facilitate relationships among other concerned stakeholders including local people. However, such investments depend on several factors.

According to Snyman and Saayman (2009), some of the factors influencing FDI are perception (local and national political stability, law and order situation, foreign exchange, and so on) and infrastructure (communication infrastructure, availability and locations of roads of airports, availability of freshwater, medical facilities, and so on), government (cooperation from the government) and policy

(policy related to investment, labor, new Black Economic Empowerment, labor cost, training, and so on), economy (economic outlook, inflation rate, expected returns, market size, GDP and its growth, and so on), competitiveness (public–private partnerships, market size, incentive schemes, entrance to new markets, ports, growth of international travels, and so on), and nature (what is the country's main tourism thrust, tourism types, and so on). Depending on these factors among many other factors of FDI has a massive influence on the development of tourism facilities, i.e., infrastructure. Having a heterogeneous nature, the tourism industry integrates various supporting industries and sectors including communication and transportation, aviation, accommodation, travel agencies, safety and security, forestry, agriculture, shipping, and so on which the tourism sector requires FDI (Jamieson, 2001).

Strategic Tourism Planning for CBT to Promote Development and Conservation

Strategic tourism planning is a process that starts with the establishment of tourism organizational goals, defines tourism strategies and policies to achieve them, and creates comprehensive plans to ensure that the CBT strategies are implemented to achieve the desired outcomes. It is the process of determining ahead of time what kind of effort will be conducted when it will be undertaken, how it will be undertaken, who will undertake it, and what will be done with the results (Steiner, 2010). Hamzah and Khalifah (2009) have developed a CBT strategic planning model to promote the development and conservation of natural resources. There are nine steps in this model (see Table 15.1).

Table 15.1. Various Steps in CBT Strategic Planning Model.

Step no.	Title of the Steps	Objectives	Main Motivations
Step 1	Assess community needs and readiness for tourism	• To know community's needs and their current situation • To understand their preparedness to launch CBT	• Satisfy the basic needs of the community • Ready to start CBT enterprise to be benefited
Step 2	Educate and prepare the community for tourism	To build the capacity of the community so that they are compatible and confident in CBT business	• Make them skilled to do their business properly • Gaining confidence to profit
Step 3	Identify and establish leadership/ local champion	To build leadership to lead the CBT business	• Growing ownership • Making the business viable

(Continued)

Table 15.1. *(Continued)*

Step no.	Title of the Steps	Objectives	Main Motivations
Step 4	Prepare and develop community organization	To develop a community organization to plan, operate, and promote CBT projects	• Transform the community • A local champion breeds a local champion • Empowerment of local people including women and youth • Manage CBT by themselves (ownership)
Step 5	Develop partnership	To increase the community's capacity in undertaking various CBT projects and increase their compatibility	• Rich and healthy destination • Leveraging limited local resources • Satisfied tourists
Step 6	Adopt an integrated approach	To ensure sustainable CBT business	• Conservation of natural resources • Gaining long-term benefits for locals • Responsible tourism • Resilient CBT
Step 7	Plan and design quality products	To prepare a detailed action plan in ensuring quality CBT products and services	• Good flow of tourists • Ensure quality CBT experiences
Step 8	Identify market demand and develop marketing strategy	• To understand the market segments and prepare a marketing strategy • To make CBT business sustainable	• Matching local products and services with potential market segments • Functional distribution channel • Use of ICT • Branded and certified local products and services

Table 15.1. *(Continued)*

Step no.	Title of the Steps	Objectives	Main Motivations
Step 9	Implement and monitor performance	• To ensure local empowerment according to the desired outputs • To achieve the targets of a CBT project	• Performance-based activities • Empowered local community

Source: Authors' compilation.

Conclusions

Tourism development creates additional revenue for the local budget, which can be used to fund future tourism development plans and the conservation of destinations, ensuring the area's long-term viability (Harun et al., 2018; Islam et al., 2011). CBT is relatively a recent concept in Bangladesh to practice at the field level. However, recently, it has gained the attention of some local communities as a source of income to improve their overall living standard. Therefore, these local communities along with some external investors (tour operators, businessmen, government, foreign investors including USAID, European Unions, GIZ, and so on) are recently motivated to invest in CBT development, particularly in the Sundarbans region being one of the key biodiversity landscapes in Bangladesh.

Such investments are trying to motivate the local people as well as concerned government and NGOs to be involved in CBT development. The outputs of these investments are changing the total landscape ecology of the Sundarbans region along with some other forest-based landscapes. Community development through improving communication and transportation facilities, education facilities for the local children, medical facilities, and so on are taking place through CBT around the Sundarbans area (under Khulna, Bagerhat, and Satkhira districts). Though the rate is slow, but the recent communication and transportation development particularly through the inauguration of the Padma bridge has created a great potential for CBT in the area as well as some other parts of south-western Bangladesh, particularly Kuakata sea beach area, Borguna, Patuakhali, Jhalkathi and some other districts.

Chottogram Hill Tracts, Hobiganj, Moulovibazar, Sylhet, Cox's Bazar, Tangail, and Jashore are some of the districts where CBT is currently practiced at least to some extent. Proper understanding of CBT and its contributions, updated tourism policy motivating CBT, integrated planning (including strategic planning), implementation, strong monitoring, and evaluation, encouraging more investors (both domestic and international), and improving law and order situation, among others, are expected to further improve the existing status of CBT at these destinations as well as to introduce CBT in many other existing and potential nature-based tourism destinations.

Bangladesh is very rich in the diversified culture of various religions and tribes along with its natural diversity which makes the country a potential CBT destination for both domestic and international tourists. A good and controlled flow of tourists for sustainable CBT enterprises can significantly facilitate community development of these destinations along with improving the conservation status of natural resources of these destinations. Such developments are expected to foster sustainable development in Bangladesh by achieving several SDGs. Therefore, the factors and motives which play crucial roles in motivating the concerned stakeholders of CBT are warranted to address seriously so that CBT can be developed and performed in a sustainable way to change the fate of the local community as well as the conservation of natural resources of these destinations. Stakeholder collaboration is required along with good relationships among themselves. Various theories, concepts, processes, components, types, and so on related to motivation should be well studied to apply in new and existing CBT projects. The knowledge will be useful to motivate different stakeholders including local people to create an effective and functional platform to develop CBT. Different techniques and tools to raise CBT motivation are warranted in Bangladesh to maximize the benefits and minimize the negative impacts of CBT development.

References

Adongo, R., Choe, J. Y., & Han, H. (2017). Tourism in Hoi An, Vietnam: Impacts, perceived benefits, community attachment and support for tourism development. *International Journal of Tourism Sciences, 17*(2), 86–106.

Alshmemri, M., Shahwan-Akl, L., & Maude, P. (2017). Herzberg's two-factor theory. *Life Science Journal, 14*(5), 12–16.

Amin, M. R. (2018). Sustainable tourism development in Sundarbans, Bangladesh (A world heritage site): Issues and actions. *Journal of Business, 39*(2), 31–52.

Ashley, C., & Garland, E. B. (1994). *Promoting community-based tourism development: Why, what, and how?* (Vol. 4). Directorate of Environmental Affairs, Ministry of Environment and Tourism.

Asker, S., Boronyak, L., Carrard, N., & Paddon, M. (2010). *Effective community based tourism: A best practice manual.* Asia-Pacific Economic Cooperation.

Baldassarre, G. (2011). *What are intrinsic motivations? A biological perspective.* In Paper presented at the *2011 IEEE International Conference on Development and Learning (ICDL)*, Frankfurt am Main, Germany.

BECA (Bangladesh Ecotourism and Conservation Alliance). (2023). https://bangladesh-ecotourism.org/about/. Accessed on October 16, 2023.

BFD (Bangladesh Forest Department). (2019). *Sundarbans – At a glance.* Sundarbans Management Assistance Project, Boyra, Khulna 9100.

Björk, P. (2000). Ecotourism from a conceptual perspective, an extended definition of a unique tourism form. *International Journal of Tourism Research, 2*(3), 189–202.

Brown, L. V. (2007). *Psychology of motivation.* Nova Publishers.

Burgos, A., & Mertens, F. (2017). Participatory management of community-based tourism: A network perspective. *Community Development, 48*(4), 546–565.

Byrd, E. T. (2007). Stakeholders in sustainable tourism development and their roles: Applying stakeholder theory to sustainable tourism development. *Tourism Review, 62*(2), 6–13.

CEGIS (Centre for Environmental and Geographic Information Services). (2021). *Strategic environmental management plan. Strategic environmental assessment of the South West Region of Bangladesh for conserving the outstanding universal value of the Sundarbans.* Dhaka, Bangladesh.

Chebus, P. (2018). Local participation on community-based tourism in Wajee Nature Park, Mukurwe-Ini, Nyeri County. *International Journal of Progressive Sciences and Technologies, 7*(2).

Cherry, K. (2022). *What is motivation?* Verywell Mind. https://www.verywellmind.com/what-is-motivation-2795378. Accessed on July 4, 2022.

Choi, H.-S. C., & Sirakaya, E. (2005). Measuring residents' attitude toward sustainable tourism: Development of sustainable tourism attitude scale. *Journal of Travel Research, 43*(4), 380–394.

Clarkson, M. E. (1995). A stakeholder framework for analyzing and evaluating corporate social performance. *Academy of Management Review, 20*(1), 92–117.

Connell, D. (1997). Participatory development. *Development in Practice, 7*(3), 248–259.

Deci, E. L. (1971). Effects of externally mediated rewards on intrinsic motivation. *Journal of Personality and Social Psychology, 18*(1), 105.

Deci, E. L., & Ryan, R. M. (2012). Self-determination theory. *Handbook of Theories of Social Psychology, 1*(20), 416–436.

Delli Paoli, A., & Addeo, F. (2019). Assessing SDGs: A methodology to measure sustainability. *Athens Journal of Social Sciences, 6,* 229–250.

Dweck, C. S. (2012). Implicit theories. *Handbook of Theories of Social Psychology, 2.*

Ezeani, J. (2015). *Impact of tourism in Ezeagu local government area of Enugu state.* https://johnp2012.blogspot.com/2016/09/impact-of-tourism-in-ezeagu-local.html. Accessed on September 8, 2015.

Forstner, K. (2004). Community ventures and access to markets: The role of intermediaries in marketing rural tourism products. *Development Policy Review, 22*(5), 497–514.

Franco, I. B., & Tracey, J. (2019). Community capacity-building for sustainable development: Effectively striving towards achieving local community sustainability targets. *International Journal of Sustainability in Higher Education, 20*(4), 691–725.

George, B. P., Nedelea, A., & Antony, M. (2007). The business of community based tourism: A multi-stakeholder approach. *Tourism Issues, 3.*

Giampiccoli, A., & Mtapuri, O. (2017). Role of external parties in community-based tourism development: Towards a new model. *African Journal of Hospitality, Tourism and Leisure, 6*(2), 1–12.

Giri, C., Zhu, Z., Tieszen, L., Singh, A., Gillette, S., & Kelmelis, J. (2008). Mangrove forest distributions and dynamics (1975–2005) of the tsunami-affected region of Asia. *Journal of Biogeography, 35*(3), 519–528.

Greer, D. C. (2016). Motivation and attention as foundations for student learning. In *From the laboratory to the classroom* (pp. 57–72). Routledge.

Hamzah, A., & Khalifah, Z. (2009). *Handbook on community based tourism: "How to develop and sustain CBT"*. APEC Secretariat.

Harmon-Jones, E., & Harmon-Jones, C. (2012). Cognitive dissonance theory. *Handbook of Motivation Science, 71*.

Harun, R., Chiciudean, G. O., Sirwan, K., Arion, F. H., & Muresan, I. C. (2018). Attitudes and perceptions of the local community towards sustainable tourism development in Kurdistan regional government, Iraq. *Sustainability, 10*(9), 2991.

Hidi, S. (2006). Interest: A unique motivational variable. *Educational Research Review, 1*(2), 69–82.

Hinds, A. L., Woody, E. Z., Drandic, A., Schmidt, L. A., Van Ameringen, M., Coroneos, M., & Szechtman, H. (2010). The psychology of potential threat: Properties of the security motivation system. *Biological Psychology, 85*(2), 331–337.

Hockenbury, D. H., & Hockenbury, S. E. (2010). *Discovering psychology*. Macmillan.

Honey, M. (2009). *Tourism in the developing world: Promoting peace and reducing poverty* (Vol. 233). United States Institute of Peace.

Huitt, W. (2001). Motivation to learn: An overview. *Educational Psychology Interactive, 12*(3), 29–36.

Imbaya, B., Nthiga, R., Sitati, N., & Lenaiyasa, P. (2019). Capacity building for inclusive growth in community-based tourism initiatives in Kenya. *Tourism Management Perspectives, 30*, 11–18.

Islam, M. W. (2010). *Community-based tourism and ecotourism are potential means to facilitate the conservation of natural resources of the Sundarbans – A theoretical perspective* (special issue, pp. 127–140). Khulna University Studies, SESB.

Islam, M. R. (2021). Community-based rural tourism development: A conceptual framework for Bangladesh. *Journal of Service Research, 7*(4), 109–117.

Islam, M. S., Abubakar, H., & Islam, M. (2011). Community-based ecotourism in the Sundarbans of Bangladesh. *Rajagiri Journal of Social Development, 3*, 31–50.

Islam, M. W., Rahman, M. M., Iftekhar, M. S., & Rakkibu, M. G. (2013). Can community-based tourism facilitate conservation of the Bangladesh Sundarbans? *Journal of Ecotourism, 12*(2), 119–129.

Jamal, T. B., & Dredge, D. (2014). Tourism and community development issues. In R. Sharpley & D. Telfer (Eds.), *Tourism and development. Concepts and issues* (2nd ed., pp. 178–204). Channel View.

Jamal, T. B., & Getz, D. (1995). Collaboration theory and community tourism planning. *Annals of Tourism Research, 22*(1), 186–204.

Jamieson, W. (2001). *Promotion of investment in tourism infrastructure*. UN ESCAP.

Johnson, P. A. (2010). Realizing rural community-based tourism development: Prospects for social economy enterprises. *Journal of Rural and Community Development, 5*(1).

Karacaoğlu, S., & Birdir, K. (2017). Success factors of community based tourism (CBT) perceived by local peoples: The case of% 100 Misia project. *Uluslararası Kırsal Turizm ve Kalkınma Dergisi (IRTAD)*, E-ISSN: 2602-4462, *1*(2), 53–61.

Kelley, H. H., & Michela, J. L. (1980). Attribution theory and research. *Annual Review of Psychology, 31*(1), 457–501.

Killeen, P. R. (1981). Incentive theory. In Paper presented at the *Nebraska Symposium on Motivation*. University of Nebraska Press.

Kostoska, O., & Kocarev, L. (2019). A novel ICT framework for sustainable development goals. *Sustainability, 11*(7), 1961.

Leballo, M. (2000). *The study of the best practice in community-based tourism initiatives.* Unpublished report prepared for the Land and Agriculture Policy Centre, Johannesburg.

Lefcourt, H. M. (2014). *Locus of control: Current trends in theory & research.* Psychology Press.

Lwoga, N. (2019). International demand and motives for African community-based tourism. *GeoJournal of Tourism and Geosites, 25,* 408–428.

Malek-Zadeh, E. (1996). The ecotourism equation: Measuring the impacts. https://elischolar.library.yale.edu/yale_fes_bulletin/101

Manyara, G., & Jones, E. (2007). Community-based tourism enterprises development in Kenya: An exploration of their potential as avenues of poverty reduction. *Journal of Sustainable Tourism, 15*(6), 628–644.

Matsumoto, M., & Hikosaka, O. (2009). Two types of dopamine neuron distinctly convey positive and negative motivational signals. *Nature, 459*(7248), 837–841.

Mbagwu, F. O., Bessong, C. D., & Anozie, O. O. (2016). Contributions of tourism to community development. *Review of European Studies, 8,* 121.

McLeod, S. (2007). Maslow's hierarchy of needs. *Simply Psychology, 1*(1–18).

Mensah, I., & Afenyo, E. (2022). Introduction: Community-based tourism and community development: The prospects, challenges and trends. In *Prospects and challenges of community-based tourism and changing demographics* (pp. xix–xxxi). IGI Global.

Miskowiak, D. (2004). *Crafting an effective plan for public participation.* The Center.

Moscardo, G. (2008). Community capacity building: An emerging challenge for tourism development. In *Building community capacity for tourism development* (pp. 1–15). CABI.

MSG. (2022). *What is motivation?* Management Guide Study. https://www.managementstudyguide.com/how-motivation-can-help-us-avoid-burnout-in-post-pandemic-age.htm. Accessed on July 4, 2022.

Mubarok, A. M., & Lokaprasidha, P. (2020). Community based tourism (CBT) as a model of tourism and self-reliance development of coastal villages in Banyuwangi. In Paper presented at the *ICO-ASCNITY 2019: Proceedings of the 1st International Conference on Applied Social Sciences, Business, and Humanity, ICo-ASCNITY, 2* November 2019, Padang, West Sumatra, Indonesia.

Myers, D. G., & Smith, S. M. (2012). *Exploring social psychology.* McGraw-Hill.

Okazaki, E. (2008). A community-based tourism model: Its conception and use. *Journal of Sustainable Tourism, 16*(5), 511–529.

Onderwater, Y. (2011). *Opportunities for community-based tourism in the Tonkolili district, Sierra Leone.* Master Thesis. Hospitality Business School Saxion, Apeldoorn.

Paper Tyari. (2022). Motivation: Process, elements, types of motivation. https://www.papertyari.com/general-awareness/management/motivation/. Accessed on July 29, 2022.

Patwary, A. K., Roy, B., Hoque, R., & Khandakar, M. S. A. (2019). Process of developing a community based tourism and identifying its economic and social impacts: An empirical study on Cox's Bazar, Bangladesh. *Pakistan Journal of Humanities and Social Sciences, 7*(1), 1–13.

Pianka, E. R. (2012). *Can human instincts be controlled?* Oasis Publisher. www. oasispub.org

Reed, M. G. (1997). Power relations and community-based tourism planning. *Annals of Tourism Research, 24*(3), 566–591.

Rozemeijer, N. (2001). *Community-based tourism in Botswana: The SNV experience in three community-tourism projects.* SNV Botswana.

Ruiz-Mallén, I., Schunko, C., Corbera, E., Rös, M., & Reyes-García, V. (2015). Meanings, drivers, and motivations for community-based conservation in Latin America. *Ecology and Society, 20*(3).

Seo, M.-G., Barrett, L. F., & Bartunek, J. M. (2004). The role of affective experience in work motivation. *Academy of Management Review, 29*(3), 423–439.

Siegling, A. B., & Petrides, K. (2016). Drive: Theory and construct validation. *PLoS One, 11*(7), e0157295.

Singh, A. (2022). Positive motivation vs negative motivation: Which one is better? https://www.lifehack.org/829873/positive-motivation. Accessed on July 29, 2022.

SNV, & University of Hawaii. (2007). *A toolkit for monitoring and managing community-based tourism.* http://www.bibalex.org/Search4Dev/files/283814/115937. pdf

Snyman, J. A., & Saayman, M. (2009). Key factors influencing foreign direct investment in the tourism industry in South Africa. *Tourism Review, 64*, 49–58.

Spenceley, A., Rylance, A., Nanabhay, S., & van der Watt, H. (2016). *Operational guidelines for community-based tourism in South Africa.* Department of Tourism: Republic of South Africa. https://tkp.tourism.gov.za/Documents/Community% 20Based%20Tourism%20Operational%20Guidelines.pdf

Steiner, G. A. (2010). *Strategic planning.* Simon and Schuster.

Stem, C. J., Lassoie, J. P., Lee, D. R., Deshler, D. D., & Schelhas, J. W. (2003). Community participation in ecotourism benefits: The link to conservation practices and perspectives. *Society & Natural Resources, 16*(5), 387–413.

Stiglitz, J. E. (2002). Participation and development: Perspectives from the comprehensive development paradigm. *Review of Development Economics, 6*(2), 163–182.

Suansri, P. (2003). *Community based tourism handbook.* Responsible Ecological Social Tour-REST Bangkok.

Sukcharoenchok, M. N. (2019). *The impacts of community-based tourism in terms of economic, social, and environmental dimensions for the local communities in Thailand.* Thammasat University.

Thompson, R. F., Bao, S., Chen, L., Cipriano, B. D., Grethe, J. S., Kim, J. J., Thompson, J. K., Tracy, J. A., Weninger, M. S., & Krupa, D. J. (1997). Associative learning. *International Review of Neurobiology, 41*, 151–189.

Tolkach, D., & King, B. (2015). Strengthening community-based tourism in a new resource-based island nation: Why and how? *Tourism Management, 48*, 386–398.

Tosun, C. (2000). Limits to community participation in the tourism development process in developing countries. *Tourism Management, 21*, 613–633.

Tosun, C. (2006). Expected nature of community participation in tourism development. *Tourism Management, 27*(3), 493–504.

Tosun, C., & Timothy, D. J. (2003). Arguments for community participation in the tourism development process. *Journal of Tourism Studies, 14*(2), 2–15.

Tranquillo, J., & Stecker, M. (2016). Using intrinsic and extrinsic motivation in continuing professional education. *Surgical Neurology International, 7*(Suppl. 7), S197.

UNDP. (2011). *Human Development Report, Sustainability and equity: A better future for all* [On line]. https//hdr.undp.org/en/reports/global/hdr201tldownloadl. Accessed on October, 2011.

Usmanovna, N. G., & Oybekovna, D. G. (2018). The importance of motivation in education. Достижения науки и образования, *16*(38), 33–35.

Wasserman, E. A., & Miller, R. R. (1997). What's elementary about associative learning? *Annual Review of Psychology, 48*, 573.

WBG, & WWF. (2014). *Getting financed: 9 tips for community joint ventures in tourism.* https://openknowledge.worldbank.org/bitstream/handle/10986/21698/ 959240WP00PUBL050NamibiaonlineFINAL.pdf?sequence=1&isAllowed=y

Wray, M. (2011). Adopting and implementing a transactive approach to sustainable tourism planning: Translating theory into practice. *Journal of Sustainable Tourism, 19*, 605–627.

Yanes, A., Zielinski, S., Diaz Cano, M., & Kim, S.-I. (2019). Community-based tourism in developing countries: A framework for policy evaluation. *Sustainability, 11*(9), 2506.

Zapata, M. J., Hall, C. M., Lindo, P., & Vanderschaeghe, M. (2011). Can community-based tourism contribute to development and poverty alleviation? Lessons from Nicaragua. *Current Issues in Tourism, 14*(8), 725–749.

Chapter 16

Strategizing the Entrepreneurial Ecosystem of Start-ups for Rebuilding Communities

Manpreet Arora and Vaishali Dhiman

Central University of Himachal Pradesh, India

Abstract

All around the world, the tourism sector was hard hit by the pandemic. Many nations across the world are majorly dependent on tourism for their gross earnings. It is the backbone of service sector and has a great potential to boost entrepreneurial and related industries. The employment generation through this sector can be enormous if proper emphasis is laid on the factors inducing entrepreneurship, like conducive start-up policies, supportive government initiatives, and adequate financial support to the budding entrepreneurs along with development of financial and societal support systems. Across the globe, many communities suffered due to pandemic and the problems associated with that. Entrepreneurship is regarded as key to business innovation and development of economies. Thereby, in order to plan for resilience strategies, it is very important to understand the peculiarities of entrepreneurial ecosystem. It becomes necessary to understand and strategize the growth of entrepreneurial ecosystem to rebuild communities. This chapter highlights the relationships between entrepreneurial ecosystems and tourism sector for the growth of economy. The major finding is that without entrepreneurial growth, no economy or no sector can revive from crises. Therefore, it is necessary to focus on building effective strategies to support the stakeholders of the entrepreneurial ecosystems so as to promote growth and revive from the damage caused by pandemic.

Keywords: Entrepreneurial ecosystem; start-ups; tourism; entrepreneur; entrepreneurship; ecosystem

Strategic Tourism Planning for Communities, 247–260
Copyright © 2024 Manpreet Arora and Vaishali Dhiman
Published under exclusive licence by Emerald Publishing Limited
doi:10.1108/978-1-83549-015-020241019

Introduction

Tourism has emerged as a driver of growth for many emerging economies: In mid-1990s, the share of low- and middle-income countries in international tourism receipts was only 17% of the world's total. By 2012, that share had grown to 28%. When development of strategic infrastructure as well as natural resources are properly managed, community welfare-oriented tourism can benefit those who often gain the least from tourism. However, tourism and infrastructure development must be carefully planned and executed to protect the value of natural assets in order to benefit the communities at large. In other words, tourism must be sustainable to be useful and profitable in the long term. This will require efforts to improve the strategies to increase tourism, manage the pressure on natural resources, and link tourism with the local economy in an effective manner. The strategies should be such that tourism proves to be a driving force for the economies and all the stakeholders concerned.

Tourism also adds to the quality of life, particularly because once we have had the experience of traveling to one or many places, we cannot remain the same person. We not only change as a human, but we also evolve and grow in a manner, that whosoever comes into contact with us also benefits from the transformation in one way or another. Life starts showing us enormous positive perspectives carrying different meanings for us. It opens up in all its colors which are characterized by beautiful and mysterious aspects of nature which can have diverse dimensions. In particular, rural tourism tends to narrow down our focus to those unexplored spaces or spots on this earth, which due to one reason or another have remained untouched and unexplored by the devastating clutches of modernization and globalization. The concept of rural tourism linked with community-oriented tourism is very old, as one can imagine as to how the first tourist traveler on the face of this earth must have behaved, and how he must have explored the little world around him and also how inadvertently he must have gotten benefited by innumerable outputs of such an activity which may have been full of dangers and risks as well. With the passage of time, the tourism not only developed as an activity but has also emerged as a profitable business sector. Tourism and related start-ups along with tourism entrepreneurship can be a possible solution for building the communities which are downtrodden and never got an opportunity to come into mainstream.

If we look at the share of major countries of the world and especially that of India in International Tourist Arrivals in 2018, 2019, and 2020, their share has decreased in the postpandemic world, but it is gradually taking momentum. Various tourism-related business-oriented activities and services within the industry have received a boost. Due to the tourist arrivals, the ventures or small start-ups get business, for example, many tourists would like to buy some souvenirs or a piece of remembrance from the place they have visited. Generally, local artisans are involved in the process of manufacturing such items which are specific to the tourist destinations. It helps the local entrepreneurs to earn business, and it also helps to keep their culture alive. The local food and destination-specific products by the tourists are always in demand which helps contributing in sustainability. Further, the local people, tribes, or rural communities get a source of income and livelihood.

Innovation and start-ups are the two pillars which contribute to the growth of economy, and entrepreneurs help to make a shift from job seeker to job creators. If anyone has an innovative idea, the execution of that idea is the key to initiate the process of business start-up. And innovation is somewhere dependent on networks, open integration, and mutual trust among people in the respective ecosystem. These all are responsible to boost the speed of innovation (Ramchandran & Ray, 2006). Such innovations in tourism industry are much needed to achieve the goals of reduction of poverty, climate control, and the holistic development of the economies. Tourism sector can be a major player in such developmental approaches across the world. Table 16.1 represents the share of major countries of the world and India in International Tourist Arrivals which gives us a hope to develop communities linking start-ups, especially in rural areas for overall community development.

Beyond any doubt in the whole world, the tourism sector was hard hit by the pandemic. A great chunk of nations across the world are highly dependent on tourism. It is the backbone of service sector and has a great potential to boost

Table 16.1. Share of Major Countries of the World and India in International Tourist Arrivals in 2018, 2019, and 2020.

S.No	Country	International Tourist Arrivals (in Millions)			Percentage (%) Share	
		2018	2019	2020 (p)	2018	2019
1.	France	89.4	–	–	6.33	–
2.	Spain	82.8	83.5	19.0	5.86	5.70
3.	United States	79.7	79.4	19.4	5.64	5.42
4.	China	62.9	65.7	–	4.45	4.48
5.	Italy	61.6	64.5	25.2	4.36	4.40
6.	Turkey	45.8	51.2	15.9	3.24	3.49
7.	Mexico	41.3	45.0	24.3	2.92	3.07
8.	Thailand	38.2	39.9	6.7	2.70	2.72
9.	Germany	38.9	39.6	12.4	2.75	2.70
10.	United Kingdom	38.7	39.4	–	2.74	2.69
11.	Other countries	851.1	975.7	–	60.23	66.56
12.	India	17.4	17.9	–	1.23	1.22
13.	World total	1413.0	1466.0	399.0	100	100

Source: Indian Tourism Statistics at a Glance: 2021 Atithidevo Bhava Incredible India.

Note: UNWTO Barometer July 2021 for other countries and Bureau of Immigration (BOI) for India P = Provisional.

entrepreneurial and related industries. The employment generation through this sector can be enormous if supportive start-up policies are made and the strategies to boost the share of tourism industry are well planned. Various local produces are not only consumed by the tourists; they are exported to diverse international markets also.

Tourism can play a significant role in the recovery of economies across the world for several reasons. It is a multifaceted industry that can have a far-reaching impact on a nation's economic well-being. Due to its labor-intensive nature, tourism has the potential to provide employment in a wide range of industries, including hospitality, transportation, food services, entertainment, and more. In economies where unemployment rates are high, job prospects in the tourism industry might be very significant. The economy becomes less dependent on a single industry as a result of tourism. An economy that is more diversified may be more resilient to shocks to the economy in other industries, like manufacturing or agriculture. Further, foreign exchange earnings are boosted by the foreign currency that foreign tourists bring into a nation. This revenue can enhance a country's trade balance and aid in currency stabilization.

Governments frequently make infrastructure development investments to build hotels, highways, and airports to accommodate tourists. These enhancements may boost associated sectors and have a favorable effect on inhabitants' general quality of life. Small and microbusinesses like bed and breakfast operators, tour guides, and local artists may find potential in tourism. Tourist-heavy locations can prove to be a great booster for small enterprises. Responsible tourism can play an important role in the preservation of natural resources and help in conserving the cultural heritage of varied destinations. The preservation of culture may be a crucial component in the revival of the economy. Governments receive tax income from tourism through a number of sources, such as sales taxes, hotel taxes, and visa fees. Infrastructure development and public services can be funded by these profits. Given that visitors frequently look for mementos and authentic local experiences, tourism can promote trade in local goods and products. Local manufacturers and artisans stand to gain from this. Here, the role of start-ups becomes significant in rebuilding the communities at different spheres.

Concept of Start-ups

Start-ups and the start-up growth has been the main focal point of research in the area of entrepreneurship (Aldrich, 1999; Brush et al., 2008; Stearns & Hills, 1996). A start-up can turn into a sustainable business by selecting right kind of business idea or plan. Start-up organizations presently are seen as growth drivers for innovation and advancement in the society and can prove to be a growth engine to any nation (Brockhoff & Guan, 1996; Dushnitsky & Lenox, 2005). Start-up brings many opportunities to the founders which they can grab from the environment and deliver a fruitful innovation and several benefits to the society. Any founder (entrepreneur) of a new venture or start-up predominantly pays attention on their idea/proposal. It is quite logical that start-ups require a course of actions as well as interventions to set a new venture. Therefore, an entrepreneur relies on the consecutive ideas and opportunities (Becker et al., 2015; Dimov, 2010; Serarols, 2008).

Economically, the start-up ecosystem of India is more progressive than other geographies; it is also very suitable for start-ups relating with community development and upliftment of rural people. Indian start-ups require moderately lower capital investments which turn them into alluring opportunity for global investors to invest in new industries which are emerging and can be promising new ventures. Start-up ecosystem of India continues to be the third largest ecosystem, globally followed by China and the United States (NASSCOM & ZINNOV, 2019). Start-up base of India has grown constantly at a steady rate of 12%–15% year by year during 2014–2019. In India, Bengaluru, Mumbai, and NCR generate about 55–58% of the overall income from the start-ups. There is significant increase in the number of incubators and accelerators in the past decade. Indian start-up ecosystem with its proactive plans can realize up to four times of its potential development and growth by 2025 (NASSCOM & ZINNOV, 2019).

Start-ups are the newly emerged business ventures started by individual or group of individuals to meet the market gap (Start-up India, 2018), and the beginning phases of any new company are very critical to its development and existence, as these new entities are very fragile and delicate. Nonetheless, these new ventures are the most fruitful part of entire economy. Indeed, new companies are the organizations set up to test the plans of action created by new ideas, typically proposed by founder or founding team members (Salamzadeh & Kesim, 2017). Start-ups are recognized as growth engines and nation builder of any country, as they create jobs and boost the economy of the nation and make a positive contribution to the country. The start-up topography in India and many other developing nations is growing at a steady pace. In order to uplift the pace of start-ups and sustain their growth, it becomes indispensable for the founders/entrepreneurs to understand the life cycle of a start-up (Start-up India, 2018).

The evolution of start-ups has been described in two fundamental phases of development in the available literature. First, a significant number of start-ups fail and leave the market soon after their entry. Second, the start-ups who do survive after entry may grow and create employment, while only a considerable small number of start-ups are able to create small portion of jobs (Fritsch & Weyh, 2006; Schindele & Weyh, 2011). The start-ups in the area of tourism are depicting a promising future, especially after pandemic period due to upsurge in tourist activities. The investment environment in start-up ecosystem has boosted significantly in the past decade due to favorable government policies (NASSCOM & ZINNOV, 2019).

Start-up Stages

Start-ups have a great potential in positively contributing toward the county's economic system (Start-up India, 2018). In most basic scenario, a start-up is a new company that has taken birth to solve the market problems with a unique idea and working toward achieving a set goal. Start-ups in India are getting more attention in recent years, and there is a decent growth in the number of start-ups in India during past few years (Korreck, 2019). Also, start-up means starting a new firm as an act of entrepreneurship, and the founders of any start-up can be new or a serial entrepreneurs, whereas the early-stage start-ups or new ventures are those who are on the verge of entering to their growth stage (Venugopal, 2018).

Every start-up firms have got different aspects, and they differ in size, form, domain, and type (Salamzadeh & Kesim, 2017). An entrepreneur sees various stages of start-up lifecycle of newly found ventures from birth to its maturity. Marmer et al. (2011) have considered six key steps for information technology (IT) start-ups, i.e., (a) Discovery, (b) Validation, (c) Efficiency, (d) Scale, (e) Sustain, and (f) Conserve. Research on start-up firms is still in its nascent stage, but the development of nation with the help of start-ups can be immense (Korreck, 2019).Every single phase in start-up brings new opportunities and challenges that an entrepreneur must learn to handle (Start-up India, 2018).There are five stages mentioned and described by start-up India initiative for a start-up, i.e., concept or idea stage, preseed or validation stage, seed or early traction stage, growth and scaling stage, and maturity or exit stage. All these stages are briefly described as:

(1) *Concept or Idea Stage:* An entrepreneur or founder of new venture firstly finds an issue/problem and then identifies an opportunity that has a potential to deliver solution to that particular problem. Mentoring support for an entrepreneur plays a key role at this stage to look after the ideation plan and other related activities; everything needs to be so well defined that it will not create problem at later stage of start-up. At this stage, there is not a lot of necessity of much funding. Normally, founders tend to be neither bootstrap nor self-funding at this stage (Start-up India, 2018).

(2) *Preseed or Validation Stage:* A start-up founder/entrepreneur forms a probable expected solution in the form of verification of concept or proto-type with appropriate assumptions. Then these assumptions are validated with a pilot testing of the product in the target market or customer and get a response/feedback. Entrepreneurs then approach incubators/mentors at this stage to get help for infrastructure, develop a viable product, and move toward early clients (Start-up India, 2018).

(3) *Seed or Early Traction Stage:* After getting the responses and feedback from mentors and early clients, demand for that product/service is identified. And the retention rate of product in the mind of customer confirms the early traction of product and its company. Start-up attracts more clients by effectively seeking funds from angel investors, crowd funding, seed grant from government, and incubators' support (Start-up India, 2018).

(4) *Growth or Scaling Stage:* At this stage, the business is established, and most of the business processes have been defined at this stage. Entrepreneurs build their potential clients/customers, identify its potential market, and exploit the

opportunities available in the environment as well as ready to expand the business to other market and geography boundaries. For expanding the business, founders get funding support from the institutional investors such as angel investors, venture capitalists (Start-up India, 2018).

(5) *Maturity or Exit, Initial Public Offering (IPO), Mergers and Acquisitions (M&A) Stage:* This is a crucial stage of a start-up, either business has to sustain and maintain their market place by adding valuable features which helps the customers to retain or else the business would decline or head toward an exit stage. Many promoters, founders, and investors look at opportunity to exit and acknowledge benefits and profits either through partial or full sale of the business entity or sometimes these declining start-ups may issue IPO or altogether sell the business venture (Start-up India, 2018).

Start-up India Flagship and the Strategies Based on Literature

According to Government of India, start-up is defined as: "An entity shall be considered as a start-up up to a period of 10 years from the date of incorporation/registration, if it is incorporated as a private limited company (as defined in the Companies Act, 2013) or registered as a partnership firm (registered under section 59 of the Partnership Act, 1932) or a limited liability partnership (under the Limited Liability Partnership Act, 2008) in India." And start-up firm's turnover should be less than 100 crores in any previous financial year, should be working toward innovation/improvement of exiting product/services and also have potential to generate employment and create wealth (as per the Department for Policy Promotion and Industry [DPITT]).

Governments around the globe are setting up bigger pools of assets and funds to catalyze unique and innovative ventures and foster the early-stage ventures (Islam et al., 2018). So is the Government of India which is putting strong efforts by encouraging the youth of the nation and potential founders to validate their ideas into execution. Also, the government is providing many schemes, funds, and all possible kind of assistance, which in turn, nurture the potential start-ups.

The road map of start-up India initiative is prepared by DPPIT, which is now renamed as the Department for Promotion of Industry and Internal Trades (DPIIT) in January 2016. In this incentive, most of the states have taken part from last couple of year, and they are putting great efforts to strengthen the start-up ecosystem (Start-up India, 2018). Currently, 22 states have exclusive start-up policy set up to provide desired fiscal and nonfiscal incentives to start-ups. Every state government is actively developing incubation facilities, mentors' network, and accelerators to provide good ecosystem to early-stage start-ups. There are 17 states, which are paying attention to start-ups founded/co-funded by women entrepreneurs and offering special incentives in the form of grant or subsidy in addition to what is provided to a start-up.

Since the launch of Start-up India Initiative, 3,000+ start-ups have been given seed funding support from state government, after the launch of Start-up India Initiative. Government of each state who participated in start-up India flagship have set up a pool of approximately 2,000+ registered mentors across the nation. More than 70 incubator supports have been provided by state governments. There is a high boost in start-up growth from 503 to 8,724 year on year, during 2016–2018. This initiative will create 1.25 lakh direct jobs (Start-up India, 2018).

Out of all states, Gujarat is a best performing state, Himachal Pradesh and Haryana comes under aspiring states, and Punjab and Uttarakhand are considered as emerging states under start-up India flagship. And the authors would like to mention here that Himachal Pradesh and Uttarakhand are majorly tourism-oriented states which provide a good hope of developing the communities based on tourism and rural development. Emerging states are those which are recognized to have fast scaling up business ecosystem. These states are effectively promoting the incubation support, simplified regulations and implement their start-up policy to imminent start-up with necessary infrastructure and intellectual support. Aspiring leaders are perceived as a state which have displayed excellent execution and are at advance phase of implementation of their start-up goals. They have effective seed funding structure for new ventures and have been continuously working on rectifying, delivery, and creation of infrastructure to empower the start-ups globally.

If we analyze the literature for start-up ecosystem, Korreck (2019) analyzed the ecosystem of Indian start-ups, their challenges, and support organizations. Primary focus of the study was technological start-ups followed by nontech, social, and micro entrepreneurs. The study showed technology start-ups play a key role for providing low cost and high impact solution to scaling up the start-ups and its exponential growth and also revealed that the ecosystem is still not so favorable for the start-ups who produce hardware or other physical products. Author has investigated the major challenges, i.e., most of the start-ups were bootstrapped, not self-sufficient and find difficulty in obtaining funds, less capable of understanding customer needs, lack of clarity about rules and regulations, and faced difficulty in hiring talented employees because majority of qualified employees were hired by big corporates. This study highlighted that with the help of support pillars such as incubators, accelerators, angel investors, and governments, start-ups were able to promote growth, employment opportunities, and had varied positive socioeconomic impacts. It thereby highlights the fact that a proper strategic initiative has to be taken at the level of policymakers in order to promote start-ups. Salamzadeh and Kesim (2017) studied the status of ecosystem of start-up companies and enterprising communities in Iran and their existing stages and challenges. The study showed that there was a significant role of incubators, accelerators, and start-ups itself for improving the enterprising communities and also reflected that there could be significant effect of informal sectors like social networks, support organization, and government interventions that can affect the start-up ecosystem as a whole. Findings of the study showed that lack of IPO possibilities, intense competition with other firms, lack of legal support, and lack of enough capacity to respond market were the most affecting challenges of Iranian start-ups. Pangarkar and Wu (2013) investigated the relationship between performance and alliance strategy of Singapore start-ups. The argument of the study was that the start-ups who make larger number of alliances and have diverse networking partners (incubators, VC, government) perform better than lesser number of alliances; by doing so, start-ups achieve high magnitude of skills and drive more benefits because of learning effect. Results showed that wide range of start-ups were having 1–3 founding members; out of them, at least one had worked as a manager before joining the start-up. Study also revealed majority of start-ups believed that alliances had a significant impact on their performance. Findings of the study showed that there was a positive impact of number of alliances which had enhanced the performance and a strong impact of diverse networking partners for better performance of Singapore start-ups, in terms of composite performance. Therefore, networking can be a good strategy or developing communities based on initial stages of start-ups. Oe and Mitsuhashi in year 2012 claimed that when founders had previous work experience in the same industry, they can reach faster at break-even point in start-ups. Authors have argued and also suggested that there was a positive effect of information distribution and interpretation on start-ups who have experience in the same industry and prior job experience. Findings of the study revealed that information distribution and interpretation variable were insignificant to previous start-up experience but significant to prior job experience and the same industry experience. The study also highlighted that start-ups founded by those founders who had experience in the same industry and prior job experience reach the break-even point faster. Fritsch and Schindele (2011) have investigated the contribution made by start-ups to regional employment. Findings of the study revealed that there was a significant positive effect of highly qualified employees and innovation activities conducted by start-ups; this provides an opportunistic environment to compete them successfully. Ramchandran and Ray (2006) examined the role of networks and resource strategies to build the strong competence of start-ups. Authors have explored the two IT start-ups, their innovativeness, dynamic resources, and network building strategies. Author argued that start-ups gain resources when they are tied up with networks, and the success relies upon the entrepreneur's capability to set up supportive relations. Result of the study showed that in the fast-changing competitive ecosystem, a steady pace and accuracy were the important factors for the success of IT start-ups industry. And also revealed entrepreneurship, capital, and technology were recognized as three most key resources for the success of any new business venture. Findings exhibits that firms were not only depend on single network but had wide range of networks. And the networking ability of entrepreneurs and resourcefulness encourages acquisition of managerial resources, capital and making smoother accomplishment of business idea and success of start-ups.

How Can Strategizing the Entrepreneurial Ecosystem of Start-ups Can Promote Rebuilding of Communities?

Promoting community reconstruction can be greatly aided by strategically managing the start-up environment. When effectively used, entrepreneurship may be a catalyst for social and economic advancement as well as a means of reviving and empowering local communities. An effective way to support community reconstruction is through planned start-up environment management. When applied skillfully, entrepreneurship has the potential to revitalize and strengthen local communities while also acting as a catalyst for social and economic growth. Access to resources is an important aspect of this process. In order to assist regional business owners and start-ups, the policymakers should make it easier for people to obtain vital resources like capital, co-working spaces, and technological infrastructure. This can involve financing, grants, or assistance from venture capitalists and angel investors, which can foster the process of rebuilding.

Mentorship and networking can play an important role in overcoming the challenges of the rebuilding process. A well-established mentorship program that can link prospective founders with seasoned professionals and entrepreneurs can be of great help. Establishing a network of advisers and mentors can aid businesses in overcoming obstacles and arriving at wise choices. Here the incubators and accelerators that offer coaching, resources, and a friendly atmosphere to companies can be of immense help. These groups can aid in the quicker growth and success of start-ups. A dynamic force behind innovation, employment creation, and economic progress is entrepreneurship. By utilizing the resources, information, and skills found in academic settings, entrepreneurship can be effectively fostered. Working together with surrounding colleges and universities is a great way to do this. These collaborations foster innovation, research, and teaching that promote entrepreneurship and benefit academic institutions as well as the larger community. Higher education institutions and entrepreneurship now have a mutually beneficial partnership in the modern world. Universities and colleges have come to understand that they can be essential not only for teaching students but also for fostering the growth of start-ups, doing research that influences business decisions, and acting as centers of innovation. Research is one of the main ways that entrepreneurship thrives when it collaborates with academic institutions. Universities are hubs for cutting-edge research, with staff and students working on projects in a variety of subject areas. These investigations may produce insightful discoveries and workable answers. Working together with business owners and entrepreneurs can help translate these insights into marketable goods and services. Access to scholarly knowledge and research can be very helpful for start-ups, giving them a competitive advantage in their respective sectors. These partnerships have advantages outside of the educational setting. They support regional economies by fostering a dynamic environment. These partnerships foster the growth of small and new companies, which attracts investment and boosts employment and economic activity. Additionally, they support the local community's revival by creating an atmosphere that brings together talent, money, and creativity.

One of the main forces behind both economic expansion and community development worldwide is the tourism sector. It may strengthen regional economies, generate job opportunities, and promote cross-cultural interactions. But in the wake of the COVID-19 pandemic, the tourism industry, like many others, encountered challenges that were previously unthinkable. Tourism suffered greatly as a result of the crisis, which had an effect on the people that depend on it for their lives. It is critical to take a thoughtful approach to encouraging entrepreneurship in the tourism sector in order to restore and revive these communities. As a diverse business, tourism has a great deal of potential to promote social and economic advancement. Its capacity to draw tourists and make money can spur efforts at collaborative restoration. However, realizing these potential calls for a carefully considered entrepreneurial ecosystem that is adapted to the particular requirements and features of the surrounding community.

Initiatives for Training and Education

Tourism-dependent communities stand to gain from training and educational initiatives that foster entrepreneurial abilities. These initiatives give locals the resources they need to establish and run tourism-related companies. Through the dissemination of knowledge in domains such as sustainable tourism practices, customer service, and hospitality, these programs enable individuals to participate actively in the business.

Assistance to Local Start-ups

One of the most important aspects of encouraging entrepreneurship in the tourism sector is resource accessibility. Communities should create support systems to help local entrepreneurs realize their tourism-related ideas, like co-working spaces, funding possibilities, and mentorship programs. These resources aid in community reconstruction by acting as stimulants for creativity and the creation of jobs.

Innovation and the Preservation of Culture

Cultural preservation has both intrinsic worth and is a subject of pride in the tourism industry. By supporting regional artists, traditional crafts, and cultural events, communities can profit from their cultural heritage in a calculated and effective way. This generates distinctive selling factors that draw tourists in addition to maintaining cultural uniqueness.

Cooperation With Academic Institutions

Establishing collaborations with local higher education institutions can play a pivotal role in fostering an entrepreneurial environment for the tourism sector. These establishments have the capacity to supply skilled labor for the tourism industry, promote research and innovation, and provide specialized instruction in tourism-related subjects. These partnerships may also result in projects that use scholarly knowledge to further eco-friendly travel strategies.

Participation of Communities and Governance

Governance and community involvement are critical to the success of entrepreneurship promotion in the tourism industry. It is important for communities to have an active role in creating solutions that meet their specific requirements and goals. For implementation to be successful, local governance institutions must be able to adapt to the opportunities and problems that the tourism sector presents.

Environmental Responsibility and Sustainability

Ecosystems and resources in the area may be impacted by tourism. As a result, an entrepreneurial ecosystem ought to support environmentally friendly and environmentally responsible tourism methods. This helps to maintain the tourist sector's long-term sustainability and enhances the community's standing as a respectable and appealing travel destination.

Market Entry and Advancement

Tourism-related entrepreneurial endeavors shouldn't function independently. In order to draw in a consistent stream of visitors, communities should endeavor to create access to both domestic and international markets by utilizing marketing and promotion techniques. A diverse revenue source from effective promotion might lessen the community's susceptibility to the seasonality of tourism.

Tracking and Assessing

Communities need to implement procedures for monitoring and evaluating the efficacy of their strategies. Data-driven methodologies facilitate the ongoing evaluation of the effects of entrepreneurial endeavors on the economic recuperation and advancement of the neighborhood. Frequent evaluations aid in strategy optimization, effective resource allocation, and learning from both triumphs and failures.

Concluding Remarks

In conclusion, deliberate encouragement of entrepreneurship in the travel and tourist industry can be a powerful catalyst for the restoration of civilizations affected by external forces such as the COVID-19 pandemic. Adapted to the specific needs and opportunities of each community, entrepreneurial ecosystems have the potential to create jobs, elevate people, preserve cultural heritage, and advance environmental sustainability. By taking this calculated risk, communities may leverage the transformative power of entrepreneurship to rehabilitate, revitalize, and define a prosperous and sustainable future. Through careful stimulation of entrepreneurship in the tourism sector, communities can become more resilient and self-sufficient. Communities can become more resilient to future economic shocks by promoting an entrepreneurial culture that lessens their reliance on outside forces and markets. In addition, as local company owners prosper and build prosperous enterprises, they serve as role models and sources of inspiration for upcoming generations, fostering an ongoing cycle of innovation and expansion. It is crucial to understand that every community is different, and that entrepreneurship promotion strategies should be customized to fit each community's particular needs and resources. Communities can maximize their potential and progressively lessen gaps in social and economic well-being by adopting this customized approach. In conclusion, there is more to the resilience of entrepreneurship in the travel and tourism sector than merely economic recovery. It is about protecting cultural identity, empowering people, and creating a more resilient and sustainable future. The process of reconstructing communities via entrepreneurship is dynamic and continuous, requiring commitment, flexibility, and cooperation from all parties involved – from local governments to academic institutions and business executives. By working together, communities may steer toward a prosperous and sustainable future in which the transformative potential of entrepreneurship turns into a long-lasting source of opportunity and optimism.

References

Aldrich, H. E. (1999). *Organizations evolving.* Sage Publications. https://books.google.co.in/books?id=pdci-4om5rIC&lpg=PR9&ots=DDZcus8DXa&dq=Aldrich%2C%20H.%20E.%20(1999).%20Organizations%20evolving.%20London%2C%20UK%3A%20Sage%20Publications.&lr&pg=PR9#v=onepage&q&f=false

Becker, A., Knyphausen-Aufseß, D. Z., & Brem, A. (2015). Beyond traditional developmental models: A fresh perspective on entrepreneurial new venture creation. *International Journal of Entrepreneurial Venturing, 7*(2), 152–172. https://doi.org/10.1504/IJEV.2015.068591

Brockhoff, K., & Guan, J. (1996). Innovation via new ventures as a conversion strategy for the Chinese defence industry. *R & D Management, 26*(1), 49–56. https://doi.org/10.1111/j.1467-9310.1996.tb00928.x

Brush, C. G., Manolova, T. S., & Edelman, L. F. (2008). Properties of emerging organizations: An empirical test. *Journal of Business Venturing, 23*(5), 547–566. https://doi.org/10.1016/j.jbusvent.2007.09.002

Dimov, D. (2010). Nascent entrepreneurs and venture emergence: Opportunity confidence, human capital, and early planning. *Journal of management studies, 47*(6), 1123–1153.

Dushnitsky, G., & Lenox, M. J. (2005). When do firms undertake R&D by investing in new ventures? *Strategic Management Journal, 26*(10), 947–965. https://doi.org/10.1002/smj.488

Fritsch, M., & Schindele, Y. (2011). The contribution of new businesses to regional employment—An empirical analysis. *Economic Geography, 87*(2), 153–180. https://doi.org/10.1111/j.1944-8287.2011.01113.x

Fritsch, M., & Weyh, A. (2006). How large are the direct employment effects of new businesses?—An empirical investigation. *Small Business Economics, 27*, 245–260. https://www.jstor.org/stable/40229501

Ghosh, D., & Natarajan, P. (2019). *Indian tech start-up ecosystem-leading tech in 20s.* NASSCOM and ZINNOV, Edition. http://10000startups.com/frontend/images/ Indian-Tech-Start-up-Ecosystem-2019-report.pdf. http://dln.jaipuria.ac.in:8080/ jspui/bitstream/123456789/10830/1/Indian-Tech-Start-up-Ecosystem-2019-report.pdf

Islam, M., Fremeth, A., & Marcus, A. (2018). Signaling by early stage startups: US government research grants and venture capital funding. *Journal of Business Venturing, 33*(1), 35–51.

Korreck, S. (2019). *The Indian start-up ecosystem: Drivers, challenges and pillars of support.* ORF Occasional Paper No. 210, September 2019. Observer Research Foundation. https://www.orfonline.org/wp-content/uploads/2019/09/ORF_ Occasional_Paper_210_Startups.pdf

Marmer, M., Herrmann, B. L., Dogrultan, E., Berman, R., Eesley, C., & Blank, S. (2011). *Startup Genome Report Extra: Premature scaling.* Startup Genome, 10. https://integral-entrepreneurship.org/wp-content/uploads/2016/07/Startup-Genome-Premature-Scaling.pdf

Oe, A., & Mitsuhashi, H. (2012). Founders' experiences for start-ups' fast break-even. *Journal of Business Research.* https://doi.org/10.1016/j.jbusres.2012.01.011

Pangarkar, N., & Wu, J. (2013). Alliance formation, partner diversity, and performance of Singapore start-ups. *Asia Pacific Journal of Management, 30*, 791–807. https://doi.org/10.1007/s10490-012-9305-9

Ramchandran, K., & Ray, S. (2006). Networking and new venture resource strategies: A study of information technology start-ups. *The Journal of Entrepreneurship, 15*, 2. https://doi.org/10.1177/097135570601500203

Salamzadeh, A., & Kesim, H. K. (2017). The enterprising communities and start-up ecosystem in Iran. *Journal of Enterprising Communities: People and Places in the Global Economy.* https://doi.org/10.1108/JEC-07-2015-0036

Schindele, Y., & Weyh, A. (2011). The direct employment effects of new businesses in Germany revisited: An empirical investigation for 1976–2004. *Small Business Economics, 36.* https://doi.org/10.1007/s11187-009-9218-2

Serarols, C. (2008). The process of business start-ups in the internet: A multiple case study. *International Journal of Technology Management, 43*(1–3), 142–159. https:// doi.org/10.1504/IJTM.2008.019412

Start-up India. (2018). *States' Start-up Ranking, Report 2018.* Start-up India. https:// www.startupindia.gov.in/

Stearns, T. M., & Hills, G. E. (1996). Entrepreneurship and new firm development: A definitional introduction. *Journal of Business Research, 36*(1), 1–4. https://doi.org/ 10.1016/0148-2963(95)00157-3

Venugopal, B. (2018). *Essays on angel investors and early-stage start-ups.* C.T. Bauer College of Business, University of Houston. http://hdl.handle.net/10657/3082

https://www.startupindia.gov.in/content/sih/en/startup-scheme/state-startup-policies/ Punjab-state-policy.html

https://www.startupindia.gov.in/

Printed in the USA
CPSIA information can be obtained
at www.ICGtesting.com
JSHW011356250624
65367JS00004B/43